THE LANGUAGE OF LITERATURE

THE *InterActive*
READER™ PLUS

McDougal Littell
A HOUGHTON MIFFLIN COMPANY

Evanston, Illinois • Boston • Dallas

Reading Consultants, *The InterActive Reader™ Plus*

Sharon Sicinski-Skeans, Ph.D. Assistant Professor of Reading, University of Houston-Clear Lake; former K–12 Language Arts Program Director, Spring Independent School District, Houston, Texas.
Olga Bautista Reading Coordinator, Will C. Wood Middle School, Sacramento, California.

Senior Consultants, *The Language of Literature*

Arthur N. Applebee Professor of Education, State University of New York at Albany; Director, National Research Center on English Learning and Achievements; Senior Fellow, Center for Writing and Literacy.
Andrea B. Bermúdez Professor of Studies in Language and Culture; Director, Research Center for Language and Culture; Chair, Foundations and Professional Studies, University of Houston-Clear Lake.
Sheridan Blau Senior Lecturer in English and Education and former Director of Composition, University of California at Santa Barbara; Director, South Coast Writing Project; Director, Literature Institute for Teachers; Past President, National Council of Teachers of English.
Rebekah Caplan Coordinator, English Language Arts K–12, Oakland Unified School District, Oakland, California; Teacher-Consultant, Bay Area Writing Project, University of California at Berkeley; served on the California State English Assessment Development Team for Language Arts.
Peter Elbow Professor of English, University of Massachusetts at Amherst; Fellow, Bard Center for Writing and Thinking.
Susan Hynds Professor and Director of English Education, Syracuse University, Syracuse, New York.
Judith A. Langer Professor of Education, State University of New York at Albany; Director, National Research Center on English Learning and Achievements; Director, Albany Institute for Research on Education.
James Marshall Professor of English and English Education, University of Iowa, Iowa City.

Acknowledgments

Jennifer Burton Bauer: "The Lost City of Akrotiri" by Jennifer Burton Bauer, from *Boys' Quest Magazine,* April/May 2001, pages 10–12. Copyright © 2001 Jennifer Burton Bauer. Reprinted by permission of the author.
Susan Bergholz Literary Services: "Eleven," from *Woman Hollering Creek* by Sandra Cisneros. Copyright © 1991 by Sandra Cisneros. Published by Vintage Books, a division of Random House, Inc., and originally in hardcover by Random House, Inc. Reprinted by permission of Susan Bergholz Literary Services, New York. All rights reserved.

Continued on page 353.

ISBN-13: 978-0-618-30985-6   ISBN-10: 0-618-30985-3

13 14 15 16 17 –VEI–08 07

Table of Contents

Introducing *The InterActive Reader™ Plus*

The InterActive Reader™ Plus is a new kind of literature book. As you will see, this book helps you become an active reader. It is a book to mark on, to write in, and to make your own. You can use it in class *and* take it home.

An Easy-to-Carry Literature Text

This book won't weigh you down—it can fit as comfortably in your hand as it can in your backpack. Yet it contains works by such important authors as . . .

Sandra Cisneros, whose story "Eleven" draws on memories of feeling awkward and shy.

Gary Paulsen, whose memoir *Woodsong* reads like an adventure novel.

Walter Dean Myers, who combines research and drama in the biography of an enslaved prince, "Abd al-Rahman Ibrahima."

You will read these selections and other great literature—plays, poems, stories, and nonfiction. In addition, you will learn how to understand the texts you use in classes, on tests, and in the real world, and you will study and practice specific strategies for taking standardized tests.

Help for Reading

Many works of literature are challenging the first time you read them. *The InterActive Reader™ Plus* helps you understand these works. Here's how.

Before-You-Read Activities The page before each literary work helps you connect the selection to your everyday life and gives you a key to understanding the selection.

Preview A preview of every selection tells you what to expect.

Reading Tips Useful, specific reading tips are provided at points where language is difficult.

Focus Each longer piece is broken into smaller "bites" or sections. A focus at the beginning of each section tells you what to look for.

Pause and Reflect At the end of each section, a quick question or two helps you check your understanding.

Read Aloud Specific passages are marked for you to read aloud. You will use your voice and ears to interpret literature.

Reread This feature directs you to passages where a lot of action, change, or meaning is packed in a few lines.

Mark It Up This feature invites you to mark your own notes and questions right on the page.

Vocabulary Support

Words to Know Important new words are underlined. Their definitions appear in a Words to Know section at the bottom of any page where they occur in the selection. You will work with these words in the Words to Know SkillBuilder pages.

Personal Word List As you read, you will want to add some words from the selections to your own vocabulary. Write these words in your Personal Word List on page 335.

SkillBuilder Pages

After each literary selection, you will find these SkillBuilder pages:

Active Reading SkillBuilder

Literary Analysis SkillBuilder

Words to Know SkillBuilder (for most selections)

These pages will help you practice and apply important skills.

Links to *The Language of Literature*

If you are using McDougal Littell's *The Language of Literature*, you will find *The InterActive Reader*™ *Plus* to be a perfect companion. The literary selections in the reader can all be found in that book. *The InterActive Reader*™ *Plus* lets you read certain core selections from *The Language of Literature* more slowly and in greater depth.

Read on to learn more!

Academic and Informational Reading

Here is a special collection of real-world examples to help you read every kind of informational material, from textbooks to technical directions. The strategies you learn will help you on tests, in other classes, and in the world outside of school. You will find strategies for the following:

Analyzing Text Features This section will help you read many different types of magazine articles and textbooks. You will learn how titles, subtitles, lists, graphics, many different kinds of visuals, and other special features work in magazines and textbooks. After studying this section you will be ready to read even the most complex material.

Understanding Visuals Tables, charts, graphs, maps, and diagrams all require special reading skills. As you learn the common elements of various visual texts, you will learn to read these materials with accuracy and skill.

Recognizing Text Structures Informational texts can be organized in many different ways. In this section you will study the following structures and learn about special key words that will help you identify the organizational patterns:

- Main Idea and Supporting Details
- Problem and Solution
- Sequence
- Cause and Effect
- Comparison and Contrast
- Argument

Reading in the Content Areas You will learn special strategies for reading social studies, science, and mathematics texts.

Reading Beyond the Classroom In this section you will encounter applications, schedules, technical directions, product information, Web pages, and other readings. Learning to analyze these texts will help you in your everyday life and on some standardized tests.

Test Preparation Strategies

In this section, you will find strategies and practice to help you succeed on many different kinds of standardized tests. After closely studying a variety of test formats through annotated examples, you will have an opportunity to practice each format on your own. Additional support will help you think through your answers. You will find strategies for the following:

Successful Test Taking This section provides many suggestions for preparing for and taking tests. The information ranges from analyzing test questions to tips for answering multiple-choice and open-ended test questions.

Reading Tests: Long Selections You will learn how to analyze the structure of a lengthy reading and prepare to answer the comprehension questions that follow it.

Reading Tests: Short Selections These selections may be a paragraph of text, a poem, a chart or graph, or some other item. You will practice the special range of comprehension skills required for these pieces.

Functional Reading Tests These real-world texts present special challenges. You will learn about the various test formats that use applications, product labels, technical directions, Web pages, and more.

Revising-and-Editing Tests These materials test your understanding of English grammar and usage. You may encounter capitalization and punctuation questions. Sometimes the focus is on usage questions such as verb tenses or pronoun agreement issues. You will become familiar with these formats through the guided practice in this section.

Writing Tests Writing prompts and sample student essays will help you understand how to analyze a prompt and what elements make a successful written response. Scoring rubrics and a prompt for practice will prepare you for the writing tests you will take.

User's Guide

The InterActive Reader™ Plus has an easy-to-follow organization, as illustrated by these sample pages from *Woodsong*.

Connect to Your Life

These activities help you see connections between your own life and what happens in the selection.

Key to the Selection

This section provides a "key" to help you unlock the selection so that you can understand and enjoy it. One of these four kinds of keys will appear:

- **What You Need to Know**— important background information.

- **What's the Big Idea?**—an introduction to key words or concepts in the selection.

- **What Do You Think?**—a preview of an important quotation from the selection.

- **What to Listen For**—a chance to examine the sound and rhythm of a piece.

Before You Read

Connect to Your Life

Think of a safety tip for dealing with wild animals or animals you don't know, for example, "Do not pet a dog you don't know." In the space below, create a sign to share your tip with others.

Key to the Memoir

WHAT DO YOU THINK? Read the following lines from *Woodsong* in which Paulsen describes the bears that live near him.

> *We started to treat them like pets.*
> *A major mistake.*

Look at the bear in the picture. Why is it a mistake to treat this animal "like a pet"?

_____

_____

_____

56

Memoir

FROM WOODSONG

BY GARY PAULSEN

PREVIEW In *Woodsong*, Gary Paulsen describes memories of his life. This type of writing is called *memoir.* He lived with his wife, Ruth, and his son, James, in the woods of Minnesota. Their cabin had no plumbing or electricity. This part of Paulsen's memoir describes one lesson he learned about the ways of the woods.

57

PREVIEW

This feature tells you what the selection is about. It may also raise a question that helps you set a purpose for reading.

And there's more!

1 **FOCUS**

Every selection is broken down into parts. A Focus introduces each part and tells you what to look for as you read.

2 **|||⟩ MARK IT UP ⟩**

This feature may appear in the Focus or in the side column next to a boxed passage. It asks you to underline or circle key details in the text.

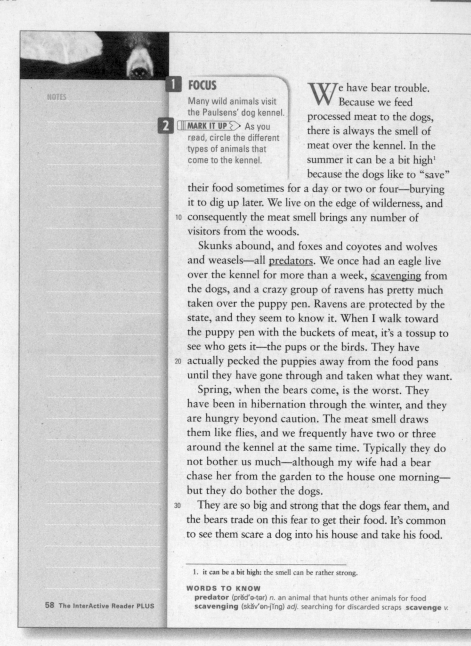

NOTES

1 **FOCUS**

Many wild animals visit the Paulsens' dog kennel.

2 **|||⟩ MARK IT UP ⟩** As you read, circle the different types of animals that come to the kennel.

We have bear trouble. Because we feed processed meat to the dogs, there is always the smell of meat over the kennel. In the summer it can be a bit high[1] because the dogs like to "save" their food sometimes for a day or two or four—burying it to dig up later. We live on the edge of wilderness, and
10 consequently the meat smell brings any number of visitors from the woods.

Skunks abound, and foxes and coyotes and wolves and weasels—all <u>predators</u>. We once had an eagle live over the kennel for more than a week, <u>scavenging</u> from the dogs, and a crazy group of ravens has pretty much taken over the puppy pen. Ravens are protected by the state, and they seem to know it. When I walk toward the puppy pen with the buckets of meat, it's a tossup to see who gets it—the pups or the birds. They have
20 actually pecked the puppies away from the food pans until they have gone through and taken what they want.

Spring, when the bears come, is the worst. They have been in hibernation through the winter, and they are hungry beyond caution. The meat smell draws them like flies, and we frequently have two or three around the kennel at the same time. Typically they do not bother us much—although my wife had a bear chase her from the garden to the house one morning— but they do bother the dogs.
30 They are so big and strong that the dogs fear them, and the bears trade on this fear to get their food. It's common to see them scare a dog into his house and take his food.

---

1. **it can be a bit high:** the smell can be rather strong.

WORDS TO KNOW
 predator (prĕd′ə-tər) *n.* an animal that hunts other animals for food
 scavenging (skăv′ən-jĭng) *adj.* searching for discarded scraps **scavenge** *v.*

58 The InterActive Reader PLUS

Twice we have had dogs killed by rough bear swats that broke their necks—and the bears took their food.

We have evolved[2] an uneasy peace with them, but there is the problem of familiarity. The first time you see a bear in the kennel it is a <u>novelty</u>, but when the same ones are there day after day, you wind up naming some of them (old Notch-Ear, Billy-Jo, etc.). There gets to be a too-
40 relaxed attitude. We started to treat them like pets.

A major mistake.

3 Pause & Reflect

FOCUS

In this section, you will meet a bear called Scarhead. Read to find out how Scarhead and the other bears act.

There was a large male around the kennel for a week or so. He had a white streak across his head, which I guessed was a wound scar from some hunter—bear hunting is allowed here. He wasn't all that bad, so we didn't mind him. He would frighten the dogs and take
50 their hidden stashes now and then, but he didn't harm them, and we became accustomed to him hanging around. We called him Scarhead, and now and again we would joke about him as if he were one of the yard animals.

At this time we had three cats, forty-two dogs, fifteen or twenty chickens, eight ducks, nineteen large white geese, a few banty hens, ten fryers which we'd raised from chicks and couldn't (as my wife put it) "snuff and eat," and six woods-wise goats.

The bears, strangely, didn't bother any of the yard
60 animals. There must have been a rule, or some order to the way they lived, because they would hit the kennel

---
2. **evolved** (ĭ-vŏlvd′): developed by a series of small changes.

5 WORDS TO KNOW
novelty (nŏv′əl-tē) n. something new and unusual

Pause & Reflect

1. Review the details you marked. Then cross out the animal below that does *not* visit the kennel. **(Clarify)**

foxes   skunks

ravens   snakes

2. What did you learn about bears? **(Summarize)**

 4 the boxed passage. How does the author feel about Scarhead at first? Use your voice to express Paulsen's relaxed attitude.

NOTES

Woodsong 59

---

3 Pause & Reflect

Whenever you see these words in the selection, stop reading. Go to the side column and answer the questions.

Pause-and-Reflect questions at the end of every section follow up the Focus activity at the beginning of each section. They give you a quick check of your understanding.

 4 This feature appears in the side column next to a boxed passage. It asks you to use your voice to interpret the passage, and to listen to the language.

5 WORDS TO KNOW

Important **Words to Know** are underlined in each section. Definitions are given at the bottom of the page.

And there's more!

Student Model

These pages show you how one student made use of
The InterActive Reader™ Plus for the selection from *Woodsong*.

Note how this student used the following symbols:

* marks a place where something is important—a main idea, topic sentence, or important detail.

? marks a place where something is unclear or confusing.

! marks a surprising or critical fact, or a turning point in the action—not just a main idea but a major event or theme.

NOTES

What does this

look like?

READ ALOUD the boxed text. Paulsen describes what it was like to see the bear coming at him. As you read, try to express the drama and danger of this scene.

62 The InterActive Reader PLUS

FOCUS
Read to find out if your prediction is right.

Scarhead had been gone for two or three days, and the breeze was right, so I went to burn the trash. I fired it off and went back into the house for a moment—not more than two minutes. When I came back out, Scarhead was in the burn area. His tracks (directly
100 through the tomatoes in the garden) showed he'd come from the south.

He was having a grand time. The fire didn't bother him. He was trying to reach a paw in around the edges of flame to get at whatever smelled so good. He had torn things apart quite a bit—ripped one side off the burn enclosure—and I was having a bad day, and it made me mad.

I was standing across the burning fire from him, and without thinking—because I was so used to him—I picked
110 up a stick, threw it at him, and yelled, "Get out of here."

I have made many mistakes in my life, and will probably make many more, but I hope never to throw a stick at a bear again.

In one rolling motion—the muscles seemed to move within the skin so fast that I couldn't take half a breath—he turned and came for me. Close. I could smell his breath and see the red around the sides of his eyes. Close on me he stopped and raised on his back legs and hung over me, his forelegs and paws hanging
120 down, weaving back and forth gently as he took his time and decided whether or not to tear my head off.

I could not move, would not have time to react. I knew I had nothing to say about it. One blow would break my neck. Whether I lived or died depended on him, on his thinking, on his ideas about me—whether I was worth the bother or not.

I did not think then.

Looking back on it, I don't remember having one coherent[5] thought when it was happening. All I knew was terrible <u>menace</u>. His eyes looked very small as he studied me. He looked down on me for what seemed hours. I did not move, did not breathe, did not think or do anything.

And he lowered.

Perhaps I was not worth the trouble. He lowered slowly and turned back to the trash, and I walked backward halfway to the house and then ran—anger growing now—and took the rifle from the gun rack by the door and came back out.

He was still there, <u>rummaging</u> through the trash. I worked the bolt and fed a cartridge in and aimed at the place where you kill bears and began to squeeze. In raw anger, I began to take up the four pounds of pull necessary to send death into him.

And stopped.

Kill him for what?

That thought crept in.

<u>Kill him for what?</u>

For not killing me? For letting me know <u>it is wrong to throw sticks at four-hundred-pound bears?</u> For not hurting me, for not killing me, I should kill him? I lowered the rifle and ejected the shell and put the gun away. I hope Scarhead is still alive. For what he taught me, I hope he lives long and is very happy, because I learned then—looking up at him while he made up his mind whether or not to end me—that when it is all boiled down, I am nothing more and nothing less than any other animal in the woods. ❖

Pause Reflect

---

5. coherent (kō-hîr′ənt): clear; logical.

WORDS TO KNOW
menace (mĕn′ĭs) *n.* a possible danger; threat
rummaging (rŭm′ĭ-jĭng) *adj.* searching thoroughly **rummage** *v.*

Pause Reflect

1. Why didn't Paulsen shoot the bear? (Draw Conclusions)

The bear didn't kill him so why should he take away the bear's life? The bear let Paulsen live. Now Paulsen should let the bear live.

2. REREAD the boxed passage. What lesson did Paulsen learn? (Question)

If he kills the bear, it would be like killing a human. Just because the bear is not a human doesn't mean that a human is better than any other animal.

CHALLENGE Do you think that Paulsen's decision not to kill the bear was a good one? Mark details in this memoir to support your answer. (Evaluate)

Woodsong 63

Before You Read

Connect to Your Life

What was turning 11 like for you? Or, what will turning 11 be like? Use the word web below to explore your thoughts. Jot down words and phrases that come to mind.

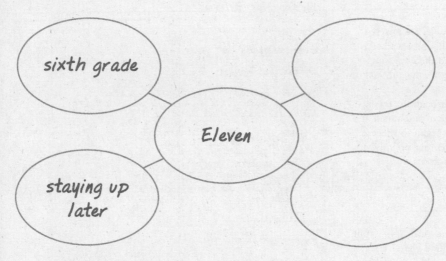

- sixth grade
- Eleven
- staying up later

Key to the Story

WHAT DO YOU THINK? Have you ever felt that time passes too slowly or that it takes too long to grow up? Read the following statement from "Eleven."

And when you wake up on your eleventh birthday you expect to feel eleven, but you don't.

What would you say to Rachel, the character in the story who feels this way? Write your response in the balloon.

ELEVEN

by Sandra Cisneros

PREVIEW   This short story tells how a girl
named Rachel feels about turning 11 years old.
What will happen on her birthday when
Rachel gets a "present" she doesn't want?

Pause & Reflect

1. Circle the best explanation of Rachel's feelings about birthdays: **(Summarize)**

On your birthday you are still all the ages that you were before.

On your birthday everything is different than it was the day before.

When you wake up on your birthday, you feel older right away.

2. Do you agree with Rachel's feelings about birthdays? **(Connect)**

YES / NO, because

FOCUS

Rachel describes what turning 11 years old is like.

MARK IT UP As you read, underline statements that tell you about Rachel's feelings. An example is highlighted.

What they don't under-stand about birthdays and what they never tell you is that when you're eleven, you're also ten, and nine, and eight, and seven, and six, and five, and four, and three, and two, and one. And when you
10 wake up on your eleventh birthday you <u>expect</u> to feel eleven, but you don't. You open your eyes and every-thing's just like yesterday, only it's today. And you don't feel eleven at all. You feel like you're still ten. And you are—underneath the year that makes you eleven.

Like some days you might say something stupid, and that's the part of you that's still ten. Or maybe some days you might need to sit on your mama's lap because you're scared, and that's the part of you that's five. And maybe one day when you're all grown up maybe you will need to cry like if you're three, and
20 that's okay. That's what I tell Mama when she's sad and needs to cry. Maybe she's feeling three.

Because the way you grow old is kind of like an onion or like the rings inside a tree trunk or like my little wooden dolls that fit one inside the other, each year inside the next one. That's how being eleven years old is.

You don't feel eleven. Not right away. It takes a few days, weeks even, sometimes even months before you say Eleven when they ask you. And you don't feel
30 smart eleven, not until you're almost twelve. That's the way it is.

Pause & Reflect

WORDS TO KNOW
expect (ĭk-spĕkt′) v. to look forward to something that is likely to occur

FOCUS

Read to find out what Mrs. Price, Rachel's teacher, does that upsets Rachel.

Only today I wish I didn't have only eleven years rattling inside me like pennies in a tin Band-Aid box. Today I wish I was one hundred and two instead of eleven because if I was one hundred and two I'd have known what to say when Mrs. Price put the red sweater on my desk. I would've known how to tell her it wasn't mine instead of just sitting there with that look on my face and nothing coming out of my mouth.

"Whose is this?" Mrs. Price says, and she holds the red sweater up in the air for all the class to see. "Whose? It's been sitting in the coatroom for a month."

"Not mine," says everybody. "Not me."

"It has to belong to somebody," Mrs. Price keeps saying, but nobody can remember. It's an ugly sweater with red plastic buttons and a collar and sleeves all stretched out like you could use it for a jump rope. It's maybe a thousand years old and even if it belonged to me I wouldn't say so.

Maybe because I'm skinny, maybe because she doesn't like me, that stupid Sylvia Saldívar says, "I think it belongs to Rachel." An ugly sweater like that, all raggedy and old, but Mrs. Price believes her. Mrs. Price takes the sweater and puts it right on my desk, but when I open my mouth nothing comes out.

"That's not, I don't, you're not . . . Not mine," I finally say in a little voice that was maybe me when I was four.

"Of course it's yours," Mrs. Price says. "I remember you wearing it once." Because she's older and the teacher, she's right and I'm not.

Pause & Reflect

NOTES

Pause & Reflect

1. **MARK IT UP** Why does Rachel wish she were 102 instead of 11? Find the answer in the text and circle it. **(Clarify)**

2. Place a check mark next to the three details below that correctly describe the sweater. **(Clarify)**
   ❏ plastic buttons
   ❏ blue
   ❏ ugly
   ❏ stretched out
   ❏ wool

FOCUS

Rachel looks at the ugly, red sweater on her desk. Notice how the sweater makes her feel.

| MARK IT UP ⟩⟩ As you read, underline details that show how Rachel reacts to the sweater.

Not mine, not mine, not mine, but Mrs. Price is already turning to page thirty-two, and math problem number four. I don't know
70 why but all of a sudden I'm feeling sick inside, like the part of me that's three wants to come out of my eyes, only I squeeze them shut tight and bite down on my teeth real hard and try to remember today I am eleven, eleven. Mama is making a cake for me for tonight, and when Papa comes home everybody will sing Happy birthday, happy birthday to you.

But when the sick feeling goes away and I open my
80 eyes, the red sweater's still sitting there like a big red mountain. I move the red sweater to the corner of my desk with my ruler. I move my pencil and books and eraser as far from it as possible. I even move my chair a little to the right. Not mine, not mine, not mine.

In my head I'm thinking how long till lunchtime, how long till I can take the red sweater and throw it over the schoolyard fence, or leave it hanging on a parking meter, or bunch it up into a little ball and toss it in the alley. <u>Except</u> when math period ends, Mrs.
90 Price says loud and in front of everybody, "Now, Rachel, that's enough," because she sees I've shoved the red sweater to the tippy-tip corner of my desk and it's hanging all over the edge like a waterfall, but I don't care.

"Rachel," Mrs. Price says. She says it like she's getting mad. "You put that sweater on right now and no more nonsense."

WORDS TO KNOW
except (ĭk-sĕpt') *prep.* other than; but

"But it's not—"

"Now!" Mrs. Price says.

100 This is when I wish I wasn't eleven, because all the years inside of me—ten, nine, eight, seven, six, five, four, three, two, and one—are pushing at the back of my eyes when I put one arm through one sleeve of the sweater that smells like cottage cheese, and then the other arm through the other and stand there with my arms apart like if the sweater hurts me and it does, all itchy and full of germs that aren't even mine.

That's when everything I've been holding in since this morning, since when Mrs. Price put the sweater 110 on my desk, finally lets go, and all of a <u>sudden</u> I'm crying in front of everybody. I wish I was <u>invisible</u> but I'm not. I'm eleven and it's my birthday today and I'm crying like I'm three in front of everybody. I put my head down on the desk and bury my face in my stupid clown-sweater arms. My face all hot and spit coming out of my mouth because I can't stop the little animal noises from coming out of me, until there aren't any more tears left in my eyes, and it's just my body shaking like when you have the hiccups, and my 120 whole head hurts like when you drink milk too fast.

But the worst part is right before the bell rings for lunch. That stupid Phyllis Lopez, who is even dumber than Sylvia Saldívar, says she remembers the red sweater is hers! I take it off right away and give it to her, only Mrs. Price pretends like everything's okay.

Today I'm eleven. There's a cake Mama's making for tonight, and when Papa comes home from work we'll eat it. There'll be candles and presents, and everybody will sing Happy birthday, happy birthday to you, 130 Rachel, only it's too late.

sudden (sŭd'n) *adj.* happening without warning
invisible (ĭn-vĭz'ə-bəl) *adj.* impossible to see; not visible

MARK IT UP > Reread the boxed passage. Circle details that help you picture Rachel. (Visualize)

NOTES

NOTES

Pause & Reflect

1. Why does Rachel feel so embarrassed? **(Infer)**

_____

_____

_____

_____

_____

2. Do you sympathize with Rachel's feelings? **(Connect)**

YES / NO, because

_____

_____

_____

_____

_____

_____

_____

_____

On page 4, Cisneros writes that "growing old is kind of like an onion." This is an example of a **simile,** a type of figurative language that compares one thing to another using *like* or *as.* Find and star other similes in the story. How do the similes help you understand Rachel's feelings? **(Analyze)**

I'm eleven today. I'm eleven, ten, nine, eight, seven, six, five, four, three, two, and one, but I wish I was one hundred and two. I wish I was anything but eleven, because I want today to be far away already, far away like a runaway balloon, like a tiny *o* in the sky, so tiny-tiny you have to close your eyes to see it. ❖

Pause & Reflect

Active Reading SkillBuilder

Connecting

When you read a story, you can connect story events or a character's actions to your own life. As you read "Eleven," think about the graphic below. Do you remember how you felt when you turned eleven, ten, or five? Jot down details about Rachel's birthday in one column, and recollections about your own birthday in the other column.

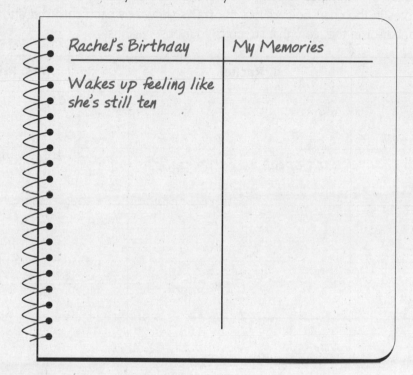

Rachel's Birthday	My Memories
Wakes up feeling like she's still ten	

1. Explain Rachel's ideas about the age eleven. Use what you read and the graphic above to help you explain your answer.

2. Are your ideas about age eleven the same as Rachel's? Why or why not?

3. Have you ever felt shy on your birthday or wished that you were older, the way Rachel does? Explain.

Literary Analysis SkillBuilder

Character

A **character** is any person, animal, or imaginary creature in a story. The **main character** is usually the focus of the action in the story and is most important. There may be one or more **minor characters,** who interact in some way with the main character to move the action along. To learn more about the characters of Rachel and Mrs. Price, take notes in the chart below. Note the **traits** shown by each character and the language or behavior in the story that supports your observations.

	Rachel	Mrs. Price
Trait	shy	
Evidence	can't speak up for herself	
Trait		
Evidence		
Trait		
Evidence		
Trait		
Evidence		

Words to Know SkillBuilder

Words to Know

except	expect	invisible	sudden

A. Circle the word that best completes each sentence.

1. Rachel wished that she were (indivisible, invisible) when Mrs. Price gave her the sweater.

2. If the incident had occurred any day (except, accept) her birthday, it would have been less upsetting.

3. She knew what to (except, expect) when she arrived home for dinner.

4. So that she would not attract attention, she avoided making (sudden, sullen) movements.

B. On the line next to each word pair, write whether the words are synonyms or antonyms. **Synonyms** are words with the same or similar meaning. **Antonyms** are words with opposite meanings.

1. assume–expect _____

2. obvious–invisible _____

3. gradual–sudden _____

4. but–except _____

C. Write a description of her day that Rachel might have given to her mother. Use **all** the Words to Know.

_____

_____

_____

_____

Before You Read

Connect to Your Life

Would you like to be an explorer? Suppose you were invited to join an expedition to the North Pole. Using what you already know about the Arctic region, make a list of items you would pack for the trip.

Important Items	Extras
compass	camera
thermometer	books
waterproof clothes	

Key to the Biography

WHAT YOU NEED TO KNOW Robert E. Peary and Matthew Henson were two of the first people to reach the North Pole. Peary said of Henson, who accompanied Peary as his servant, "I can't get along without him."

WHO: Matthew Henson was an adventurous African American living in a racially segregated, or divided, society.

WHEN: In 1891 Henson agreed to accompany Peary on a journey.

WHERE: On their way to the North Pole, Peary and Henson undertook five expeditions, or journeys, into harsh Arctic regions.

MATTHEW HENSON AT THE TOP OF THE WORLD

by Jim Haskins

PREVIEW   As a child, Matthew Henson first lost his mother and then other close family members. Later, he overcame poverty and racial prejudice to become one of the first explorers to attempt to reach the North Pole.

READING TIP **Primary Sources**
Slow down when
you see sections
such as the boxed paragraph
on this page, set off in
quotation marks or *italic* type.
Mark important words or
phrases within them.

NOTES

─────────────

─────────────

─────────────

─────────────

─────────────

─────────────

─────────────

▥ **MARK IT UP** ⟩ **KEEP TRACK**
Remember to use these
marks to keep track of your
reading.

  ✳ This is important.

  ? I have a question about
     this.

  ! This is a surprise.

FOCUS
Read to find out about
Matthew Henson's early
life in Maryland.

While the explorers of the American West faced many dangers in their travels, at least game and water were usually plentiful; and if winter with its cold and snow overtook them, they could, in time, expect warmth and spring. For Matthew Henson, in his explorations with Robert Peary at the North Pole, this was hardly the case. In many ways, to forge ahead into

10 the icy Arctic took far greater <u>stamina</u> and courage than did the earlier explorers' travels, and Henson possessed such hardiness. As Donald MacMillan, a member of the expedition, was later to write: "Peary knew Matt Henson's real worth. . . . Highly respected by the Eskimos,[1] he was easily the most popular man on board ship. . . . Henson . . . was of more real value to our Commander than [expedition members] Bartlett, Marvin, Borup, Goodsell, and myself all put together. Matthew Henson went to the Pole with Peary because he was a

20 better man than any one of us."

Matthew Henson was born on August 8, 1866, in Charles County, Maryland, some forty-four miles south of Washington, D.C. His parents were poor, free tenant farmers[2] who barely eked a living from the sandy soil. The Civil War had ended the year before Matthew was born, bringing with it a great deal of bitterness on the part of former slave-owners. One manifestation of this hostility was the terrorist activity on the part of the Ku Klux Klan[3] in Maryland. Many

30 free and newly freed blacks had suffered at the hands

---

1. **Eskimos:** a term used in this account to refer to the native peoples of the Arctic; the Eskimos of Greenland, such as those who traveled on Peary's expeditions, call themselves Inuit.
2. **tenant farmers:** people who farm land rented from others.
3. **Ku Klux Klan** (kōō´ klŭks klăn´): a secret society, organized in the South after the Civil War, that used terrorism against minorities to show the power of whites.

WORDS TO KNOW
  stamina (stăm´ə-nə) *n.* the strength to withstand hardship

of this band of night riders.[4] Matthew's father, Lemuel Henson, felt it was only a matter of time before the Klan turned its vengeful eyes on his family. That, and the fact that by farming he was barely able to support them, caused him to decide to move north to Washington, D.C.

Pause & Reflect

FOCUS

In this section, you will read about the hardships Henson faces in his youth.

MARK IT UP As you read, underline examples of these hardships. One has been highlighted for you.

At first things went well for the Henson family, but then Matthew's mother died and
40 his father found himself unable to care for Matthew. The seven-year-old boy was sent to live with his uncle, a kindly man who welcomed him and enrolled him in the N Street School. Six years later, however, another blow fell; his uncle himself fell upon hard times and could no longer support Matthew. The boy couldn't return to his father, because Lemuel
50 had recently died. Alone, homeless, and penniless, Matthew was forced to fend for himself.

Matthew Henson was a bright boy and a hard worker, although he had only a sixth-grade education. Calling upon his own resourcefulness, he found a job as a dishwasher in a small restaurant owned by a woman named Janey Moore. When Janey discovered that Matthew had no place to stay, she fixed a cot for him in the kitchen; Matthew had found a home again.

---

4. **night riders:** mounted and usually masked white men who committed acts of terror against African Americans.

Pause & Reflect

1. Why did young Matthew Henson's father move his family to Washington, D.C.? Cross off the *wrong* answer below. **(Cause and Effect)**

   to escape poverty

   to escape the raids of the Ku Klux Klan

   to take a job with the government

   to find new work

2. **REREAD** the boxed text on page 14. What was Donald MacMillan's opinion of Matthew Henson? Circle four words below. **(Clarify)**

   brave   respected

   popular   handsome

   humble   hardy

NOTES

Matthew Henson didn't want to spend his life
60 waiting on people and washing dishes, however, no
matter how kind Janey was. He had seen enough of
the world through his schoolbooks to want more, to
want adventure. This desire was reinforced by the men
who frequented the restaurant—sailors from many
ports, who spun tales of life on the ocean and of
strange and wonderful places. As Henson listened,
wide-eyed, to their stories, he decided, as had so many
boys before him, that the life of a sailor with its
adventures and dangers was for him. Having made up
70 his mind, the fourteen-year-old packed up what little
he owned, bade good-bye to Janey, and was off to
Baltimore to find a ship.

Although Matthew Henson's early life seems harsh,
in many ways he was very lucky. When he arrived in
Baltimore, he signed on as a cabin boy on the *Katie
Hines*, the master of which was a Captain Childs. For
many sailors at that time, life at sea was brutal and
filled with hard work, <u>deprivation</u>, and a "taste of the
cat": whipping. The captains of many vessels were
80 petty despots,[5] ruling with an iron hand and having
little regard for a seaman's health or safety. Matthew
was fortunate to find just the opposite in Childs.

Captain Childs took the boy under his wing.
Although Matthew of course had to do the work he
was assigned, Captain Childs took a fatherly interest
in him. Having an excellent private library on the ship,
the captain saw to Matthew's education, insisting that
he read widely in geography, history, mathematics, and
literature while they were at sea.

---

5. **petty despots:** mean, harsh persons in charge of small companies or territories.

WORDS TO KNOW
   deprivation (dĕp′rə-vā′shən) *n.* a lack of what is needed for survival or
   comfort

90　　The years on the *Katie Hines* were good ones for
Matthew Henson. During that time he saw China, Japan,
the Philippines, France, Africa, and southern Russia; he
sailed through the Arctic to Murmansk. But in 1885 it all
ended; Captain Childs fell ill and died at sea. Unable to
face staying on the *Katie Hines* under a new skipper,
Matthew left the ship at Baltimore and found a place on
a fishing schooner bound for Newfoundland. Now, for
the first time, Henson encountered the kind of unthinking
cruelty and tyranny so often found on ships at that time.
100 The ship was filthy, the crew surly and resentful of their
black shipmate, and the captain a dictator. As soon as he
was able, Matthew left the ship in Canada and made his
way back to the United States, finally arriving in
Washington, D.C., only to find that things there had
changed during the years he had been at sea.

Pause & Reflect

FOCUS

Read to find out how
Henson's life changes
when he meets the
explorer Robert E. Peary.

Opportunities for blacks
had been limited when
Henson had left Washington
in 1871, but by the time he
110 returned they were almost
nonexistent. Post–Civil War
reconstruction[6] had failed, bringing with its failure a
great deal of bitter resentment toward blacks. Jobs
were scarce, and the few available were menial ones.

---

6. **reconstruction:** The period (1865–1877) during which the states of the defeated
Confederacy were controlled by the federal government before being readmitted
to the Union.

WORDS TO KNOW
tyranny (tĭr′ə-nē) *n.* an extremely harsh or unjust government or authority
resentful (rĭ-zĕnt′fəl) *adj.* angry due to a feeling of being treated unfairly
menial (mē′nē-əl) *adj.* fit for a servant

Pause & Reflect

1. What do you think was
the greatest hardship
Matthew Henson faced
in his youth? (Evaluate)

2. Why did Henson decide to
go to sea? (Infer)

3. **REREAD** the boxed text
on this page.
What happened
to Matthew after Captain
Childs died? (Clarify)

Matthew finally found a job as a stock clerk[7] in a clothing and hat store, B. H. Steinmetz and Sons, bitterly wondering if this was how he was to spend the rest of his life. But his luck was still holding.

Steinmetz recognized that Matthew Henson was
120 bright and hard working. One day Lieutenant Robert E. Peary, a young navy officer, walked into the store, looking for tropical hats. After being shown a number of hats, Peary unexpectedly offered Henson a job as his personal servant. Steinmetz had recommended him, Peary said, but the job wouldn't be easy. He was bound for Nicaragua to head an engineering survey team.[8] Would Matthew be willing to put up with the discomforts and hazards of such a trip? Thinking of the adventure and opportunities offered, Henson
130 eagerly said yes, little realizing that a partnership had just been formed that would span years and be filled with exploration, danger, and fame.

Robert E. Peary was born in Cresson, Pennsylvania, in 1856 but was raised in Maine, where his mother had returned after his father's death in 1859. After graduating from Bowdoin College, Peary worked as a surveyor for four years and in 1881 joined the navy's corps of civil engineers. One result of his travels for the navy and of his reading was an ardent desire for
140 adventure. "I shall not be satisfied," Peary wrote to his mother, "until my name is known from one end of the earth to the other." This was a goal Matthew Henson could understand. As he later said, "I recognized in [Peary] the qualities that made me willing to engage myself in his service." In November 1887, Henson and

REREAD the boxed passage. What do Robert Peary and Matthew Henson have in common? (Compare and Contrast)

---

7. **stock clerk:** a person in an office or store who keeps track of merchandise.
8. **engineering survey team:** a group knowledgable in the planning, construction, and management of land and land boundaries.

WORDS TO KNOW
surveyor (sər-vā'ər) *n.* a person who determines land boundaries by measuring angles and distances
ardent (är'dnt) *adj.* full of enthusiasm or devotion

Peary set sail for Nicaragua, along with forty-five other engineers and a hundred black Jamaicans.

Peary's job was to study the feasibility[9] of digging a canal across Nicaragua (that canal that would later be 150 dug across the Isthmus of Panama).[10] The survey took until June of 1888, when the surveying party headed back to the United States. Henson knew he had done a good job for Peary, but even as they started north, Peary said nothing to him about continuing on as his servant. It was a great surprise, then, when one day Peary approached Henson with a <u>proposition</u>. He wanted to try to raise money for an expedition to the Arctic, and he wanted Henson to accompany him. Henson quickly accepted, saying he would go whether 160 Peary could pay him or not.

"It was in June, 1891, that I started on my first trip to the Arctic regions, as a member of what was known as the 'North Greenland Expedition,'" Matthew Henson later wrote. So began the first of five expeditions on which Henson would accompany Peary.

Pause & Reflect

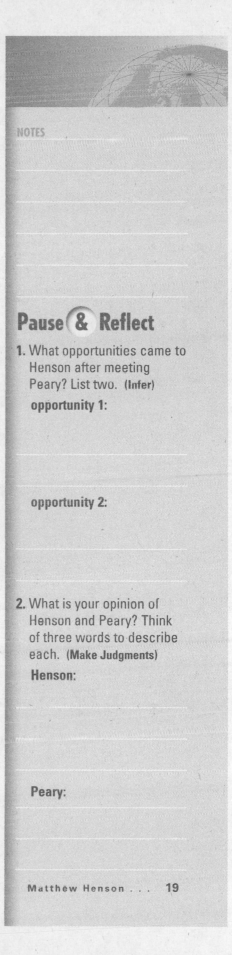

NOTES

Pause & Reflect

1. What opportunities came to Henson after meeting Peary? List two. **(Infer)**

   opportunity 1:

   opportunity 2:

2. What is your opinion of Henson and Peary? Think of three words to describe each. **(Make Judgments)**

   Henson:

   Peary:

---

9. **feasibility** (fē′zə-bĭl′ĭ-tē): the possibility of being completed successfully.

10. **Isthmus** (ĭs′məs) **of Panama:** a narrow strip of land connecting the North and South American continents.

WORDS TO KNOW
proposition (prŏp′ə-zĭsh′ən) *n.* a plan offered for acceptance

FOCUS

Henson begins his adventure with Peary.

▐▌**MARK IT UP** ⬦ As you read, underline details that tell you about the challenges they meet.

During this first trip to Greenland, on a ship named *Kite*, Peary discovered how

170 valuable Henson was to any expedition. He reported that Henson was able to establish "a friendly relationship with the Eskimos, who believed him to be somehow related to them because of his brown skin. . . ." Peary's expedition was also greatly aided by Henson's expert handling of the Eskimos, dogs, and equipment. Henson also hunted with the Eskimos for meat for the expedition and cooked under the supervision of Josephine Peary, Robert's wife.

180 On the expedition's return to New York, September 24, 1892, Peary wrote, "Henson, my faithful colored[11] boy, a hard worker and <u>apt</u> at anything, . . . showed himself . . . the equal of others in the party."

This first expedition to the Arctic led to several others, but it was with the 1905 expedition that Peary first tried to find that mystical point,[12] the North Pole, the sole goal of the 1908 expedition.

On July 6, 1908, the *Roosevelt* sailed from New York City. Aboard it were the supplies and men for an

190 expedition to reach the North Pole. Accompanying Peary were Captain Robert Bartlett and Ross Marvin, who had been with Peary on earlier expeditions; George Borup, a young graduate from Yale and the youngest member of the group; Donald MacMillan, a teacher; and a doctor, J. W. Goodsell. And, of course, Matthew Henson. In Greenland the group was joined by forty-one Eskimos and 246 dogs, plus the supplies. "The ship," Henson wrote, "is now in a most perfect

---

11. **colored:** Peary's use of this term to describe Matthew Henson as a non-white was common during the period. It is now considered offensive and racist.

12. **mystical point:** a place with a sense of sacredness and mystery.

WORDS TO KNOW
   apt (ăpt) *adj.* quick to learn or understand

state of dirtiness." On September 5, the *Roosevelt*
200 arrived at Cape Sheridan, and the group began
preparing for their journey, moving supplies north to
Cape Columbia by dog sled to establish a base camp.
Peary named the camp Crane City in honor of Zenas
Crane, who had contributed $10,000 to the expedition.

The plan was to have two men, Bartlett and Borup, go
ahead of the rest of the group to cut a trail stretching
from the base camp to the North Pole. On February 28,
the two men set out, and on March 1, the remainder of
the expedition started north, following the trail Bartlett
210 and Borup had cut the day before. At first, trouble
seemed to plague them. On the first day, three of the
sledges[13] broke, Henson's among them. Fortunately,
Henson was able to repair them, despite the fact that it
was nearly 50 degrees below zero.

As the days passed, further trouble came the way of
the expedition. Several times they encountered leads—
open channels of water—and were forced to wait until
the ice closed over before proceeding. On March 14,
Peary decided to send Donald MacMillan and Dr.
220 Goodsell back to the base camp. MacMillan could
hardly walk, because he had frozen a heel when his
foot had slipped into one of the leads. Dr. Goodsell
was exhausted. As the expedition went on, more men
were sent back due to exhaustion and frostbite.
George Borup was sent back on March 20, and, on the
26th, so was Ross Marvin.

Pause & Reflect

---

13. **sledges:** sleds pulled by dogs.

Pause & Reflect

1. How did Henson show his value to the expedition? Check three phrases below. **(Main Idea and Details)**
   ❑ repairing the sleds
   ❑ hunting with the Eskimos
   ❑ taking care of the sick
   ❑ handling the dogs

2. Do you think the expeditions would have been successful without Henson? **(Evaluate)**
   YES / NO, because

NOTES

the boxed passage. As you read, try to picture the journey. How might you feel in such conditions? **(Connect)**

FOCUS

Henson and Peary struggle to reach the North Pole. Read to find out about their journey.

Although the expedition had encountered problems with subzero temperatures, 230 with open water, and in handling the dogs, they had had no real injuries. On Ross Marvin's return trip to the base camp, however, he met with tragedy. On his journey, Marvin was accompanied by two Eskimos. He told them that he would go ahead to scout the trail. About an hour later, the Eskimos came upon a hole in the ice; floating in it was Marvin's coat. Marvin had gone through thin ice and, unable to save himself, had drowned or frozen. 240 The Peary expedition had suffered its first—and fortunately its last—fatality.

By April 1, Peary had sent back all of the original expedition except for four Eskimos and Matthew Henson. When Bartlett, the last man to be sent back, asked Peary why he didn't also send Henson, Peary replied, "I can't get along without him." The remnant of the original group pushed on.

> *We had been travelling eighteen to twenty hours out of every twenty-four. Man, that was killing work!* 250 *Forced marches all the time. From all our other expeditions we had found out that we couldn't carry food for more than fifty days, fifty-five at a pinch. . . .*
>
> *We used to travel by night and sleep in the warmest part of the day. I was ahead most of the time with two of the Eskimos.*

So Matthew Henson described the grueling journey. Finally, on the morning of April 6, Peary called a halt. Henson wrote: "I was driving ahead and was swinging around to the right. . . . The Commander, who was 260 about 50 feet behind me, called to me and said we would go into camp. . . ." In fact, both Henson and Peary felt they might have reached the Pole already.

That day, Peary took readings with a sextant[14] and determined that they were within three miles of the Pole. Later he sledged ten miles north and found he was traveling south; to return to camp, Peary would have to return north and then head south in another direction—something that could only happen at the North Pole. To be absolutely sure, the next day Peary

270 again took readings from solar observations. It was the North Pole, he was sure.

On that day Robert Peary had Matthew Henson plant the American flag at the North Pole. Peary then cut a piece from the flag and placed it and two letters in a glass jar that he left at the Pole. The letters read:

> *90 N. Lat., North Pole*
> *April 6, 1909*

Arrived here today, 27 marches from C. Columbia.
I have with me 5 men, Matthew Henson, colored,
280 *Ootah, Egingwah, Seegloo, and Ooqueah, Eskimos;*
5 sledges and 38 dogs. My ship, the S.S. Roosevelt, *is in winter quarters at Cape Sheridan, 90 miles east of Columbia.*

The expedition under my command which has succeeded in reaching the Pole is under the auspices[15] of the Peary Arctic Club of New York City, and has been fitted out and sent north by members and friends of the Club for the purpose of securing this geographical prize, if possible, for the honor and
290 *prestige[16] of the United States of America.*

READING TIP This letter, written by Peary, is a **primary source** used by the author. To prove he got there first, Peary left the document at the North Pole. He wrote the letter in the style of a report, or business letter. The footnotes may help you understand it.

NOTES

---

14. **sextant:** an instrument used to measure the positions of heavenly bodies.

15. **auspices:** protection and support.

16. **prestige:** high standing or esteem.

1. Why did Peary keep Henson with him rather than sending him back to base camp with the others? **(Clarify)**

2. ⫍‖‖‖ MARK IT UP ⟩ How did Peary know that he had reached the North Pole? Circle details on page 23 that tell the answer. **(Main Idea and Details)**

NOTES

The officers of the Club are Thomas H. Hubbard of New York, President; Zenas Crane, of Mass., Vice-president; Herbert L. Bridgman, of New York, Secretary and Treasurer.

I start back for Cape Columbia tomorrow.

                      Robert E. Peary
                      United States Navy

                  90 N. Lat., North Pole
                  April 6, 1909

300   I have today hoisted the national ensign of the United States of America at this place, which my observations indicate to be the North Polar axis of the earth, and have formally taken possession of the entire region, and adjacent,[17] for and in the name of the President of the United States of America.

I leave this record and United States flag in possession.

                      Robert E. Peary
                      United States Navy

FOCUS

Read to find out about the journey from the North Pole and Henson's later years.

⫍‖‖‖ MARK IT UP ⟩ As you read, circle details that tell you what happens to Henson.

310   Having accomplished their goal, the small group set out on the return journey. It was, Matthew Henson wrote, "17 days of haste, toil, and misery. . . . We crossed lead after lead, sometimes like a bareback rider in the circus, balancing on cake after cake of ice." Finally they

---

17. **adjacent** (ə-jā′sənt): close to, nearby, next to.

reached the *Roosevelt,* where they could rest and eat
320 well at last. The Pole had been conquered!

During the return trip to New York City, Henson
became increasingly puzzled by Peary's behavior. "Not
once in [three weeks]," Henson wrote, "did he speak a
word to me. Then he . . . ordered me to get to work.
Not a word about the North Pole or anything
connected with it." Even when the *Roosevelt* docked
in New York in September of 1909, Peary remained
withdrawn and silent, saying little to the press and
quickly withdrawing to his home in Maine.

330 The ostensible[18] reason for his silence was that when
the group returned to New York, they learned that Dr.
Frederick A. Cook was claiming that *he* had gone to
the North Pole—and done so before Peary reached it.
Peary told his friends that he wished to wait for his
own proofs to be <u>validated</u> by the scientific societies
before he spoke. He felt sure that Cook would not be
able to present the kinds of evidence that he could
present, and so it proved.

On December 15, Peary was declared the first to
340 reach the North Pole; Cook could not present
adequate evidence that he had made the discovery.
Peary and Bartlett were awarded gold medals by the
National Geographic Society; Henson was not.
Because Henson was black, his contributions to the
expedition were not recognized for many years.

After 1909, Henson worked in a variety of jobs.
For a while, he was a parking-garage attendant in
Brooklyn, and at the age of forty-six, he became a
clerk in the U.S. customshouse in Lower Manhattan.
350 In the meantime, friends tried again and again to have
his contributions to the expedition recognized. At last,

---

18. **ostensible** (ŏ-stĕn′sə-bəl): claimed, but not necessarily true.

WORDS TO KNOW
  validate (văl′ĭ-dāt′) *v.* to show to be correct

Pause & Reflect

1. Which two phrases below are true of Matthew Henson after returning from the North Pole? Circle them. **(Summarize)**

worked different jobs

awarded a gold medal by the National Geographic Society

proved that Cook had reached the North Pole first

honored by the state of Maryland after his death

2. What most impressed you about Matthew Henson? **(Evaluate)**

CHALLENGE Do you think Peary treated Henson fairly? Underline places in the text that support your opinion. **(Analyze)**

in 1937, nearly thirty years after the expedition, he was invited to join the Explorers Club in New York, and in 1944, Congress authorized a medal for all of the men on the expedition, including Matthew Henson.

After his death in New York City on March 9, 1955, another lasting tribute[19] was made to Henson's endeavors.[20] In 1961, his home state of Maryland placed a bronze tablet in memory of him in the state
360 house. It reads, in part:

MATTHEW ALEXANDER HENSON
Co-discoverer of the North Pole
with Admiral Robert Edwin Peary
April 6, 1909

Son of Maryland, exemplification of courage, fortitude, and patriotism, whose valiant deeds of noble devotion under the command of Admiral Robert Edwin Peary, in pioneer Arctic exploration and discovery, established everlasting prestige and
370 *glory for his state and country* ❖

Pause & Reflect

---

19. **tribute:** a gift, payment, or other sign of gratitude, respect, or admiration.

20. **endeavors:** efforts to do or accomplish something.

Active Reading SkillBuilder

Identifying Main Ideas and Details

Identifying the **main ideas** of a selection helps you understand the key points the author is trying to make. Supporting details add weight to each main idea. Use the following chart to note the main idea and **details** of a few important paragraphs in "Matthew Henson at the Top of the World."

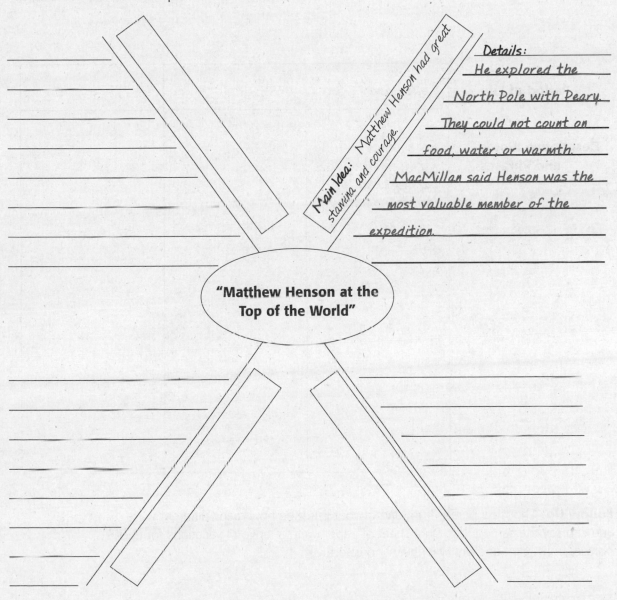

Main Idea: Matthew Henson had great stamina and courage.

Details:
He explored the
North Pole with Peary.
They could not count on
food, water, or warmth.
MacMillan said Henson was the
most valuable member of the
expedition.

"Matthew Henson at the Top of the World"

Literary Analysis SkillBuilder

Biography

A **biography** is the story of one person's life, told by another person. Biographers try to turn facts into a **narrative,** or a story, by using vivid language. Use the following chart to list descriptive words and phrases in three interesting passages of "Matthew Henson at the Top of the World."

Period of Life	Childhood		
Descriptive Words and Phrases	free tenant-farmers who barely eked a living from the sandy soil		

Follow Up: Choose a phrase from one of your lists. See how many different ways you can say the same thing. On a sheet of paper, write a range of variations for each phrase, from short and dry to lengthy and colorful.

Words to Know SkillBuilder

Words to Know

apt	deprivation	proposition	stamina	tyranny
ardent	menial	resentful	surveyor	validate

A. On each blank line, write the Word to Know that the rhyme describes.

When someone cuts in line and makes you wait and wait and wait,
You may feel this; it's how you feel toward many things you hate. _____ (1)

To keep on keeping on when life is hard and things are rough,
You must have some of this. Successful people have enough. _____ (2)

When kings are mean or queens are cruel or bosses are unfair,
The folks they rule object to this. (The rulers, though, don't care.) _____ (3)

Just where does my land end, I wonder. Where does yours begin?
To help us find the answers, this is who we could call in. _____ (4)

This could be "Let's go fishing!" or "Let's vote for So-and-So."
And people who agree say "Yes," and those who don't say "No." _____ (5)

If this describes the audience where rock stars are appearing,
Besides the music, you will hear an awful lot of cheering. _____ (6)

Scrubbing floors is this, and shining shoes, and digging, too.
In all our lives, this word describes a lot of things we do. _____ (7)

People who suffer from this are in need.
It may be a serious problem, indeed. _____ (8)

If you're described as being this, it means that you have skills,
Perhaps at writing, fixing cars, or raising daffodils. _____ (9)

If you do this to check a fact so it is not a guess,
And someone asks, "Can you support that?" you can then say "Yes." _____ (10)

B. On a separate sheet of paper, write a letter to Matthew Henson. Ask him about his experiences, or tell him what you admire about him. Use at least **five** of the Words to Know in your letter.

Before You Read

Connect to Your Life

What do you know about wilderness fires? Use the chart below.
Fill in the first and second columns before you read. Fill in the third
column after you have finished reading.

What I Know	What I Want to Learn	What I Learned
Wilderness fires can spread quickly.		

Key to the Informative Article

WHAT YOU NEED TO KNOW
In wilderness areas, fires can be started by lightning as well as by
humans. Park managers must decide whether to let fires burn or put
them out.

WHY Fires are not entirely harmful. Burned plants and trees renew
nutrients in the soil, and fires can clear away old branches. Many
animals, from ants to bears, find a new source of food in the plants
that grow in the rich after-fire soil.

HOW In the summer of 1988, Yellowstone rangers let small fires burn
while they waited for the "summer rains" to come. But the fires
raged out of control, and the rain held off all the way into September.

SUMMER OF FIRE

by Patricia Lauber

PREVIEW Large fires can destroy huge areas of forest and threaten people who live or work nearby. That is what happened in Yellowstone National Park during the very dry summer of 1988. How much of the park was saved from burning? What were the effects of the fires? In this informative article, Patricia Lauber relates the dramatic details.

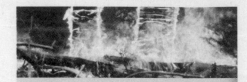

FOCUS

In this section you will find out how the "summer of fire" gets started.

▐▐▐ **MARK IT UP** ⟩ As you read, underline the details that tell you what the summer of 1988 was like. An example is shown.

The summer of 1988 was hot and dry in much of the United States. Above plains and prairies, the sun blazed out of an ever blue sky, baking fields and <u>withering</u> crops. Ponds and streams dried up. Rivers shrank. In places the very
10 earth cracked open as underground water supplies dwindled away.

Farther west, forests were <u>tinder</u> dry. Sometimes skies grew dark with storm clouds. Thunder growled and lightning crackled, but little rain fell. Lightning strikes started forest fires that raged across the Rockies and other ranges with the roar of jumbo jets on take-off. Night skies turned red and yellow where flames soared 300 feet into the air. Smoke, carried on the winds, darkened skies as far away as Spokane and
20 Minneapolis–St. Paul. Airline passengers, flying high above the fires, could smell the smoke. Before the rains and snows of autumn came, 2,600,000 acres had burned in the West and Alaska, an area twice the size of Delaware.

In Yellowstone the fire season started on May 24, when lightning struck a tree in the northeastern part of the park. The fire stayed small. Rain fell later in the day and put it out. That was what usually happened. In Yellowstone, winters are long and cold, summers
30 short and often rainy. Many people thought you couldn't set fire to the forest if you tried.

On June 23 lightning started a fire near Shoshone Lake in the southern part of the park. On June 25

WORDS TO KNOW
withering (wĭth′ər-ĭng) *adj.* causing to dry out and shrivel up; wilting
  wither *v.*
tinder (tĭn′dər) *n.* a material, such as dry twigs, that is used to start a fire because it burns easily

another bolt of lightning started a fire in the northwest. These fires did not go out, and no one tried to put them out. Park policy was to let wildfires burn unless they <u>threatened</u> lives or property. Also, there seemed no reason to worry about the fires. Although winters in the 1980s had been dry, with little snow, 40 summers had been unusually wet. The summer of 1988 was expected to be wet too.

Pause & Reflect

FOCUS

Read to find out what causes the fires in Yellowstone to spread.

But in 1988 the rains of summer did not come. The Shoshone and other fires blazed and spread. By mid-July, 8,600 acres had burned. Park officials decided that all fires should be put out, no matter whether they were wildfires or caused by human carelessness.

50   Fire fighters arrived by the hundreds to attack fires from the ground. Helicopters and airplanes attacked from above. But new fires started in the park. In 1988 Yellowstone had more than 50 lightning strikes, twice the normal number. Fires in neighboring national forests swept into the park. Old fires burned on. And still the rains did not come.

Cold fronts passed through, bringing winds of hurricane force with gusts of 60 to 80 miles an hour. Winds whipped and spread the fires and fed them 60 <u>oxygen</u>, which fires must have to keep burning. Big fires met, <u>merged</u>, and became even bigger fires. In forests flames galloped through the tops, or crowns, of

WORDS TO KNOW
threaten (thrĕt′n) *v.* to be a danger to
oxygen (ŏk′sĭ-jən) *n.* one of the gases that make up air, needed for nearly all burning
merge (mûrj) *v.* to combine or unite

Pause & Reflect

1. Circle two phrases below that are true of the summer of 1988. **(Main Idea and Details)**

   dry farmland

   clear air

   overflowing rivers

   lightning fires

2. |||**MARK IT UP** Why didn't rangers try to put out the fires in Yellowstone National Park? Circle the sentences on this page that give the answer. **(Cause and Effect)**

NOTES

trees, through the <u>canopy</u>. Snags—dead trees that are still standing—burned like Roman candles.[1] Boulders exploded in the heat. Sheets of flame leaped forward. Gigantic clouds of smoke ringed the horizon, looking like thunderheads,[2] only bigger. There were days when the sun was no brighter than a full moon.

Fires jumped rivers, roads, canyons, parking lots. 70 Glowing <u>embers</u>, some the size of a man's fist, shot a mile or more ahead, starting new fires. Flames were roaring through the park at a rate of four or five miles a day. One fire ran 14 miles in only four hours. On August 20, a day known as Black Saturday, more than 150,000 acres burned inside the park and in neighboring forests. The 2,000 fire fighters could no more put out these fires than they could have stopped a hurricane. But what they could do was defend the park communities—the information centers and the 80 buildings where people slept, ate, and shopped.

By September 6 fire fighters were moving in to defend the area around the park's most famous <u>geyser</u>, Old Faithful. The geyser itself could not be harmed by fire, but the buildings around it could. One of them, the Old Faithful Inn, was the world's largest log building. Now one of the eight major fires in the park was <u>bearing</u> down on it.

Called the North Fork fire, it had started in the Targhee National Forest on July 22, when a careless 90 woodcutter threw away a lighted cigarette. Driven by shifting winds, the fire raced into Yellowstone, turned

REREAD the boxed passage. Why do you think the area around Old Faithful was particularly vulnerable to the danger of fire? **(Infer)**

---

1. **Roman candles:** fireworks that shoot out showers of sparks and balls of fire.
2. **thunderheads:** the spreading upper parts of thunderclouds.

WORDS TO KNOW
canopy (kăn′ə-pē) *n.* a rooflike cover; the covering formed by the branches and leaves of trees in a forest
ember (ĕm′bər) *n.* a small glowing bit of burning wood or coal
geyser (gī′zər) *n.* a natural hot spring that at times spouts water and steam into the air
bear (bâr) *v.* to move forcefully; push

back into Targhee, neared the town of West Yellowstone, then <u>veered</u> back into the park. There it jumped roads and rivers, snarling its way through the crossroads at Madison on August 15. By the afternoon of September 7 it was approaching Old Faithful. Long before they could see the flames, fire fighters heard the fire's deep rumble and saw a churning wall of dark smoke towering skyward.

Pause & Reflect

FOCUS

Read to find out how the changes in the weather affected the fires.

⬛▌MARK IT UP ⬦> As you read, circle details that tell you about the changes in the weather.

100   Planes dropped chemicals to damp down fires. On the ground weary fire fighters were wetting down buildings.

The fire came on, a mass of red flames whipped by winds gusting up to 50 miles an hour. Sparks and embers were everywhere, flying over the inn, parking lots, and geyser, and setting fire to the woods beyond. At the last moment 110 the wind shifted and the fire turned to the northeast, away from Old Faithful.

Saturday, September 10, began as another bad day. One arm of the North Fork fire was threatening park headquarters at Mammoth Hot Springs, and another arm was a quarter of a mile from Tower Junction. The forecast was for winds of up to 60 miles an hour. But the sky was thick with clouds, and the temperature was falling.

By early afternoon, September 10 had turned into a day of hope. Rain was drenching the area around Old 120 Faithful. The next morning snow blew along the streets of West Yellowstone. It sifted through

WORDS TO KNOW
veer (vîr) *v.* to turn aside; swerve

Pause & Reflect

1. Write the numbers 1, 2, 3, 4, or 5 to show the order in which the events below occurred. **(Chronological Order)**

___ Fire approached the Old Faithful Inn.

___ A lighted cigarette started a fire at Targhee National Forest.

___ Park officials decided that all fires must be put out.

___ Cold fronts with high winds spread the fires.

___ Black Saturday marked a day of defeat for firefighters.

2. What details in this section helped you **visualize** the spreading fires?

NOTES

Pause & Reflect

1. What changes in the weather helped to put out the fires? (Summarize)

2. **READ ALOUD** the boxed passage. Then restate the main idea in your own words. (Paraphrase)

CHALLENGE What, if anything, might be done to prevent such fires in the future? Mark passages in the selection to support your views. (Cause and Effect)

blackened forests and dusted herds of bison and elk. Scattered islands of fire would burn until November blanketed them in snow. But the worst was over.

At long last the summer of fire had ended. During it, eight major fires and many smaller ones had burned in Yellowstone. To people who had watched the fires on television news, it seemed the park must lie in ruins. But this was not so. The geysers, steam vents, 130 and hot springs were unharmed. Park communities had been saved. Nearly two-thirds of the park had not even been touched by fire.

It was true that many once-green areas were now black and gray. Yet it was also true that they were not ruined. Instead, they were beginning again, starting over, as they had many times in the past. Fire has always been part of the Yellowstone region. Wildfire has shaped the landscape and renewed it. ❖

Pause & Reflect

Active Reading SkillBuilder

Chronological Order

Chronological order refers to the time sequence in which events occur. Transition words such as *next, then, after, before, during,* or *until* help show chronological order. Words showing numerical order such as *first* or *second,* and the use of dates or times also help. Write important events from the selection in the chart below. Arrange them in the order in which they occurred, and write the word or phrase that shows the time order at the top of the box.

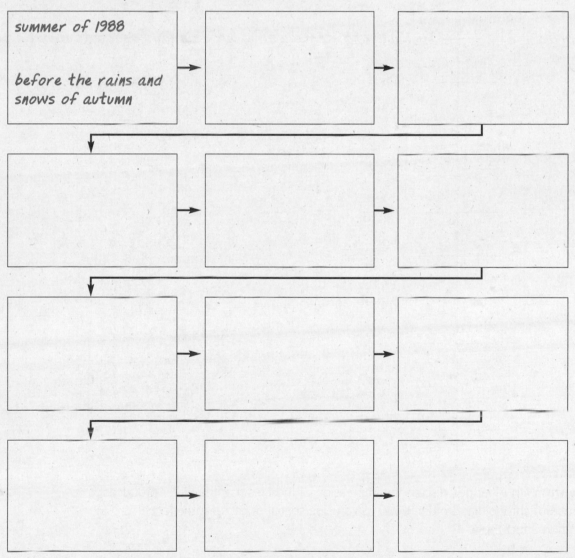

summer of 1988

before the rains and snows of autumn

Literary Analysis SkillBuilder

Informative Nonfiction

Informative nonfiction is writing that provides factual information about real people, places, and events. It can be organized in various ways. Writers may choose *chronological, spatial, cause-and-effect,* or *compare-and-contrast* organization. "Summer of Fire" is organized chronologically. Fill out the time line below with events and dates to trace the progress of the fires.

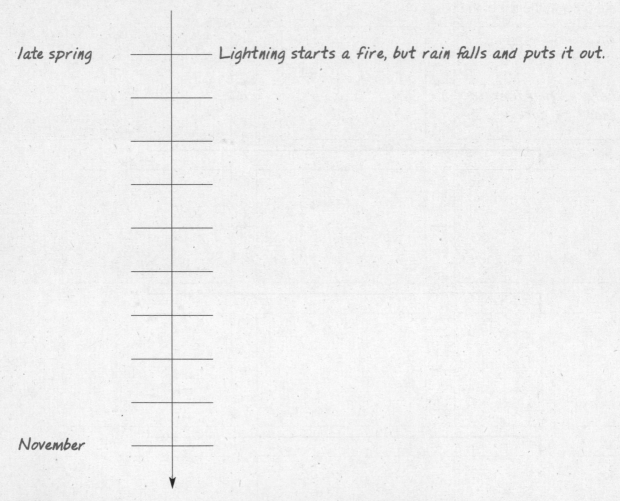

late spring ——————— Lightning starts a fire, but rain falls and puts it out.

November ———————

Follow Up: With a partner, discuss the impression of the fires that the writer produces by the use of chronological order. How would using spatial or cause-and-effect organization affect the text?

Words to Know SkillBuilder

Words to Know

bear	ember	merge	threaten	veer
canopy	geyser	oxygen	tinder	withering

A. Write the letter of the word or phrase that is most nearly **opposite** in meaning to the underlined word as it is used in each sentence below.

_____ 1. The fires <u>merged</u>, doubling their area of destruction.

    a. combined   b. divided   c. blurred

_____ 2. The <u>canopy</u> of trees was quickly demolished.

    a. undergrowth   b. roof   c. collection

_____ 3. The officials did not want the fire close enough to <u>threaten</u> the buildings.

    a. save   b. warp   c. endanger

_____ 4. The road <u>veers</u> slightly to avoid the geyser.

    a. narrows   b. swerves   c. straightens

_____ 5. We watched the fire <u>bear</u> down on our position.

    a. move toward   b. retreat from   c. lean

B. Complete each analogy with one of the Words to Know. In an **analogy,** the last two words must be related in the same way that the first two are related.

1. GROWING : DYING : : thriving : _____

2. CAR : KEY : : fire : _____

3. ICE : GLACIER : : hot water : _____

4. CAKE : FLOUR : : air : _____

C. On a separate sheet of paper, write a brief news report for August 20, 1988, about the fire in Yellowstone National Park. Use at least **four** of the Words to Know in your report.

Before You Read

Connect to Your Life

Think of someone you know or have read about who you think displays bravery, or courage. What courageous actions has he or she taken? What dreams or ideas made this person take risks? In the chart below, write down information about this courageous person. An example is shown.

Person's Name	Courageous Action(s)	Why He or She Did This
Matthew Henson	expedition to North Pole	loved adventure and exploring

Key to the Story

WHAT'S THE BIG IDEA? Think of words related to **danger**. Write them in the boxes below. Then use each word in a sentence about the sea.

1. risk

The captain knew taking his boat out in the storm was a risk.

2.

3.

Ghost
of the
Lagoon

by Armstrong Sperry

PREVIEW This short story is set on Bora Bora, an island in the southern Pacific Ocean. Mako, a young boy, has heard many stories about a terrifying shark in the waters near his home. He vows to slay the shark and win the reward offered by the king. Will Mako have the chance to test his courage?

Pause & Reflect

1. What are your impressions of Mako? (Infer)

2. **| MARK IT UP** ▷ Underline vivid details about the island where Mako lives. Would you like to live on Bora Bora? (Visualize)

   YES / NO, because

FOCUS

As the story opens, you meet Mako and learn about the island where he lives.

| MARK IT UP ▷ As you read, circle details that help you get to know Mako. An example is highlighted.

The island of Bora Bora, where Mako lived, is far away in the South Pacific. It is not a large island—you can paddle around it in a single day—but the main body of it rises straight out of the sea, very high into the air, like a castle. Waterfalls trail down

10 the faces of the cliffs. As you look upward, you see wild goats leaping from crag to crag.

   Mako had been born on the very edge of the sea, and most of his waking hours were spent in the waters of the lagoon, which was nearly enclosed by the two outstretched arms of the island. He was very clever with his hands; he had made a harpoon that was as straight as an arrow and tipped with five pointed iron spears. He had made a canoe, hollowing it out of a tree. It wasn't a very big canoe—only a little longer

20 than his own height. It had an outrigger, a sort of balancing pole, fastened to one side to keep the boat from tipping over. The canoe was just large enough to hold Mako and his little dog, Afa. They were great companions, these two.

Pause & Reflect

WORDS TO KNOW
   lagoon (lə-gōōn´) *n.* a shallow body of water separated from a sea by sandbars or coral reefs
   harpoon (här-pōōn´) *n.* a spearlike weapon used to hunt large fish

FOCUS

Mako's grandfather tells him about Tupa, the "ghost" of the lagoon.

MARK IT UP > As you read, underline words and phrases that tell about this creature and how the islanders feel about him.

One evening Mako lay stretched at full length on the pandanus mats, listening to Grandfather's voice. Overhead, stars shone in the

30 dark sky. From far off came the thunder of the surf on the <u>reef</u>.

The old man was speaking of Tupa, the ghost of the lagoon. Ever since the boy could remember, he had heard tales of this terrible monster. Frightened fishermen, returning from the reef at midnight, spoke of the ghost. Over the evening fires, old men told endless tales about the monster.

Tupa seemed to think the lagoon of Bora Bora

40 belonged to him. The natives left presents of food for him out on the reef: a dead goat, a chicken, or a pig. The presents always disappeared mysteriously, but everyone felt sure that it was Tupa who carried them away. Still, in spite of all this food, the nets of the fishermen were torn during the night, the fish stolen. What an appetite Tupa seemed to have!

Not many people had ever seen the ghost of the lagoon. Grandfather was one of the few who had.

"What does he really look like, Grandfather?" the

50 boy asked, for the hundredth time.

The old man shook his head solemnly. The light from the cook fire glistened on his white hair. "Tupa lives in the great caves of the reef. He is longer than this house. There is a sail on his back, not large but terrible to see, for it burns with a white fire. Once, when I was fishing beyond the reef at night, I saw him come up right under another canoe—"

WORDS TO KNOW
reef (rēf) *n.* a ridge of rocks, sand, or coral near the surface of the water

"What happened then?" Mako asked. He half rose on one elbow. This was a story he had not heard
60 before.

The old man's voice dropped to a whisper. "Tupa dragged the canoe right under the water—and the water boiled with white flame. The three fishermen in it were never seen again. Fine swimmers they were, too."

Grandfather shook his head. "It is bad fortune even to speak of Tupa. There is evil in his very name."

"But King Opu Nui has offered a reward for his capture," the boy pointed out.

70 "Thirty acres of fine coconut land, and a sailing canoe as well," said the old man. "But who ever heard of laying hands on a ghost?"

Mako's eyes glistened. "Thirty acres of land and a sailing canoe. How I should love to win that reward!"

Grandfather nodded, but Mako's mother scolded her son for such foolish talk. "Be quiet now, son, and go to sleep. Grandfather has told you that it is bad fortune to speak of Tupa. Alas, how well we have learned that lesson! Your father—" She stopped
80 herself.

"What of my father?" the boy asked quickly. And now he sat up straight on the mats.

"Tell him, Grandfather," his mother whispered.

The old man cleared his throat and poked at the fire. A little shower of sparks whirled up into the darkness.

"Your father," he explained gently, "was one of the three fishermen in the canoe that Tupa destroyed." His words fell upon the air like stones dropped into a deep
90 well.

Mako shivered. He brushed back the hair from his damp forehead. Then he squared his shoulders and cried fiercely, "I shall slay Tupa and win the king's reward!" He rose to his knees, his slim body tense, his eyes flashing in the firelight.

"Hush!" his mother said. "Go to sleep now. Enough of such foolish talk. Would you bring trouble upon us all?"

Mako lay down again upon the mats. He rolled over 100 on his side and closed his eyes, but sleep was long in coming.

The palm trees whispered above the dark lagoon, and far out on the reef the sea thundered.

Pause & Reflect

Pause & Reflect

1. Why do the people of Bora Bora fear Tupa? (Clarify) Cross out the *wrong* answer below.

   He tears the fishing nets.

   He attacks children.

   He killed three fishermen.

   He has a terrible sail on his back.

2. **MARK IT UP** What does Mako learn about his father from his grandfather's story? Underline the sentence on page 44 that tells the answer. (Clarify)

NOTES

FOCUS

The next day, Mako and his dog go to another island. Read to find out what Mako sees along the way.

MARK IT UP As you read, circle details that help you visualize what Mako sees.

The boy was slow to wake up the next morning. The ghost of Tupa had played through his dreams, making him restless. And so it was almost noon before Mako sat 110 up on the mats and stretched himself. He called Afa, and the boy and his dog ran down to the lagoon for their morning swim.

When they returned to the house, wide-awake and hungry, Mako's mother had food ready and waiting.

"These are the last of our bananas," she told him. "I wish you would paddle out to the reef this afternoon and bring back a new bunch."

The boy agreed eagerly. Nothing pleased him more 120 than such an errand, which would take him to a little island on the outer reef, half a mile from shore. It was one of Mako's favorite playgrounds, and there bananas and oranges grew in great plenty.

"Come, Afa," he called, gulping the last mouthful.

"We're going on an <u>expedition</u>." He picked up his long-bladed knife and seized his spear. A minute later, he dashed across the white sand, where his canoe was drawn up beyond the water's reach.

Afa barked at his heels. He was all white except for
130 a black spot over each eye. Wherever Mako went, there went Afa also. Now the little dog leaped into the bow of the canoe, his tail wagging with delight. The boy shoved the canoe into the water and climbed aboard. Then, picking up his paddle, he thrust it into the water. The canoe shot ahead. Its sharp bow cut through the green water of the lagoon like a knife through cheese. And so clear was the water that Mako could see the coral gardens, forty feet below him, growing in the sand. The shadow of the canoe moved
140 over them.

A school of fish swept by like silver arrows. He saw scarlet rock cod with ruby eyes and the head of a conger eel peering out from a cavern in the coral. The boy thought suddenly of Tupa, ghost of the lagoon. On such a bright day it was hard to believe in ghosts of any sort. The fierce sunlight drove away all thought of them. Perhaps ghosts were only old men's stories, anyway!

Mako's eyes came to rest upon his spear—the spear
150 that he had made with his own hands—the spear that was as straight and true as an arrow. He remembered his vow of the night before. Could a ghost be killed with a spear? Some night, when all the village was sleeping, Mako swore to himself that he would find out! He would paddle out to the reef and challenge Tupa! Perhaps tonight. Why not? He caught his breath at the thought. A shiver ran down his back. His hands were tense on the paddle.

READ ALOUD the boxed passage. Vary the tone and volume of your voice to express Mako's feelings.

WORDS TO KNOW
expedition (ĕk′spĭ-dĭsh′ən) *n.* a journey with a goal or purpose

As the canoe drew away from shore, the boy saw
160 the coral reef that, above all others, had always
interested him. It was of white coral—a long slim
shape that rose slightly above the surface of the water.
It looked very much like a shark. There was a ridge on
the back that the boy could pretend was a dorsal fin,
while up near one end were two dark holes that
looked like eyes!

Times without number the boy had practiced
spearing this make-believe shark, aiming always for
the eyes, the most vulnerable[1] spot. So true and
170 straight had his aim become that the spear would pass
right into the eyeholes without even touching the sides
of the coral. Mako had named the coral reef Tupa.

This morning, as he paddled past it, he shook his
fist and called, "Ho, Mister Tupa! Just wait till I get
my bananas. When I come back, I'll make short work
of you!"

Afa followed his master's words with a sharp bark.
He knew Mako was excited about something.

Pause & Reflect

FOCUS

Mako and Afa reach the island where bananas grow. Find out what Mako does in the jungle.

The bow of the canoe
180 touched the sand of the little
island where the bananas
grew. Afa leaped ashore and
ran barking into the jungle,
now on this trail, now on that. Clouds of sea birds
whirled from their nests into the air with angry cries.

Mako climbed into the shallow water, waded
ashore, and pulled his canoe up on the beach. Then,
picking up his banana knife, he followed Afa. In the

---

1. vulnerable (vŭl´ nər-ə-bəl): open to physical injury.

Pause & Reflect

1. [MARK IT UP] Review the details you circled as you read. Star the ones that you feel are the most vivid. (Evaluate)

2. Do you think Mako will kill Tupa? (Predict)
   YES / NO, because

3. Check the phrase that best completes the following sentence. (Clarify)
   Mako often practices killing Tupa by spearing a
   ❏ banana tree.
   ❏ wild pig.
   ❏ coral reef.

NOTES

jungle the light was so dense and green that the boy
190 felt as if he were moving underwater. Ferns grew
higher than his head. The branches of the trees formed
a green roof over him. A flock of parakeets fled on
swift wings. Somewhere a wild pig crashed through
the undergrowth while Afa dashed away in pursuit.
Mako paused anxiously. Armed only with his banana
knife, he had no desire to meet the wild pig. The pig,
it seemed, had no desire to meet him, either.

Then, ahead of him, the boy saw the broad green
blades of a banana tree. A bunch of bananas, golden
200 ripe, was growing out of the top.

At the foot of the tree he made a nest of soft leaves
for the bunch to fall upon. In this way the fruit
wouldn't be crushed. Then with a swift slash of his
blade he cut the stem. The bananas fell to the earth
with a dull thud. He found two more bunches.

Then he thought, "I might as well get some oranges
while I'm here. Those little rusty ones are sweeter than
any that grow on Bora Bora."

So he set about making a net out of palm leaves to
210 carry the oranges. As he worked, his swift fingers
moving in and out among the strong green leaves, he
could hear Afa's excited barks off in the jungle. That
was just like Afa, always barking at something: a bird,
a fish, a wild pig. He never caught anything, either.
Still, no boy ever had a finer companion.

The palm net took longer to make than Mako had
realized. By the time it was finished and filled with
oranges, the jungle was dark and gloomy. Night comes
quickly and without warning in the islands of the
220 tropics.

Mako carried the fruit down to the shore and
loaded it into the canoe. Then he whistled to Afa. The
dog came bounding out of the bush, wagging his tail.

"Hurry!" Mako scolded. "We won't be home before the dark comes."

The little dog leaped into the bow of the canoe, and Mako came aboard. Night seemed to rise up from the surface of the water and swallow them. On the distant shore of Bora Bora, cook fires were being lighted. The 230 first star twinkled just over the dark mountains. Mako dug his paddle into the water, and the canoe leaped ahead.

Pause & Reflect

FOCUS

Read to find out what Mako sees near the coral reef on his way home.

The dark water was alive with <u>phosphorus</u>. The bow of the canoe seemed to cut through a pale liquid fire. Each dip of the paddle trailed streamers of light. As the canoe approached the coral reef, the boy called, "Ho, Tupa! It's too late tonight to 240 teach you your lesson. But I'll come back tomorrow." The coral shark glistened in the darkness.

And then, suddenly, Mako's breath caught in his throat. His hands felt weak. Just beyond the fin of the coral Tupa, there was another fin—a huge one. It had never been there before. And—could he believe his eyes? It was moving.

The boy stopped paddling. He dashed his hand across his eyes. Afa began to bark furiously. The great white fin, shaped like a small sail, glowed with 250 phosphorescent light. Then Mako knew. Here was Tupa—the real Tupa—ghost of the lagoon!

WORDS TO KNOW
  phosphorus (fŏs′fər-əs) *n.* a substance that glows with a yellowish or white light

Pause & Reflect

1. The list below describes things that Mako and Afa do on the island. Number the statements in the order in which they occur in the story. **(Sequence of Events)**

__ Afa chases a wild pig.

__ Mako loads the fruit into his canoe.

__ Mako picks three bunches of bananas.

__ Mako makes a nest of leaves.

2. How does Mako feel about his dog, Afa? **(Infer)**

NOTES

1. In the space below, draw a picture of what Mako sees in the dark near the reef. **(Visualize)**

2. Will Mako be able to save Afa from the shark? Write down your **prediction**.

YES / NO, because

_____

_____

_____

_____

NOTES

_____

_____

_____

_____

_____

_____

_____

His knees felt weak. He tried to cry out, but his voice died in his throat. The great shark was circling slowly around the canoe. With each circle, it moved closer and closer. Now the boy could see the phosphorescent glow of the great shark's sides. As it moved in closer, he saw the yellow eyes, the gill slits in its throat.

Afa leaped from one side of the canoe to the other. 260 In sudden anger Mako leaned forward to grab the dog and shake him soundly. Afa wriggled out of his grasp as Mako tried to catch him, and the shift in weight tipped the canoe on one side. The outrigger rose from the water. In another second they would be overboard. The boy threw his weight over quickly to balance the canoe, but with a loud splash Afa fell over into the dark water.

Mako stared after him in dismay. The little dog, instead of swimming back to the canoe, had headed 270 for the distant shore. And there was the great white shark—very near.

"Afa! Afa! Come back! Come quickly!" Mako shouted.

Pause & Reflect

FOCUS

Read to find out if your prediction is right.

The little dog turned back toward the canoe. He was swimming with all his strength. Mako leaned forward. Could Afa make it? Swiftly the boy seized his spear. Bracing himself, he stood upright. There was no 280 weakness in him now. His dog, his companion, was in danger of instant death.

Afa was swimming desperately to reach the canoe. The white shark had paused in his circling to gather speed for the attack. Mako raised his arm, took aim. In that instant the shark charged. Mako's arm flashed forward. All his strength was behind that thrust. The spear drove straight and true, right into the great shark's eye. Mad with pain and rage, Tupa whipped about, lashing the water in fury. The canoe rocked

290 back and forth. Mako struggled to keep his balance as he drew back the spear by the cord fastened to his wrist.

He bent over to seize Afa and drag him aboard. Then he stood up, not a moment too soon. Once again the shark charged. Once again Mako threw his spear, this time at the other eye. The spear found its mark. Blinded and weak from loss of blood, Tupa rolled to the surface, turned slightly on his side. Was he dead?

Mako knew how clever sharks could be, and he was

300 taking no chances. Scarcely daring to breathe, he paddled toward the still body. He saw the faintest motion of the great tail. The shark was still alive. The boy knew that one flip of that tail could overturn the canoe and send him and Afa into the water, where Tupa could destroy them.

Swiftly, yet calmly, Mako stood upright and braced himself firmly. Then, murmuring a silent prayer to the shark god, he threw his spear for the last time. Downward, swift as sound, the spear plunged into a

310 white shoulder.

Peering over the side of the canoe, Mako could see the great fish turn over far below the surface. Then slowly, slowly, the great shark rose to the surface of the lagoon. There he floated, half on one side.

Tupa was dead.

Mako flung back his head and shouted for joy. Hitching a strong line about the shark's tail, the boy

Pause & Reflect

1. **MARK IT UP** Why does Mako attack Tupa? Find the answer on page 50 and underline it. **(Cause and Effect)**

2. What was your reaction to Mako's fight with Tupa? **(Connect)**

CHALLENGE Now that you have read the ending, look back through the story. Star events or details that suggest that Mako will encounter Tupa later in the story. **(Analyze)**

began to paddle toward the shore of Bora Bora. The dorsal fin, burning with the white fire of phosphorus, 320 trailed after the canoe.

Men were running down the beaches of Bora Bora, shouting as they leaped into their canoes and put out across the lagoon. Their cries reached the boy's ears across the water.

"It is Tupa—ghost of the lagoon," he heard them shout. "Mako has killed him!"

That night, as the tired boy lay on the pandanus mats listening to the distant thunder of the sea, he heard Grandfather singing a new song. It was the song 330 which would be sung the next day at the feast which King Opu Nui would give in Mako's honor. The boy saw his mother bending over the cook fire. The stars leaned close, winking like friendly eyes. Grandfather's voice reached him now from a great distance, "Thirty acres of land and a sailing canoe. . . ." ❖

Pause & Reflect

Active Reading SkillBuilder

Predicting

An active reader makes **predictions**—ideas about what will happen next—while reading. Writers of adventure stories use suspenseful language to keep the reader wondering what will happen.

Consider each of the situations from "Ghost of the Lagoon," listed below. Write two different predictions that you think make sense at this point in the story.

Situation	Predictions: Two Things That Might Happen
1. Mako listens to his Grandfather's stories about the "ghost" Tupa.	*Mako will meet Tupa.*
2. Mako vows to kill the shark and win the reward.	
3. Mako and his dog, Afa, land on a reef to pick bananas.	
4. Mako and Afa start home in the canoe at night.	
5. Mako kills the shark to protect Afa.	

Literary Analysis SkillBuilder

Conflict

In almost every story, the main character faces a **conflict,** or struggle. Sometimes conflict is **internal;** that is, the struggle may take place in a character's mind, such as when the character has to make a big decision. Other times conflict is **external,** and the character struggles against an outside force, such as nature. As you read "Ghost of the Lagoon," use the chart below to keep track of the conflicts that Mako faces. Decide whether each conflict is internal or external. An example is provided.

Conflict	Type of Conflict
Mako wants to avenge his father's death but fears the shark.	internal

Follow Up: Discuss which conflict is the main conflict of the story. How do the minor conflicts relate to the resolution of the main conflict?

Words to Know SkillBuilder

Words to Know

expedition   harpoon   lagoon   phosphorus   reef

A. On each blank line, write the Word to Know that the rhyme describes.

This is sharp; and one might use it to get fish to cook.
Yes, it's pointed (like I said), and, no, it's not a hook.

_____
(1)

To cross a sandbar and go wading, that is what my wish is.
This is where I want to go to spy on little fishes.

_____
(2)

This may keep a ship from sailing all the way to shore.
It sticks up kind of like a hill to raise the ocean floor.

_____
(3)

If you see the water shining and you think that you
    are dreaming,
Perhaps you are, or maybe it is this stuff you see gleaming.

_____
(4)

To go on one of these, try driving, flying, biking, rowing,
Or take a train or walk, just have a purpose for your going.

_____
(5)

B. Fill in each blank with the correct Word to Know.

I had to walk across a _____ to get to the shallow water
(1)

of the _____ with a _____ in my
(2)   (3)

hand, while trying to avoid the places where there was _____
(4)

in the water. Who ever said an _____ had to be easy?
(5)

Before You Read

Connect to Your Life

Think of a safety tip for dealing with wild animals or animals you don't know, for example, "Do not pet a dog you don't know." In the space below, create a sign to share your tip with others.

Key to the Memoir

WHAT DO YOU THINK? Read the following lines from *Woodsong* in which Paulsen describes the bears that live near him.

> *We started to treat them like pets.*
> *A major mistake.*

Look at the bear in the picture. Why is it a mistake to treat this animal "like a pet"?

_____

_____

_____

FROM WOODSONG

BY GARY PAULSEN

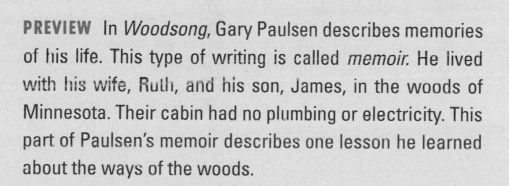

PREVIEW In *Woodsong*, Gary Paulsen describes memories of his life. This type of writing is called *memoir*. He lived with his wife, Ruth, and his son, James, in the woods of Minnesota. Their cabin had no plumbing or electricity. This part of Paulsen's memoir describes one lesson he learned about the ways of the woods.

FOCUS

Many wild animals visit the Paulsens' dog kennel.

MARK IT UP > As you read, circle the different types of animals that come to the kennel.

We have bear trouble. Because we feed processed meat to the dogs, there is always the smell of meat over the kennel. In the summer it can be a bit high[1] because the dogs like to "save" their food sometimes for a day or two or four—burying it to dig up later. We live on the edge of wilderness, and

10 consequently the meat smell brings any number of visitors from the woods.

Skunks abound, and foxes and coyotes and wolves and weasels—all <u>predators</u>. We once had an eagle live over the kennel for more than a week, <u>scavenging</u> from the dogs, and a crazy group of ravens has pretty much taken over the puppy pen. Ravens are protected by the state, and they seem to know it. When I walk toward the puppy pen with the buckets of meat, it's a tossup to see who gets it—the pups or the birds. They have

20 actually pecked the puppies away from the food pans until they have gone through and taken what they want.

Spring, when the bears come, is the worst. They have been in hibernation through the winter, and they are hungry beyond caution. The meat smell draws them like flies, and we frequently have two or three around the kennel at the same time. Typically they do not bother us much—although my wife had a bear chase her from the garden to the house one morning—but they do bother the dogs.

30 They are so big and strong that the dogs fear them, and the bears trade on this fear to get their food. It's common to see them scare a dog into his house and take his food.

---

1. **it can be a bit high:** the smell can be rather strong.

WORDS TO KNOW
predator (prĕd′ə-tər) *n.* an animal that hunts other animals for food
scavenging (skăv′ən-jĭng) *adj.* searching for discarded scraps **scavenge** *v.*

Twice we have had dogs killed by rough bear swats that broke their necks—and the bears took their food.

We have evolved[2] an uneasy peace with them, but there is the problem of familiarity. The first time you see a bear in the kennel it is a <u>novelty</u>, but when the same ones are there day after day, you wind up naming some of them (old Notch-Ear, Billy-Jo, etc.). There gets to be a too-
40 relaxed attitude. We started to treat them like pets.

A major mistake.

Pause & Reflect

FOCUS

In this section, you will meet a bear called Scarhead. Read to find out how Scarhead and the other bears act.

There was a large male around the kennel for a week or so. He had a white streak across his head, which I guessed was a wound scar from some hunter—bear hunting is allowed here. He wasn't all that bad, so we didn't mind him. He would frighten the dogs and take
50 their hidden stashes now and then, but he didn't harm them, and we became accustomed to him hanging around. We called him Scarhead, and now and again we would joke about him as if he were one of the yard animals.

At this time we had three cats, forty-two dogs, fifteen or twenty chickens, eight ducks, nineteen large white geese, a few banty hens, ten fryers which we'd raised from chicks and couldn't (as my wife put it) "snuff and eat," and six woods-wise goats.

The bears, strangely, didn't bother any of the yard
60 animals. There must have been a rule, or some order to the way they lived, because they would hit the kennel

---

2. **evolved** (ĭ-vŏlvd′): developed by a series of small changes.

WORDS TO KNOW
novelty (nŏv′əl-tē) *n.* something new and unusual

Pause & Reflect

1. Review the details you marked. Then cross out the animal below that does *not* visit the kennel. **(Clarify)**

   foxes   skunks
   ravens   snakes

2. What did you learn about bears? **(Summarize)**

 READ ALOUD the boxed passage. How does the author feel about Scarhead at first? Use your voice to express Paulsen's relaxed attitude.

NOTES

Pause & Reflect

1. Why are the bears attracted by the burning trash? Complete the **cause-and-effect** chart below.

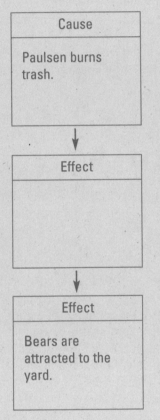

Cause
Paulsen burns trash.

↓

Effect

↓

Effect
Bears are attracted to the yard.

2. What do you think is going to happen "one July morning" when the bears arrive from the south? **(Predict)**

and steal from the dogs but leave the chickens and goats and other yard stock completely alone—although you would have had a hard time convincing the goats of this fact. The goats spent a great deal of time with their back hair up, whuffing and blowing snot at the bears—and at the dogs, who would *gladly* have eaten them. The goats never really believed in the truce.

70 There is not a dump or landfill to take our trash to, and so we separate it—organic, inorganic[3]—and deal with it ourselves. We burn the paper in a screened enclosure, and it is fairly efficient; but it's impossible to get all the food particles off wrapping paper, so when it's burned, the food particles burn with it.

And give off a burnt food smell.

And nothing draws bears like burning food. It must be that they have learned to understand human dumps—where they spend a great deal of time foraging. And they learn amazingly fast. In Alaska, for instance, the bears 80 already know that the sound of a moose hunter's hunt means there will be a fresh gut pile when the hunter cleans the moose. They come at a run when they hear the shot. It's often a close race to see if the hunter will get to the moose before the bears take it away. . . .

Because we're on the south edge of the wilderness area, we try to wait until there is a northerly breeze before we burn, so the food smell will carry south, but it doesn't always help. Sometimes bears, wolves, and other predators are already south, working the sheep farms 90 down where it is more settled—they take a terrible toll[4] of sheep—and we catch them on the way back through.

That's what happened one July morning.

Pause & Reflect

---

3. **organic** (ôr-găn′ĭk), **inorganic** (ĭn′ôr-găn′ĭk): on the one hand, things made of plant or animal material; and on the other, things made of material that has never been alive.

4. **take a terrible toll:** destroy a large number.

Scarhead had been gone for two or three days, and the breeze was right, so I went to burn the trash. I fired it off and went back into the house for a moment—not more than two minutes. When I came back out, Scarhead was in the burn area. His tracks (directly through the tomatoes in the garden) showed he'd come from the south.

He was having a grand time. The fire didn't bother him. He was trying to reach a paw in around the edges of flame to get at whatever smelled so good. He had torn things apart quite a bit—ripped one side off the burn enclosure—and I was having a bad day, and it made me mad.

I was standing across the burning fire from him, and without thinking—because I was so used to him—I picked up a stick, threw it at him, and yelled, "Get out of here."

I have made many mistakes in my life, and will probably make many more, but I hope never to throw a stick at a bear again.

In one rolling motion—the muscles seemed to move within the skin so fast that I couldn't take half a breath—he turned and came for me. Close. I could smell his breath and see the red around the sides of his eyes. Close on me he stopped and raised on his back legs and hung over me, his forelegs and paws hanging down, weaving back and forth gently as he took his time and decided whether or not to tear my head off.

I could not move, would not have time to react. I knew I had nothing to say about it. One blow would break my neck. Whether I lived or died depended on him, on his thinking, on his ideas about me—whether I was worth the bother or not.

I did not think then.

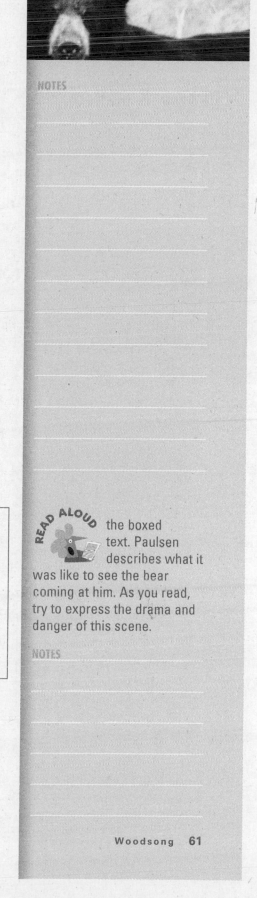

READ ALOUD the boxed text. Paulsen describes what it was like to see the bear coming at him. As you read, try to express the drama and danger of this scene.

NOTES

Pause & Reflect

1. Why didn't Paulsen shoot the bear? (Draw Conclusions)

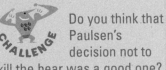

2. REREAD the boxed passage. What lesson did Paulsen learn? (Question)

CHALLENGE Do you think that Paulsen's decision not to kill the bear was a good one? Mark details in this memoir to support your answer. (Evaluate)

Looking back on it, I don't remember having one coherent⁵ thought when it was happening. All I knew
130 was terrible <u>menace</u>. His eyes looked very small as he studied me. He looked down on me for what seemed hours. I did not move, did not breathe, did not think or do anything.

And he lowered.

Perhaps I was not worth the trouble. He lowered slowly and turned back to the trash, and I walked backward halfway to the house and then ran—anger growing now—and took the rifle from the gun rack by the door and came back out.

140 He was still there, <u>rummaging</u> through the trash. I worked the bolt and fed a cartridge in and aimed at the place where you kill bears and began to squeeze. In raw anger, I began to take up the four pounds of pull necessary to send death into him.

And stopped.

Kill him for what?

That thought crept in.

Kill him for what?

For not killing me? For letting me know it is wrong
150 to throw sticks at four-hundred-pound bears? For not hurting me, for not killing me, I should kill him? I lowered the rifle and ejected the shell and put the gun away. I hope Scarhead is still alive. For what he taught me, I hope he lives long and is very happy, because I learned then—looking up at him while he made up his mind whether or not to end me—that when it is all boiled down, I am nothing more and nothing less than any other animal in the woods. ❖

Pause & Reflect

---

5. **coherent** (kō-hîr′ənt): clear; logical.

WORDS TO KNOW
menace (měn′ĭs) *n.* a possible danger; threat
rummaging (rŭm′ĭ-jĭng) *adj.* searching thoroughly **rummage** *v.*

Active Reading SkillBuilder

Questioning

The process of raising questions while reading is called **questioning.** Good readers ask questions in an effort to understand characters and events. After questioning, always look for answers as you continue to read. Use the question frame to help you ask and answer important questions about this selection from *Woodsong*.

Problem

Who had the problem? *Gary Paulsen*

What was the problem? *A bear was tearing up his trash pit.*

Why was it a problem? _____

Solution

What attempt was made to solve the problem? _____

_____

_____

Results

Did this attempt succeed? _____

What happened? _____

_____

_____

Then what happened? _____

_____

_____

Literary Analysis SkillBuilder

Memoir

A **memoir** is a type of autobiography. It is a writer's own account of one or more important events and is usually told in the first person.

Use the spider map to collect details from this selection that could only be told by the person who experienced them.

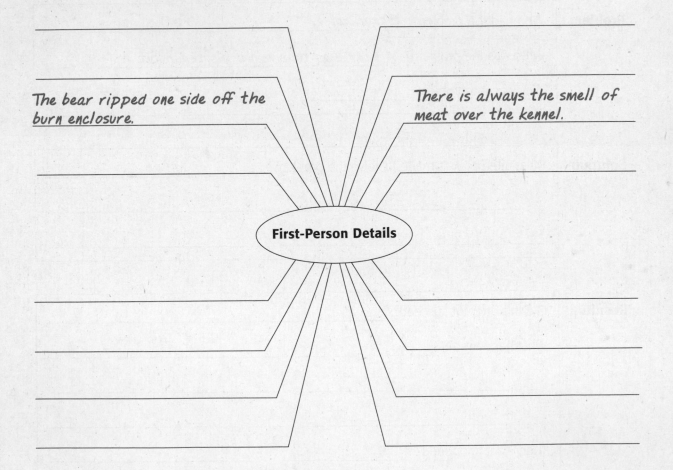

The bear ripped one side off the burn enclosure.

There is always the smell of meat over the kennel.

First-Person Details

Follow Up: In a small group, compare the details you collected. What kinds of details can only be told by a first-person narrator? Group the details into categories such as those that relate to the five senses, to daily life, and so on.

Words to Know SkillBuilder

Words to Know

menace   novelty   predator   rummaging   scavenging

A. On each blank line, write the Word to Know that the rhyme describes.

Although the car's a common sight, not odd to you or me,
A hundred years ago, it was indeed a (1).

_____
(1)

One animal's trash may be another animal's treasure
And explains why (2) animals may do it for pleasure.

_____
(2)

(3) through closets and a drawer,
Prunella found what she was looking for.

_____
(3)

A (4)'s a (5) to its prey.
Each watches for the other every day.

_____
(4)

_____
(5)

B. Fill in each set of blanks with the correct Word to Know. (Not all words will be used.) Then use the boxed letters to complete the sentence below the puzzle.

1. A wolf or a spider is this; a cow or a giraffe is not. ☐ __ __ __ __ __ __ __

2. Some examples of this are a vicious dog,
   a speeding driver, and a hurricane. __ __ __ __ __ ☐

3. This is what the elephant was
   to the first Europeans who saw one. __ __ __ __ __ ☐ __

4. This describes raccoons looking for food
   in people's garbage cans. ☐ __ __ __ __ __ __ __ __ __

Complete the following sentence with the word that the boxed letters spell out.

5. Gary Paulsen says that bears are not _____ .

Before You Read

Connect to Your Life

The story you are about to read is set in a place where it rains all the time. How would you feel if the rain never stopped? How do different types of weather affect you? Write your reactions in the diagram below. For the last section, fill in a type of weather and add a drawing of that weather.

When it is raining,
I feel . . .
_____ *quiet* _____

When it is sunny,
I feel . . .
_____

When it is _____,
I feel . . .
_____

Key to the Story

WHAT DO YOU THINK? Read the following sentence from "All Summer in a Day." Notice how the author creates distance between "they" and "she."

> *So after that, dimly, dimly, she sensed it; she was different, and they knew her difference and kept away.*

Why do children sometimes keep away from a child who seems different? Jot down reasons on the lines provided.

1. They want to be part of the "in crowd."
_____
_____
_____

ALL SUMMER IN A DAY

BY RAY BRADBURY

PREVIEW "All Summer in a Day" is science fiction. It is set in the future, on the planet Venus. In this story, it rains most of the time on Venus—except for one hour every seven years. Margot, the main character, is the only student in her class who remembers what life was like on Earth.

READING TIP **Dialogue**
The story begins with a conversation between several classmates.

NOTES

FOCUS

As the story opens, something big is about to happen on Venus. Read to find out what the children are waiting for.

MARK IT UP As you read, circle vivid details that help you picture the weather on Venus. An example is highlighted.

"Ready?"

"Ready."

"Now?"

"Soon."

"Do the scientists really know? Will it happen today, will it?"

"Look, look; see for yourself!"

10   The children pressed to each other like so many roses, so many weeds, intermixed, peering out for a look at the hidden sun.

It rained.

It had been raining for seven years; thousands upon thousands of days compounded and filled from one end to the other with rain, with the drum and gush of water, with the sweet crystal fall of showers and the <u>concussion</u> of storms so heavy they were tidal waves come over the islands. A thousand forests had been

20 crushed under the rain and grown up a thousand times to be crushed again. And this was the way life was forever on the planet Venus, and this was the schoolroom of the children of the rocket men and women who had come to a raining world to set up civilization and live out their lives.

"It's stopping, it's stopping!"

"Yes, yes!"

Margot stood apart from them, from these children who could never remember a time when there wasn't

30 rain and rain and rain. They were all nine years old, and if there had been a day, seven years ago, when the sun came out for an hour and showed its face to the stunned world, they could not recall. Sometimes, at

WORDS TO KNOW
concussion (kən-kŭsh′ən) *n.* a strong shaking

night, she heard them stir, in remembrance, and she knew they were dreaming and remembering gold or a yellow crayon or a coin large enough to buy the world with. She knew that they thought they remembered a warmness, like a blushing in the face, in the body, in the arms and legs and trembling hands. But then they always awoke to the tatting drum, the endless shaking down of clear bead necklaces upon the roof, the walk, the gardens, the forest; and their dreams were gone.

All day yesterday they had read in class about the sun, about how like a lemon it was and how hot. And they had written small stories or essays or poems about it:

"I think the sun is a flower,
That blooms for just one hour."

That was Margot's poem, read in a quiet voice in the still classroom while the rain was falling outside.

"Aw, you didn't write that!" protested one of the boys.

"I did," said Margot. "I *did*."

"William!" said the teacher.

But that was yesterday. Now, the rain was slackening, and the children were crushed to the great thick windows.

"Where's teacher?"

"She'll be back."

"She'd better hurry; we'll miss it!"

They turned on themselves, like a feverish wheel, all tumbling spokes.

Pause & Reflect

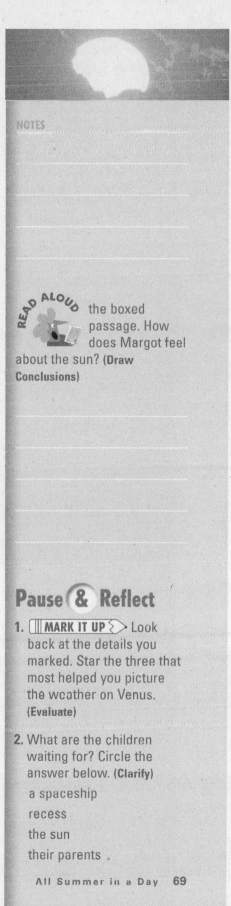

NOTES

READ ALOUD the boxed passage. How does Margot feel about the sun? (Draw Conclusions)

Pause & Reflect

1. **MARK IT UP** Look back at the details you marked. Star the three that most helped you picture the weather on Venus. (Evaluate)

2. What are the children waiting for? Circle the answer below. (Clarify)

   a spaceship

   recess

   the sun

   their parents

FOCUS

In this section, you will learn more about Margot and her classmates.

▥ **MARK IT UP** ⟩ As you read, underline the details that tell you why the other children dislike Margot.

Margot stood alone. She was a very frail girl who looked as if she had been lost in the rain for years, and the rain had washed out the blue from her eyes and the red from her mouth and the 70 yellow from her hair. She was an old photograph dusted from an album, whitened away; and if she spoke at all, her voice would be a ghost. Now she stood, separate, staring at the rain and the loud, wet world beyond the huge glass.

"What're *you* looking at?" said William.

Margot said nothing.

"Speak when you're spoken to." He gave her a shove. But she did not move; rather, she let herself be moved only by him and nothing else.

80 They edged away from her; they would not look at her. She felt them go away. And this was because she would play no games with them in the echoing tunnels of the underground city. If they tagged her and ran, she stood blinking after them and did not follow. When the class sang songs about happiness and life and games, her lips barely moved. Only when they sang about the sun and the summer did her lips move as she watched the drenched windows.

And then, of course, the biggest crime of all was 90 that she had come here only five years ago from Earth, and she remembered the sun and the way the sun was and the sky was when she was four, in Ohio. And they, they had been on Venus all their lives, and they had been only two years old when last the sun came out and had long since forgotten the color and heat of it and the way that it really was. But Margot remembered.

"It's like a penny," she said once, eyes closed.

"No, it's not!" the children cried.

100   "It's like a fire," she said, "in the stove."

"You're lying; you don't remember!" cried the children.

But she remembered and stood quietly apart from all of them and watched the patterning windows. And once, a month ago, she had refused to shower in the school shower rooms, had clutched her hands to her ears and over her head, screaming the water mustn't touch her head. So after that, dimly, dimly, she sensed it; she was different, and they knew her difference and 110 kept away.

There was talk that her father and mother were taking her back to Earth next year; it seemed vital to her that they do so, though it would mean the loss of thousands of dollars to her family. And so, the children hated her for all these reasons, of big and little consequence. They hated her pale, snow face, her waiting silence, her thinness, and her possible future.

"Get away!" The boy gave her another push. "What're you waiting for?"

120   Then, for the first time, she turned and looked at him. And what she was waiting for was in her eyes.

"Well, don't wait around here!" cried the boy, savagely. "You won't see nothing!"

Her lips moved.

"Nothing!" he cried. "It was all a joke, wasn't it?" He turned to the other children. "Nothing's happening today. *Is* it?"

They all blinked at him and then, understanding, laughed and shook their heads. "Nothing, nothing!"

NOTES

REREAD the boxed passage. Why does William tell Margot that nothing is going to happen? **(Infer)**

Pause & Reflect

1. Why do the children dislike Margot? Cross out the *wrong* answer. **(Clarify)**

   She remembers seeing the sun.

   She gets the best grades.

   She doesn't play with them.

   She is going back to Earth next year.

2. Do you think Margot will get out of the closet in time to see the sun? **(Predict)**

   YES / NO, because

NOTES

130 "Oh, but," Margot whispered, her eyes helpless. "But, this is the day, the scientists predict, they say, they *know*, the sun . . ."

"All a joke!" said the boy and seized her roughly. "Hey, everyone, let's put her in a closet before teacher comes!"

"No," said Margot, falling back.

They surged about her, caught her up, and bore her, protesting and then pleading and then crying, back into a tunnel, a room, a closet, where they slammed 140 and locked the door. They stood looking at the door and saw it tremble from her beating and throwing herself against it. They heard her muffled[1] cries. Then, smiling, they turned and went out and back down the tunnel, just as the teacher arrived.

Pause & Reflect

FOCUS

Read to find out what the children do when the rain stops.

MARK IT UP As you read, circle words and phrases that describe what they do in the sun.

"Ready, children?" She glanced at her watch.

"Yes!" said everyone.

"Are we all here?"

"Yes!"

The rain slackened still more.

150 They crowded to the huge door.

The rain stopped.

It was as if, in the midst of a film concerning an avalanche, a tornado, a hurricane, a volcanic eruption, something had, first, gone wrong with the sound apparatus, thus muffling and finally cutting off all noise, all of the blasts and repercussions[2] and

---

1. **muffled** (mŭf′ əld): made softer in volume.

2. **repercussions** (rē′ pər-kŭsh′ əns): echoes.

WORDS TO KNOW
apparatus (ăp′ə-rā′təs) *n.* a device or set of equipment used for a specific purpose

thunders, and then, secondly, ripped the film from the projector and inserted in its place a peaceful tropical slide which did not move or tremor.[3] The world ground to a standstill. The silence was so immense[4] and unbelievable that you felt that your ears had been stuffed or you had lost your hearing altogether. The children put their hands to their ears. They stood apart. The door slid back, and the smell of the silent, waiting world came in to them.

The sun came out.

It was the color of flaming bronze, and it was very large. And the sky around it was a blazing blue tile color. And the jungle burned with sunlight as the children, released from their spell, rushed out, yelling, into the summertime.

"Now, don't go too far," called the teacher after them. "You've only one hour, you know. You wouldn't want to get caught out!"

But they were running and turning their faces up to the sky and feeling the sun on their cheeks like a warm iron; they were taking off their jackets and letting the sun burn their arms.

"Oh, it's better than the sun lamps, isn't it?"

"Much, much better!"

They stopped running and stood in the great jungle that covered Venus, that grew and never stopped growing, <u>tumultuously</u>, even as you watched it. It was a nest of octopuses, clustering up great arms of fleshlike weed, wavering, flowering in this brief spring. It was the color of rubber and ash, this jungle, from the many years without sun. It was the color of stones and white cheeses and ink.

---

3. **tremor** (trĕm′ ər): shake or vibrate.

4. **immense** (ĭ-mĕns′): extremely large; huge.

WORDS TO KNOW
tumultuously (tōō-mŭl′chōō-əs-lē) *adv.* in a wild and disorderly way

MARK IT UP In the boxed passage, underline the details that help you picture the jungle on Venus. (Visualize)

NOTES

190   The children lay out, laughing, on the jungle mattress and heard it sigh and squeak under them, <u>resilient</u> and alive. They ran among the trees, they slipped and fell, they pushed each other, they played hide-and-seek and tag; but most of all they squinted at the sun until tears ran down their faces, they put their hands up at that yellowness and that amazing blueness, and they breathed of the fresh, fresh air and listened and listened to the silence which suspended them in a blessed sea of no sound and no motion.

200   They looked at everything and <u>savored</u> everything. Then, wildly, like animals escaped from their caves, they ran and ran in shouting circles. They ran for an hour and did not stop running.

   And then—

   In the midst of their running, one of the girls wailed.

   Everyone stopped.

   The girl, standing in the open, held out her hand.

   "Oh, look, look," she said, trembling.

   They came slowly to look at her opened palm.

210   In the center of it, cupped and huge, was a single raindrop.

   She began to cry, looking at it.

   They glanced quickly at the sky.

   "Oh. Oh."

Pause & Reflect

1. Check four items in the list below that describe what the children do in the sun. **(Visualize)**

❑ run

❑ take off their jackets

❑ play hide-and-seek

❑ fight

❑ squint at the sun

❑ draw pictures

2. Why does the girl begin to cry? Circle the answer. **(Infer)**

The girl realizes that the rain is about to start again.

The girl wishes the children had not locked Margot in the closet.

Pause & Reflect

WORDS TO KNOW
resilient (rĭ-zĭl′yənt) *adj.* flexible and springy
savor (sā′vər) *v.* to take great pleasure in

FOCUS

In this section, the rain returns. How do you think the story will end? Read to find out.

A few cold drops fell on their noses and their cheeks and their mouths. The sun faded behind a stir of mist. A wind blew cool around them.

220 They turned and started to walk back toward the underground house, their hands at their sides, their smiles vanishing away.

A boom of thunder startled them, and like leaves before a new hurricane, they tumbled upon each other and ran. Lightning struck ten miles away, five miles away, a mile, a half mile. The sky darkened into midnight in a flash.

They stood in the doorway of the underground for a moment until it was raining hard. Then they closed 230 the door and heard the gigantic sound of the rain falling in tons and avalanches everywhere and forever.

"Will it be seven more years?"

"Yes. Seven."

Then one of them gave a little cry.

"Margot!"

"What?"

"She's still in the closet where we locked her."

"Margot."

They stood as if someone had driven them, like so 240 many stakes, into the floor. They looked at each other and then looked away. They glanced out at the world that was raining now and raining and raining steadily. They could not meet each other's glances. Their faces were solemn and pale. They looked at their hands and feet, their faces down.

"Margot."

One of the girls said, "Well . . . ?"

No one moved.

"Go on," whispered the girl.

NOTES

⫿⫿⫿ MARK IT UP ⇒ How do the children feel when they remember Margot? Underline the details in the boxed passage that tell you. (Question)

NOTES

They walked slowly down the hall in the sound of cold rain. They turned through the doorway to the room, in the sound of the storm and thunder, lightning on their faces, blue and terrible. They walked over to the closet door slowly and stood by it.

Behind the closet door was only silence.

They unlocked the door, even more slowly, and let Margot out. ❖

Pause & Reflect

Pause & Reflect

1. Why do the other children forget about Margot? Complete the **cause-and-effect** chart below.

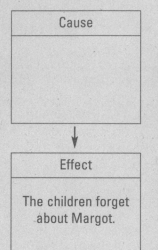

Cause

↓

Effect
The children forget about Margot.

2. How would you feel if you were Margot? **(Connect)**

_____

_____

_____

_____

 With a small group, discuss the abrupt ending of "All Summer in a Day." What do you think of the way that Bradbury chose to describe the opening of the closet door, but not what happens next? **(Evaluate)**

MARK IT UP In this story, the sun is described as a "lemon," a "penny," and a "flower." Choose your own **image** to represent the sun, and draw it in the space below.

Active Reading SkillBuilder

Evaluating

When you **evaluate** a story, you make a judgment about it. Use this diagram to record your opinions on the plot, setting, characters, and theme of this story. Support your opinions. Be sure your ideas are based on information in the story as well as on your own knowledge and experience.

SETTING	CHARACTERS
Believable?　　　**Interesting?** **Reason for my opinion:**	**Believable?**　　　**Interesting?** **Reason for my opinion:**

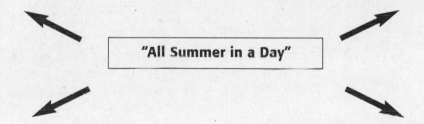

"All Summer in a Day"

PLOT	THEME
Believable?　　　**Interesting?** **Reason for my opinion:**	**Believable?** *yes*　　**Interesting?** *yes* **Reason for my opinion:** *It is true in real life just as it is in this story that people are sometimes mean to people they don't understand.*

Literary Analysis SkillBuilder

Science Fiction

Science fiction stories are based on scientific or technological developments—either real or futuristic. Many of these stories combine fantastic, imaginary details with realistic, concrete details. Often science fiction stories deal with issues that people today face. The stories also look to the future, imagining "what if?" As you read, note the fantastic and realistic details you find.

Fantastic Details	Realistic Details
takes place on Venus	*kids tease each other*

Follow Up: How is this future similar to the present? How is it different?

_____

_____

_____

_____

_____

Words to Know SkillBuilder

Words to Know

apparatus   concussion   resilient   savor   tumultuously

A. Decide which Word to Know is suggested by each description. Then write
the word on the blank line on the right.

The students ran through the museum, shrieking and
banging into displays.   _____
                                                                                                     (1)

The soft moss near the pond won't give you as much bounce
as a trampoline. Still, it's a great place to play.   _____
                                                                                                     (2)

When a truck comes down the road, the house
trembles, and new cracks open in the plaster walls.   _____
                                                                                                     (3)

In the science lab, we used to have only one microscope,
but now we have dozens of them, plus test tubes, and glass slides. _____
                                                                                                     (4)

The advice, "Stop and smell the roses," warns us that we miss
many of life's delights if we rush about.   _____
                                                                                                     (5)

B. Fill in each blank with the correct Word to Know.

1. Pots and pans are part of a cook's _____ .

2. Springs under a mattress make a bed more _____ .

3. When one bumper car hits another, the _____ that
   results can almost loosen your teeth.

4. Because frightened people often react _____ , fire
   drills are important and practical.

5. It takes longer to eat if you _____ every bite, but it is
   a healthier, more pleasant way to dine.

C. How do you think the children of Venus would react if they could spend one
summer afternoon at an ordinary playground on Earth? On a separate sheet of
paper, describe their afternoon, using at least **two** of the Words to Know.

Before You Read

Connect to Your Life

On the grid below, draw a simple map of your neighborhood or local area. Use the symbols in the key to identify places and landmarks. If you need additional symbols, create your own and add them to the key.

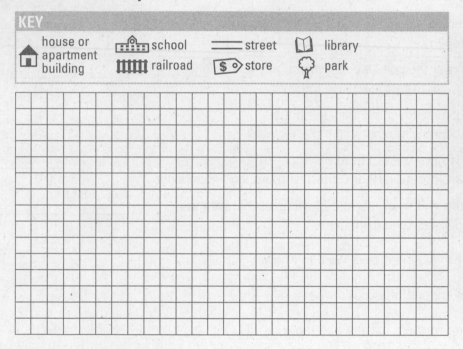

KEY

🏠 house or apartment building   🏫 school   ══ street   📖 library

🚃 railroad   🏷 store   🌳 park

Key to the Memoir

WHAT YOU NEED TO KNOW Thousands of Chinese immigrants came to San Francisco, California, during the gold rush that started in 1849. Many others came to work on the Central Pacific Railroad in the 1860s. As the Chinese-American population grew, many people believed that the newcomers were taking jobs away from whites. Laws were passed to restrict Chinese immigration. Other laws forced Chinese Americans to live only in limited areas called Chinatowns. These unfair laws remained in effect until the 1960s.

Chinatown

from *The Lost Garden*

by Laurence Yep

PREVIEW This selection is a chapter from Laurence Yep's memoir *The Lost Garden*. Yep grew up in San Francisco. Although Yep is Chinese American, he sometimes felt like an outsider in San Francisco's Chinatown. In this excerpt Yep struggles to understand his feelings about not fitting in.

READING TIP

Figures of Speech In the first sentence, the "pieces of the puzzle" are the different parts of Yep's identity. Exploring Chinatown is one way Yep tries to learn about his heritage.

NOTES

MARK IT UP **KEEP TRACK**
Remember to use these marks to keep track of your reading:

* This is important.

? I have a question about this.

! This is a surprise.

FOCUS
Read to find out about Chinatown and how it has changed over the years.

MARK IT UP As you read, underline details about Chinatown. An example is highlighted.

If Uncle Francis and other members of our family left Chinatown to explore America, my experience was the reverse because I was always going into Chinatown to explore the streets and perhaps find the key to the pieces of the puzzle. But the search only seemed to increase the number of pieces.

10 When I was a boy, Chinatown was much more like a small town than it is now. It was small not only in terms of population but in physical area as well. Its boundaries were pretty well set by Pacific Avenue on the north next to the Italian neighborhood of North Beach, Kearny Street on the east, Sacramento Street on the south, and Stockton Street on the west—an area only of a few city blocks.

There is a <u>stereotype</u> that the Chinese lived in Chinatown because they wanted to. The fact was that 20 before the fair housing laws[1] they often had no choice.

For years there was a little cottage on an ivy-covered hill in the southwest corner of Chinatown just above the Stockton tunnel. There was—and still is—very little plant life in Chinatown, so the only color green I saw was the paint on my school. The kind of green that is alive—lawns, bushes, and trees—was something I had to leave Chinatown to see, except for that ivy-covered slope. On windy days, the ivy itself would stir and move like a living sea; and overlooking the ivy was 30 a cottage that was charm itself. However, as much as I admired the house—on occasion I was disloyal enough to the Pearl Apartments to want to live in it—I knew it

---

1. **fair housing laws:** the civil rights acts of 1964 and 1968, which outlawed racial discrimination in the sale and rental of property, private as well as public.

WORDS TO KNOW
stereotype (stĕr′ē-ə-tīp′) *n.* a fixed idea, especially about the way a group of people looks or acts

wasn't for us. My Auntie Mary had once tried to rent it and had been refused because she was Chinese.

Out of some forty-five or so students in my class, I was one of the few who lived outside of Chinatown. Now, thanks to the fair housing laws that were passed in the 1960s, almost none of my former classmates live there; and Chinatown itself has spilled out of its
40 traditional boundaries.

Pause & Reflect

When I was a boy, though, we could see the results of white money and power on three sides of us. To the east we could stare up at the high-rise office buildings of the business district; and to the west, up the steep streets, were the fancy hotels of Nob Hill.[2] Southward lay
50 downtown and the fancy department stores.

Grant Avenue led directly to downtown; but for years I always thought of the Stockton tunnel as the symbolic[3] end to Chinatown. When it had been cut right through a hill, my father and his young friends had held foot races through it after midnight, hooting and hollering so that the echoes seemed to be the cheers of a huge crowd. The rich white world began just on the other side of the tunnel.

There were also invisible barriers that separated the
60 wealthy whites from the Chinese who cleaned their apartments or waited on their tables. The Chinese could see and even touch the good life; but they could not join in.

---

2. **Nob Hill:** a wealthy neighborhood in northeastern San Francisco. It is noted for its large luxury hotels.

3. **symbolic** (sĭm-bŏl'ĭk): expressed by an object that represents something invisible.

Pause & Reflect

1. How was Chinatown different from the parts of San Francisco where whites lived? **(Compare and Contrast)**

2. **REREAD** the boxed passage. Imagine you are the author. How would you feel walking through the fancy hotel with Harold? **(Connect)**

One of my classmates, Harold, had a paper route on Nob Hill. I still find it hard to believe that, up hills that angled some forty degrees or so, he carried a kind of poncho loaded with papers in front and back. But he did that every afternoon. Once I went along with him; and

70 I followed him into one of the fanciest hotels on Nob Hill, past the elaborately uniformed doorman, over the plush carpets, under the ornate chandeliers, and around in back, down concrete hallways as bleak as the ones in the Chinatown housing projects that were painted a cheap, <u>gaudy</u> yellow—a shade which my friend referred to as "landlord yellow." Harold would deliver the afternoon newspapers to the laundrymen and other workers. And with my friend that day, I wandered all around the roots of that <u>palatial</u> dream of wealth.

When the poncho was flat, my friend and I returned

80 to his <u>tenement</u> apartment where there was only one toilet to a floor; and the toilet lacked both a door and toilet paper. When you went, you brought in your own toilet paper. Nothing could be done about the door except changing your attitude about privacy.

Pause & Reflect

FOCUS

In this section, Yep describes a classmate named Paul.

MARK IT UP > As you read, circle details that help you get to know Paul. Put an exclamation point next to surprising statements about him.

Many of my schoolmates lived in the Chinatown projects, and I wasn't sure if life was any better in them than life in the projects near

90 our store. Another newspaper carrier named Paul lived there. As the oldest boy, Paul

WORDS TO KNOW
gaudy (gô'dē) *adj.* bright and showy in a way that displays bad taste
palatial (pə-lā'shəl) *adj.* large and richly decorated, like a palace
tenement (tĕn'ə-mənt) *n.* a crowded, rundown apartment building

was expected to look after his younger brothers and sisters while his parents worked—a common practice among many Chinese families. However, as a result, Paul had failed to develop many social skills let alone improve his English. I remember the nun sending him out on an errand and then asking the rest of the class to act as his special friend—which was easy for her to 100 say because she was an adult.

As far as I knew, he hung around with his own group in the projects rather than with anyone from school. His group, though, must have been pretty rough because one of them threw a knife that "accidentally" hit Paul in the eye. Fortunately, there was a charity that arranged an operation; and he was given a new eye from someone who had recently died.

We never knew the identity of the donor, but Paul amused himself by claiming it was a rich white. First, 110 he would clap a hand over his new eye and roll his remaining Chinese eye around. Then he would put his hand over his old one and gaze around elaborately with his new American eye. And then he would announce to us that the world looked just the same whether it was a Chinese eye or an American one.

Paul had shot up early and was a giant compared to the rest of us. When he ran, he looked like an ostrich with arms. He would kick out his legs explosively while his arms flailed the air, so it was hard not to laugh; but 120 we didn't because he was also <u>immensely</u> strong.

The playground at St. Mary's was only a concrete basketball court below. Up above, there was a kind of patio between the convent and the school where the younger children could play. However, the nuns were so worried about our knocking one another down that they forbade us to run during recess. About the only thing we could play under those conditions was a kind of slow-motion tag.

At noon, we could go across the street to the
130 Chinese Playground—the playground where my father had once been the director. In those days, it consisted of levels. The first level near the alley that became known as Hang Ah Alley was a volleyball and a tennis court. Down the steps was the next level with a sandbox (which was usually full of fleas), a small director's building, a Ping-Pong table, an area covered by tan bark that housed a slide, a set of bars, and a set of swings and other simple equipment. The level next to the Chinese Baptist church was the basketball court.

140 We had Physical Education once a week there. The playground director taught the boys, and I suppose the nun handled the girls. Sometimes it was calisthenics; other times it was baseball played with a tennis ball on the tennis court. There was no pitcher. Rather, the "batter" threw up the ball and hit it with his fist. Because of his size and added arm strength from his own paper route, Paul could hit a home run almost every time, sending the tennis ball flying over the high wire mesh fence.

Pause & Reflect

FOCUS

Read to find out how Yep felt about playing sports when he was young.

150 However, my experience was frequently the reverse. Because the present director knew that my father had once been the director of the playground, he was always urging me on to one disaster after another.

The worst happened when he wasn't present, though. In third grade, we had a very sweet nun, Sister Bridget, who used to play kickball with us. Kickball was like

Pause & Reflect

1. Cross out the phrase below that is *not* true of Paul. **(Clarify)**

   has good social skills

   looks after his younger brothers and sisters

   lives in the Chinatown projects

   is tall and strong

2. How does the author feel about Paul? **(Infer)**

baseball except that the pitcher bowled a ball the size of a basketball over the ground and the "batter" kicked it. One time someone kicked a ball so that it rolled foul. Retrieving it, I threw it to Sister; but as fate would have it, she had turned her head right at that moment to look at something else. I wound up hitting her in the head; and though there was no physical harm, I broke her glasses. Even though my parents paid for replacements, the rest of my class treated me as if I were <u>taboo</u> for striking a nun. I learned what it meant to be <u>shunned</u> and to be invisible.

The experience also reinforced my belief that I was terrible at sports. Despite all the practice and coaching from my father, I was hopeless when it came to catching any ball in any shape or size. Nor could I dribble a basketball, even though my father sometimes kept me practicing in the little courtyard until it was almost too dark to see.

The only sport that I was <u>remotely</u> good at was football. Having worked and lifted crates in the store made me fairly strong. As a result, I was a good lineman at blocking and rushing—like my hero, Leo Nomellini. However, I was still hopeless at catching a pass. I still remember one game where I dropped three touchdown passes in a row. I was so bad that our opponents stopped covering me. Our quarterback, unable to resist a wide-open target, persisted in throwing to me—and I dropped yet a fourth pass that could have been a touchdown.

The fact that my whole family was athletic only added to my disgrace. My father had played both basketball and football. My mother had also played basketball as well as being a track star, winning gold

MARK IT UP > What details help you **visualize** the kind of athlete Yep was? Circle the details on this page that stand out in your mind.

NOTES

WORDS TO KNOW
taboo (tə-bōō') *adj.* not to be noticed or mentioned
shunned (shŭnd) *adj.* avoided; shut out **shun** *v.*
remotely (rĭ-mōt'lē) *adv.* to a small degree; slightly

Pause & Reflect

1. How does Yep feel after he accidentally breaks the teacher's glasses during a kickball game? Why does he feel this way? **(Clarify)**

2. Why was Yep so unhappy about being bad at sports? **(Infer)**

NOTES

medals at the Chinese Olympics—a track event held for Chinese Americans. My brother was also excellent at basketball as well as bowling. Even worse, my father had coached championship teams when he had been a director at Chinese Playground—the very site of most of my failures. I often felt as if I were a major disappointment to my family.

Pause & Reflect

FOCUS

In this section, Yep explains why he felt like an outsider in Chinatown.

MARK IT UP As you read, circle details that help you understand why he felt different.

Moreover, my lack of
200 Chinese made me an outsider in Chinatown—sometimes even among my friends. Since it was a Catholic school taught by nuns, my friends would always tell dirty jokes in Chinese so the nuns wouldn't understand. However, neither did I, so I missed out on a good deal of humor when I was a boy. What Chinese I did pick up was the Chinese that
210 got spoken in the playground—mostly insults and <u>vulgar</u> names.

There were times even with a good friend like Harold when I felt different. Though Harold and I would go see American war movies, he could also open up a closet and show me the exotic Chinese weapons his father, a gardener, would fashion in his spare time, and I could sense a gulf between my experience and that of Harold. It was as if we belonged to two different worlds.

Even my friends' games and entertainments in
220 Chinatown could sometimes take their own different spin. They weren't quite like the games I saw American

WORDS TO KNOW
vulgar (vŭl′gər) *adj.* crudely disrespectful and displaying bad taste

boys playing on television or read about in Homer Price.[4]
Handball was played with the all-purpose tennis ball
against a brick wall in the courtyard.

Nor do I remember anyone ever drawing a circle
with chalk and shooting marbles in the American way.
Instead, someone would set up marbles on one side of
the basketball court at St. Mary's and invite the others
to try to hit them. If they did, they got the marbles. If
230 they didn't, the boy would quickly snatch up their
shooters. The ideal spot, of course, was where
irregularities in the paving created bumps or dips to
protect the owner's marbles. At times, one edge of the
courtyard would resemble a bazaar with different boys
trying to <u>entice</u> shooters to try their particular setup
with various shouted jingles.

Other times, they would set up baseball or football
cards. Trading cards weren't meant to be collector's
items but were used like marbles. In the case of cards,
240 the shooter would send a card flying with a flick of
the wrist. Mint cards[5] did not always fly the truest;
and certain cards with the right bends and folds
became deadly treasures.

But that sense of being different became sharpest the
time I was asked to sing. Our school had a quartet
that they sent around to build goodwill. The two girls
and two boys dressed up in outfits that were meant to
be Chinese: the girls in colored silk pajamas and
headdresses with pom-poms, the boys in robes with
250 black vests and caps topped by red knobs.

However, one day in December, one of the boys
took sick, so the nuns chose me to take his place.
Musical ability was not a consideration; the fit of the

---

4. **Homer Price:** a series of children's books by Robert McCloskey about a boy
   who has unusual adventures, published starting in 1943.

5. **mint cards:** freshly unwrapped trading cards, not yet damaged by handling.

WORDS TO KNOW
   entice (ĕn-tīs') v. to lure; to attract with promise of some reward

Pause & Reflect

1. Why does Yep feel like an outsider? Check three phrases below. (Clarify)

❏ is not used to the games played in Chinatown

❏ is given a costume that does not fit

❏ cannot understand Chinese

❏ does poorly in the singing performance

2. **REREAD** the boxed passage. Why did Yep no longer enjoy wearing costumes? (Paraphrase)

_____

_____

_____

_____

_____

_____

CHALLENGE Describe the main **conflict** that the author experienced growing up. Is this conflict shared by other young people in different times and places? Star passages in the selection to support your views. (Analyze)

_____

_____

costume was the important thing. We were brought to sing before a group of elderly people. I can remember following a cowboy with an accordion and a cowgirl with a short, spangled skirt who sang Christmas carols with a country twang.

Then we were ushered out on the small stage and I
260 could look out at the sea of elderly faces. I think they were quite charmed with the costumed Chinese children. Opening their mouths, the others began to sing in Chinese. Now during all this, no one had bothered to find out if I could sing, let alone sing in Chinese. I recognized the tune as "Silent Night" but the words were all in Chinese. I tried to fake it, but I was always one note and one pretend-syllable behind the others. Then they swung into "It Came Upon a Midnight Clear." This time they sang in English, so I
270 tried to sing along and ranged all over the musical scale except the notes I was supposed to be singing. Finally, one of the girls elbowed me in the ribs and from the side of her mouth, she whispered fiercely, "Just mouth the words."

Up until then I had enjoyed putting on costumes and even had a variety of hats, including cowboy and Robin Hood outfits as well as a French Foreign Legion hat and a Roman helmet; but the experience cured me of wanting to dress up and be something else. How
280 could I pretend to be somebody else when I didn't even know who I was?

In trying to find solutions, I had created more pieces to the puzzle: the athlete's son who was not an athlete, the boy who got "A's" in Chinese school without learning Chinese, the boy who could sing neither in key nor in Chinese with everyone else. ❖

Pause & Reflect

Active Reading SkillBuilder

Distinguishing Fact from Opinion

A **fact** is a statement that can be proved. In contrast, an **opinion** is a statement that expresses a person's feelings or beliefs.

Fact: Unlike most of his classmates, Laurence Yep lived outside of Chinatown.

Opinion: When Yep was a boy, Chinatown was like a small town.

Although an opinion cannot be proved, it can be supported by facts in the selection.

Supporting Facts: Chinatown had an area of only a few city blocks. Its population was fairly small.

For each of these opinions in the selection, find some supporting facts.

Author's Opinion	Supporting Facts
1. His friend Paul was good at sports.	*Paul was immensely strong.*
2. Yep was terrible at sports.	
3. He felt like an outsider in Chinatown.	

4. Do you agree or disagree with the following statement?

> Laurence Yep was right to feel that he didn't really "fit in" in Chinatown.

Write your opinion below. Then support it with facts from the selection.

My opinion: _____

_____

Supporting facts: _____

_____

Literary Analysis SkillBuilder

Primary Source

A **primary source** gives information from someone who has firsthand experience. Examples of primary sources include diaries, letters, autobiographies, and memoirs. A **secondary source** gives information from someone who does not have firsthand experience with the subject matter.

Choose a sentence from "Chinatown" and write it in the first column of the chart below. Then in the second column, become a "secondary source" and rewrite the sentence in your own words.

Primary Source	Secondary Source

Now write a "primary source" description of one of your own memories. Exchange books with a partner. Have your partner write a "secondary source" retelling of your memory in his or her own words.

My Memory (Primary Source)	My Partner's Retelling (Secondary Source)

Words to Know SkillBuilder

Words to Know

entice	immensely	remotely	stereotype	tenement
gaudy	palatial	shunned	taboo	vulgar

A. Beside each word write a word from the list above that is **either** a synonym **or** an antonym for the word. Then circle "synonyms" or "antonyms" to describe the word pair.

1. barely _____ synonyms/antonyms

2. luxurious _____ synonyms/antonyms

3. welcomed _____ synonyms/antonyms

4. tasteful _____ synonyms/antonyms

5. mansion _____ synonyms/antonyms

B. Fill in each set of blanks with the correct Word to Know. Then use the boxed letters to complete the sentence below the puzzle.

1. Some stores use coupons and advertisements to do this to customers.

__ __ __ __ ☐ __

2. A gross or tasteless joke might be described in this way.

__ __ __ __ ☐ __

3. The statement "Everyone from that town is careless" could be categorized as this.

__ __ __ ☐ __ __ __ __ __ __

4. This might be what you would call a topic that you are forbidden to discuss.

__ __ __ ☐ __

5. The team is losing 23–0. They are not even this close to winning.

__ __ __ __ __ ☐ __

Yep could not sing a single _____ in Chinese.

Before You Read

Connect to Your Life

Have you or someone you know ever had to move to a new place? How would frequent moves affect your feelings, schooling, and friendships? Record your thoughts in the chart below.

A Move to a New Home	
What Happens	**Why This Is Hard**
packing	I have to get rid of stuff I like.

Key to the Short Story

WHAT YOU NEED TO KNOW

WHO: This story is about a family of migrant farm workers, laborers who migrate—or move—from one area to another in search of work.

WHERE: This story is set in California, a state with a lot of farmland. Migrant farm workers also work in nearly every U.S. state.

WHY: Some crops—such as strawberries, grapes, and lettuce—are too fragile to be picked by machine. They must be picked by hand.

WHEN: Different areas of the country have different growing seasons. Migrant workers travel year-round, following the harvest.

The Circuit

by
Francisco Jiménez

PREVIEW Panchito's family moves often in search of work, and Panchito must help in the fields at certain times of the year. This prevents him from attending school regularly. When Panchito begins sixth grade, a teacher at his new school becomes an important friend.

READING TIP In this story, you will notice some text in italics. These are Spanish words and phrases. Panchito and his family are from Mexico; Spanish is their first language. Use the footnotes at the bottom of the page to help you with the meaning and pronunciation of the Spanish words.

NOTES

FOCUS

As the story opens, Panchito describes the end of the strawberry-picking season.

MARK IT UP As you read, underline words and phrases that tell how Panchito feels about the end of the season and his family's upcoming move. An example is highlighted.

It was that time of year again. Ito, the strawberry sharecropper,[1] did not smile. It was natural. The peak of the strawberry season was over and the last few days the workers, most of them *braceros*,[2] were not picking as many boxes as they had during
10 the months of June and July.

As the last days of August disappeared, so did the number of *braceros*. Sunday, only one—the best picker—came to work. I liked him. Sometimes we talked during our half-hour lunch break. That is how I found out he was from Jalisco,[3] the same state in Mexico my family was from. That Sunday was the last time I saw him.

When the sun had tired and sunk behind the mountains, Ito signaled us that it was time to go
20 home. "*Ya esora*,"[4] he yelled in his broken Spanish. Those were the words I waited for twelve hours a day, every day, seven days a week, week after week. And the thought of not hearing them again saddened me.

As we drove home, Papa did not say a word. With both hands on the wheel, he stared at the dirt road. My older brother, Roberto, was also silent. He leaned his head back and closed his eyes. Once in a while he cleared from his throat the dust that blew in from outside.

Yes, it was that time of year. When I opened the
30 front door to the shack, I stopped. Everything we owned was neatly packed in cardboard boxes. Suddenly I felt even more the weight of hours, days,

---

1. **sharecropper:** a person who farms rented land, paying for the use of the fields with a share of the crops raised.

2. *braceros* (brə-sâr´ōs) *Spanish:* Hispanic farm workers.

3. **Jalisco** (hä-lēs´kô).

4. *Ya esora:* a made-up spelling for the sharecropper's pronunciation of the Spanish expression *Ya es hora* (yä´ĕs-ô´rä), which means "It is time."

weeks, and months of work. I sat down on a box. The thought of having to move to Fresno and knowing what was in store for me there brought tears to my eyes.

That night I could not sleep. I lay in bed thinking about how much I hated this move.

Pause & Reflect

FOCUS

The family packs up and drives to Fresno. Read to find out what their new home is like.

MARK IT UP As you read, circle details that help you picture their new home.

A little before five o'clock in the morning, Papa woke 40 everyone up. A few minutes later, the yelling and screaming of my little brothers and sisters, for whom the move was a great adventure, broke the silence of dawn. Shortly, the barking of the dogs accompanied them.

While we packed the breakfast dishes, Papa went outside to start the "Carcanchita."[5] That was the name 50 Papa gave his old '38 black Plymouth. He bought it in a used-car lot in Santa Rosa in the winter of 1949. Papa was very proud of his car. "*Mi Carcanchita*," my little jalopy, he called it. He had a right to be proud of it. He spent a lot of time looking at other cars before buying this one. When he finally chose the "Carcanchita," he checked it thoroughly before driving it out of the car lot. He examined every inch of the car. He listened to the motor, tilting his head from side to side like a parrot, trying to detect any noises 60 that spelled car trouble. After being satisfied with the looks and sounds of the car, Papa then insisted on

---

5. Carcanchita (kär-kän-chē′tä) *Spanish:* jalopy.

WORDS TO KNOW
jalopy (jə-lŏp′ē) *n.* a shabby old car

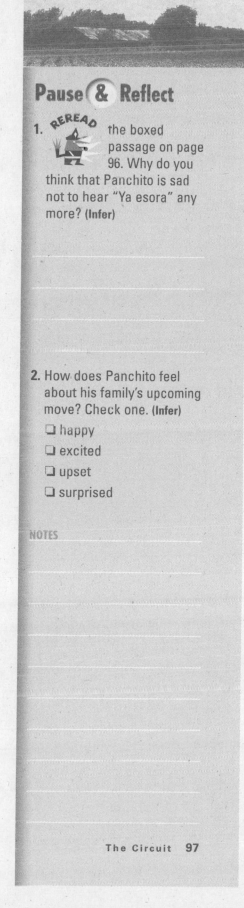

Pause & Reflect

1. **REREAD** the boxed passage on page 96. Why do you think that Panchito is sad not to hear "Ya esora" any more? **(Infer)**

2. How does Panchito feel about his family's upcoming move? Check one. **(Infer)**
   - ❑ happy
   - ❑ excited
   - ❑ upset
   - ❑ surprised

NOTES

knowing who the original owner was. He never did find out from the car salesman. But he bought the car anyway. Papa figured the original owner must have been an important man, because behind the rear seat of the car he found a blue necktie.

Papa parked the car out in front and left the motor running. "*Listo*,"[6] he yelled. Without saying a word, Roberto and I began to carry the boxes out to the car. 70 Roberto carried the two big boxes and I carried the smaller ones. Papa then threw the mattress on top of the car roof and tied it with ropes to the front and rear bumpers.

Everything was packed except Mama's pot. It was an old large galvanized pot she had picked up at an army <u>surplus</u> store in Santa Maria the year I was born. The pot was full of dents and nicks, and the more dents and nicks it had, the more Mama liked it. "*Mi olla*,"[7] she used to say proudly.

80 I held the front door open as Mama carefully carried out her pot by both handles, making sure not to spill the cooked beans. When she got to the car, Papa reached out to help her with it. Roberto opened the rear car door, and Papa gently placed it on the floor behind the front seat. All of us then climbed in. Papa sighed, wiped the sweat off his forehead with his sleeve, and said wearily: "*Es todo*."[8]

As we drove away, I felt a lump in my throat. I turned around and looked at our little shack for the 90 last time.

At sunset we drove into a labor camp near Fresno. Since Papa did not speak English, Mama asked the camp foreman if he needed any more workers. "We

---

6. *Listo* (lē'stô) *Spanish:* ready.
7. *Mi olla* (mē ô'yä) *Spanish:* my pot.
8. *Es todo* (ĕs tô'dô) *Spanish:* That's everything.

WORDS TO KNOW
surplus (sûr'pləs) *n.* extra material or supplies; leftovers

don't need no more," said the foreman, scratching his head. "Check with Sullivan down the road. Can't miss him. He lives in a big white house with a fence around it."

When we got there, Mama walked up to the house. She went through a white gate, past a row of rose
100 bushes, up the stairs to the front door. She rang the doorbell. The porch light went on and a tall husky man came out. They exchanged a few words. After the man went in, Mama clasped her hands and hurried back to the car. "We have work! Mr. Sullivan said we can stay there the whole season," she said, gasping and pointing to an old garage near the stables.

The garage was worn out by the years. It had no windows. The walls, eaten by termites, strained to support the roof full of holes. The loose dirt floor,
110 populated by earthworms, looked like a gray road map.

That night, by the light of a kerosene lamp, we unpacked and cleaned our new home. Roberto swept away the loose dirt, leaving the hard ground. Papa plugged the holes in the walls with old newspapers and tin can tops. Mama fed my little brothers and sisters. Papa and Roberto then brought in the mattress and placed it in the far corner of the garage. "Mama, you and the little ones sleep on the mattress. Roberto,
120 Panchito, and I will sleep outside under the trees," Papa said.

Pause & Reflect

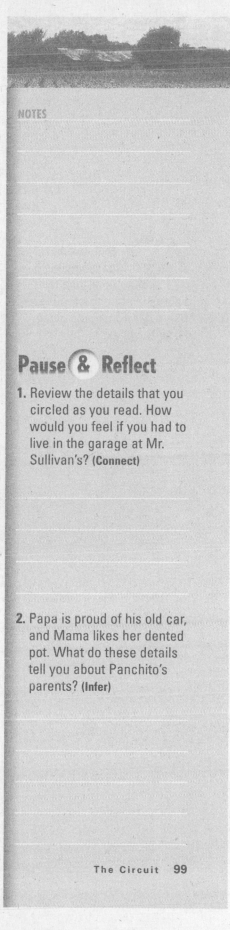

Pause & Reflect

1. Review the details that you circled as you read. How would you feel if you had to live in the garage at Mr. Sullivan's? **(Connect)**

2. Papa is proud of his old car, and Mama likes her dented pot. What do these details tell you about Panchito's parents? **(Infer)**

FOCUS

Panchito, his father, and his older brother begin work picking grapes.

⬚ **MARK IT UP** ⬚ As you read, circle words and phrases that describe what this work is like.

READ ALOUD the boxed passage. Vary your tone to express Panchito's feelings. Use a different voice when Roberto speaks.

NOTES

Early next morning Mr. Sullivan showed us where his crop was, and after breakfast, Papa, Roberto, and I headed for the <u>vineyard</u> to pick.

Around nine o'clock the temperature had risen to almost one hundred degrees. I

130 was completely soaked in sweat, and my mouth felt as if I had been chewing on a handkerchief. I walked over to the end of the row, picked up the jug of water we had brought, and began drinking. "Don't drink too much; you'll get sick," Roberto shouted. No sooner had he said that than I felt sick to my stomach. I dropped to my knees and let the jug roll off my hands. I remained motionless with my eyes glued on the hot, sandy ground. All I could hear was the drone of insects. Slowly I began to recover. I poured water over

140 my face and neck and watched the black mud run down my arms and hit the ground.

I still felt a little dizzy when we took a break to eat lunch. It was past two o'clock and we sat underneath a large walnut tree that was on the side of the road. While we ate, Papa jotted down the number of boxes we had picked. Roberto drew designs on the ground with a stick. Suddenly I noticed Papa's face turn pale as he looked down the road. "Here comes the school bus," he whispered loudly in alarm. Instinctively,

150 Roberto and I ran and hid in the vineyards. We did not want to get in trouble for not going to school. The yellow bus stopped in front of Mr. Sullivan's house. Two neatly dressed boys about my age got off. They carried books under their arms. After they crossed the street, the bus drove away. Roberto and I came out

WORDS TO KNOW
vineyard (vĭn′yerd) *n.* an area where grapevines have been planted

from hiding and joined Papa. "*Tienen que tener cuidado,*"[9] he warned us.

After lunch we went back to work. The sun kept beating down. The buzzing insects, the wet sweat, and
160 the hot dry dust made the afternoon seem to last forever. Finally the mountains around the valley reached out and swallowed the sun. Within an hour it was too dark to continue picking. The vines blanketed the grapes, making it difficult to see the bunches. "*Vámonos,*"[10] said Papa, signaling to us that it was time to quit work. Papa then took out a pencil and began to figure out how much we had earned our first day. He wrote down numbers, crossed some out, wrote down some more. "*Quince,*"[11] he murmured.

170 When we arrived home, we took a cold shower underneath a waterhose. We then sat down to eat dinner around some wooden crates that served as a table. Mama had cooked a special meal for us. We had rice and tortillas with *carne con chile,*[12] my favorite dish.

The next morning I could hardly move. My body ached all over. I felt little control over my arms and legs. This feeling went on every morning for days, until my muscles finally got used to the work.

Pause & Reflect

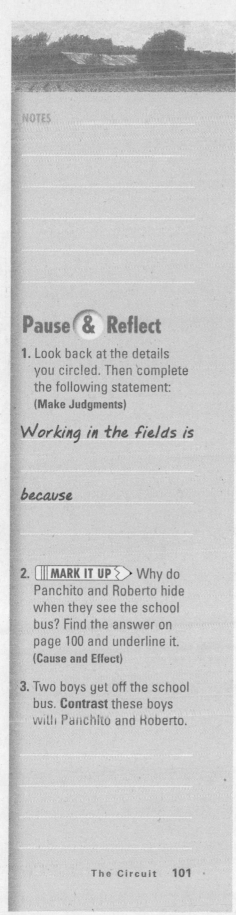

NOTES

Pause & Reflect

1. Look back at the details you circled. Then complete the following statement: **(Make Judgments)**

Working in the fields is

because

2. ▐▌▌ **MARK IT UP** ▷ Why do Panchito and Roberto hide when they see the school bus? Find the answer on page 100 and underline it. **(Cause and Effect)**

3. Two boys get off the school bus. **Contrast** these boys with Panchito and Roberto.

---

9. *Tienen que tener cuidado* (tyě-něn′ kě tě-něr′ kwē-dä′dô) *Spanish:* you have to be careful.

10. *Vámonos* (vä′mô-nôs) *Spanish:* Let's go.

11. *Quince* (kěn′sě) *Spanish:* fifteen.

12. *carne con chile* (kär′ně kôn chē′lě) *Spanish:* a mixture of meat and spicy red peppers.

FOCUS

The grape season ends. Panchito can now start sixth grade. Read to find out how Panchito feels as he enters a new school.

180   It was Monday, the first week of November. The grape season was over and I could now go to school. I woke up early that morning and lay in bed, looking at the stars and savoring the thought of not going to work and of starting sixth grade for the first time that year. Since I could not sleep, I decided to get up and join Papa and Roberto at breakfast. I sat at the table across from

190 Roberto, but I kept my head down. I did not want to look up and face him. I knew he was sad. He was not going to school today. He was not going tomorrow, or next week, or next month. He would not go until the cotton season was over, and that was sometime in February. I rubbed my hands together and watched the dry, acid-stained skin fall to the floor in little rolls.

When Papa and Roberto left for work, I felt relief. I walked to the top of a small grade next to the shack and watched the "Carcanchita" disappear in the

200 distance in a cloud of dust.

Two hours later, around eight o'clock, I stood by the side of the road waiting for school bus number twenty. When it arrived I climbed in. No one noticed me. Everyone was busy either talking or yelling. I sat in an empty seat in the back.

When the bus stopped in front of the school, I felt very nervous. I looked out the bus window and saw boys and girls carrying books under their arms. I felt empty. I put my hands in my pants pockets and

210 walked to the principal's office. When I entered I heard a woman's voice say: "May I help you?" I was startled. I had not heard English for months. For a few seconds I remained speechless. I looked at the lady who waited for an answer. My first <u>instinct</u> was to

WORDS TO KNOW
instinct (ĭn′stĭngkt′) *n.* a natural or automatic way of behaving

answer her in Spanish, but I held back. Finally, after struggling for English words I managed to tell her that I wanted to enroll in the sixth grade. After answering many questions, I was led to the classroom.

Mr. Lema, the sixth-grade teacher, greeted me and
220 assigned me a desk. He then introduced me to the class. I was so nervous and scared at that moment when everyone's eyes were on me that I wished I were with Papa and Roberto picking cotton. After taking roll, Mr. Lema gave the class the assignment for the first hour. "The first thing we have to do this morning is finish reading the story we began yesterday," he said enthusiastically. He walked up to me, handed me an English book, and asked me to read. "We are on page 125," he said politely. When I heard this, I felt my
230 blood rush to my head; I felt dizzy. "Would you like to read?" he asked <u>hesitantly</u>. I opened the book to page 125. My mouth was dry. My eyes began to water. I could not begin. "You can read later," Mr. Lema said understandingly.

For the rest of the reading period, I kept getting angrier and angrier with myself. I should have read, I thought to myself.

Pause & Reflect

FOCUS

Panchito receives two surprises. Read to find out about each one.

During recess I went into the restroom and opened my
240 English book to page 125. I began to read in a low voice, pretending I was in class. There were many words I did not know. I closed the book and headed back to the classroom.

WORDS TO KNOW
hesitantly (hĕz′ĭ-tənt-lē) *adv.* with pauses or uncertainty

Pause & Reflect

1. **REREAD** the boxed passage on page 102. How does Panchito feel about starting school? **(Infer)**

2. **MARK IT UP** Why does Panchito get angry at himself during reading period? Underline details on this page that tell you. **(Clarify)**

3. What **questions** do you have about the story so far? Write one or two.

Pause & Reflect

1. What surprise does Mr. Lema have for Panchito? Find the answer on this page and circle it. **(Clarify)**

2. What kind of person is Mr. Lema? Circle three words below that describe him. **(Draw Conclusions)**

understanding   noisy

pushy   scary

gentle   kind

3. **READ ALOUD** the boxed passage. How did the end of the story make you feel? Why? **(Connect)**

_____

_____

_____

_____

_____

How does the author show that Panchito is thoughtful and sensitive? Mark descriptions, dialogue, and actions in the story that help you understand Panchito's character. **(Analyze)**

Mr. Lema was sitting at his desk correcting papers. When I entered he looked up at me and smiled. I felt better. I walked up to him and asked if he could help me with the new words. "Gladly," he said.

The rest of the month I spent my lunch hours
250 working on English with Mr. Lema, my best friend at school.

One Friday during lunch hour, Mr. Lema asked me to take a walk with him to the music room. "Do you like music?" he asked me as we entered the building.

"Yes, I like Mexican *corridos*,"[13] I answered. He then picked up a trumpet, blew on it and handed it to me. The sound gave me goose bumps. I knew that sound. I had heard it in many Mexican *corridos*. "How would you like to learn how to play it?" he
260 asked. He must have read my face, because before I could answer, he added: "I'll teach you how to play it during our lunch hours."

That day I could hardly wait to get home to tell Papa and Mama the great news. As I got off the bus, my little brothers and sisters ran up to meet me. They were yelling and screaming. I thought they were happy to see me, but when I opened the door to our shack, I saw that everything we owned was neatly packed in cardboard boxes. ❖

Pause & Reflect

---

13. *corridos* (kô-rē′dôs) *Spanish:* slow, romantic songs.

Active Reading SkillBuilder

Making Inferences

Making an **inference** is forming an understanding beyond what is directly stated. It is often called "reading between the lines." One way readers form inferences is by connecting details from the text to experiences or to prior knowledge. Fill in the chart below with details from the story that provide the basis for your inferences about each of the characters. An example is shown.

Character	Details	Inference
Panchito	"I was completely soaked in sweat, and my mouth felt as if I had been chewing on a handkerchief."	Panchito is hot, tired, and thirsty.
Panchito		
Papa		
Mama		
Roberto		
Mr. Lema		

Literary Analysis SkillBuilder

Description

Some stories contain vivid **descriptions,** or details that help readers form strong mental pictures. These images may be of characters, settings, or events, and they always appeal to one or more of the five senses. In the story "The Circuit," the author uses descriptions that allow the reader to experience the lives of migrant farm workers. Fill in the chart below with details from the story. Identify the senses they appeal to. Then write whether they describe a person, a place, or an action.

Details	Senses Used	Describes
drone of insects	hearing	a place

Words to Know SkillBuilder

Words to Know

hesitantly   instinct   jalopy   surplus   vineyard

A. For each word in the first column, find the definition in the second column.
Write the letter of the definition in the blank.

_____ 1. instinct

_____ 2. vineyard

_____ 3. hesitantly

_____ 4. jalopy

_____ 5. surplus

A. with uncertainty

B. leftover materials

C. where grapevines have been planted

D. an urge to behave a certain way

E. a shabby automobile

B. Write the Word to Know that can replace the underlined word or phrase in
each sentence.

1. He read aloud <u>with frequent pauses</u>. _____

2. They saved the <u>extra</u> boxes for their next move. _____

3. The <u>field of grapevines</u> seemed immense to Panchito. _____

4. When they heard the bus, their <u>automatic reaction</u> was
   to duck. _____

5. Papa took care of the <u>old car</u> so that it would last. _____

Connect to Your Life

To what place would you most like to travel? Why? How would you get there—by car, bus, train, plane, or some other way? Write down your ideas in the wheel.

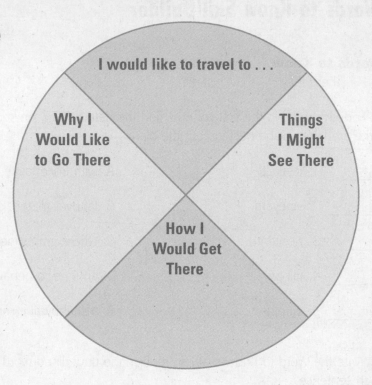

I would like to travel to . . .

Why I Would Like to Go There

Things I Might See There

How I Would Get There

Key to the Poems

WHAT TO LISTEN FOR Poetry is like words and music all rolled up in to one package. Rhythm, the pattern of heavy (ˊ) and light (˘) stresses, is one way poets add this musical quality. "Night Journey" is about a person riding on a train. Read the following lines:

> Bĕyónd thĕ móuntaĭn páss
> Mĭst déepĕns ŏn thĕ páne,
> Wĕ rúsh ĭntŏ ă ráin
> Thăt ráttlĕs dóublĕ gláss.

Notice how the rhythm is the same in each line. The regular "beat" gives the feeling of a train's motion.

WESTERN WAGONS

by Stephen Vincent Benét

NIGHT JOURNEY

by Theodore Roethke

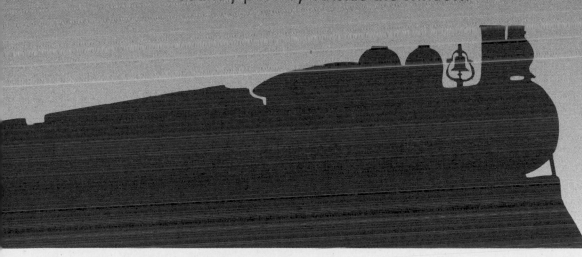

PREVIEW These two poems describe experiences of travelers to the American West. "Western Wagons" is about settlers in the 1800s.

About a century later, in "Night Journey," a passenger on a train watches the country pass by outside the window.

 Pronouns In the first three lines of the poem, the word *they* refers to the pioneers. In the rest of the poem, the speakers are often the pioneers themselves.

 the boxed passage. Would you have left your home to move west? (Connect)

YES / NO, because

FOCUS

The speaker tells about the pioneers, who went west. Read to find out why they did so.

MARK IT UP > As you read, underline words and phrases that help you understand why settlers went west. An example is highlighted.

Western Wagons

by Stephen Vincent Benét

They went with axe and rifle, when the trail
　　was still to blaze,
They went with wife and children, in the
　　prairie-schooner[1] days,
With banjo and with frying pan—Susanna,
　　don't you cry![2]
For I'm off to California to get rich out there
　　or die!

5 We've broken land and cleared it, but we're
　　tired of where we are.
They say that wild Nebraska is a better place
　　by far.
There's gold in far Wyoming, there's black
　　earth in Ioway,
So pack up the kids and blankets, for we're
　　moving out today!

---

1. **prairie-schooner:** a term comparing a covered wagon to a schooner, or large sailing ship, and the waving prairies to the sea.

2. **Susanna, don't you cry!:** a line from the American folk song "Oh! Susanna" by Stephen Foster. The song was popular among pioneers in the mid-1800s.

The cowards never started and the weak died on the road,

10 And all across the continent the endless campfires glowed.

We'd taken land and settled—but a traveler passed by—

And we're going West tomorrow—Lordy, never ask us why!

We're going West tomorrow, where the promises can't fail.

O'er the hills in legions, boys, and crowd the dusty trail!

15 We shall starve and freeze and suffer. We shall die, and tame the lands.

But we're going West tomorrow, with our fortune in our hands.

Pause & Reflect

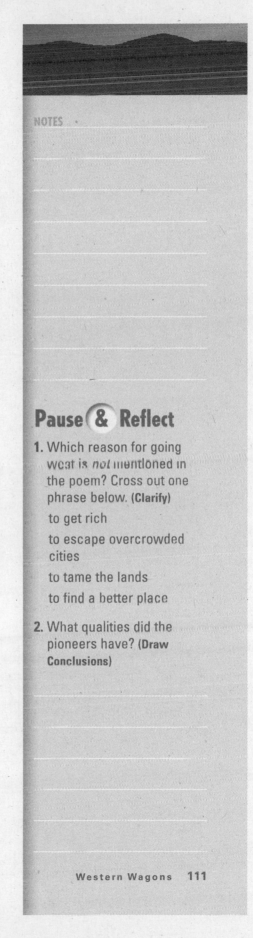

Pause & Reflect

1. Which reason for going west is *not* mentioned in the poem? Cross out one phrase below. **(Clarify)**

   to get rich

   to escape overcrowded cities

   to tame the lands

   to find a better place

2. What qualities did the pioneers have? **(Draw Conclusions)**

FOCUS

FOCUS

The speaker of this poem is traveling west on a train at night. Read to find out what he or she senses on this journey.

MARK IT UP As you read, circle details that describe what the speaker sees, hears, or feels.

Night Journey
by Theodore Roethke

Now as the train bears west,
Its rhythm rocks the earth,
And from my Pullman berth[1]
I stare into the night
5 While others take their rest.
Bridges of iron lace,
A suddenness of trees,
A lap of mountain mist
All cross my line of sight,
10 Then a bleak wasted place,
And a lake below my knees.
Full on my neck I feel
The straining at a curve;
My muscles move with steel,
15 I wake in every nerve.

 READ ALOUD the boxed passage. Then restate the last line in your own words. **(Paraphrase)**

---

1. **Pullman berth:** a fold-away bed in a train's sleeping car.

I watch a beacon[2] swing
From dark to blazing bright,
We thunder through ravines[3]
And gullies washed with light.
20 Beyond the mountain pass
Mist deepens on the pane,
We rush into a rain
That rattles double glass.
Wheels shake the roadbed stone,
25 The pistons[4] jerk and shove,
I stay up half the night
To see the land I love.

Pause & Reflect

Pause & Reflect

1. MARK IT UP > Look back at the details you circled as you read. Star the details that most helped you imagine yourself on the train. (Evaluate)

2. Would you like to be on this train ride? (Connect)

YES / NO, because

_____

_____

_____

_____

_____

_____

_____

"Western Wagons" captures the spirit of the pioneers. How would you describe that spirit? Does this spirit live on in the speaker of "Night Journey"? Explain. (Compare and Contrast)

_____

_____

_____

_____

_____

2. **beacon** (bē′kən): a light that signals the driver of a train.
3. **ravines** (rə-vēnz′): narrow valleys carved out of the earth by running water.
4. **pistons** (pĭs′tənz): devices that turn the wheels of the locomotive on a steam train.

Active Reading SkillBuilder

Reading Aloud

Very often, the key to fully appreciating poems is to read them aloud. Take turns reading the two poems aloud with a partner. In the chart, record pairs of rhyming lines and explain what effect these lines have on the poem.

Poem	Rhyming Lines	Effect
"Western Wagons"	. . . promises can't fail. . . . crowd the dusty trail!	The lines stress the feeling of eagerness.
"Night Journey"		

Literary Analysis SkillBuilder

Sound Devices

Poets use **sound devices** such as repetition, rhyme, and rhythm to create mood and to convey meaning. **Rhythm,** one of the most common poetic sound devices, is a pattern of stressed and unstressed syllables. When the poem is read aloud, the rhythm can be heard in the greater emphasis on some syllables than on others. Choose four lines from each poem. Write them in each chart below. Indicate the rhythmical pattern that you hear by marking the stressed (´) and unstressed (˘) syllables.

"Western Wagons"

They wěnt wǐth áxe ǎnd rífle̋, whěn thě tráil wǎs stíll tǒ bláze,

"Night Journey"

Follow Up: With a small group of classmates, discuss the effect of the rhythm of each poem.

Connect to Your Life

We are all unique. Think of some things that make you special. List them on the lines below. Then imagine how you would feel if these important things were all taken away from you.

My Identity

my name: _____

my language: _____

other: _____

_____

_____

Key to the Biography

WHAT YOU NEED TO KNOW The Songhai Empire dominated West Africa for about 125 years, reaching its peak in the 1500s. Most of the wealth and power of the large empire came from gold. Timbuktu, a bustling city located within the bounds of the empire, became a magnet for merchants and scholars. Find the empire and its major city on the map. Notice their central location within West Africa.

AFRICA

SAHARA

TIMBUKTU

SONGHAI EMPIRE

Rain Forest

Rain Forest

Abd al-Rahman Ibrahima

from NOW IS YOUR TIME!

by Walter Dean Myers

PREVIEW Abd al-Rahman Ibrahima was a real person. He was raised as a prince in West Africa. Suddenly his life changed forever. He was captured in his homeland and was forcibly shipped to America. As an enslaved person, he lost his name, his traditions, and his rights.

READING TIP In this true story, the author uses some names that are hard to pronounce. Don't worry if you are not familiar with them. Mainly, focus on keeping track of the events that the author describes.

NOTES

_____

_____

_____

_____

_____

_____

_____

_____

_____

_____

_____

_____

_____

_____

MARK IT UP **KEEP TRACK**
Remember to use these marks to keep track of your reading. Pay special attention to dates and key events.

* This is important.

? I have a question about this.

! This is a surprise.

. . . The Africans came from many countries, and from many cultures. Like the Native Americans, they established their territories based on centuries of tradition. Most, but not all, of the Africans who were brought to the colonies came from central and West Africa. Among them was a man named Abd al-Rahman Ibrahima.

FOCUS
Meet Ibrahima, the son of a Moslem chieftain in 18th-century West Africa.
MARK IT UP As you read, circle the details that help you understand Ibrahima's world. An example is highlighted.

The European invaders, along with those Africans 10 who cooperated with them, had made the times dangerous. African nations that had lived peacefully together for centuries now eyed each other warily. Slight insults led to major battles. Bands of outlaws roamed the countryside attacking the small villages, kidnapping those unfortunate enough to have wandered from the protection of their people. The 20 stories that came from the coast were frightening. Those kidnapped were taken to the sea and sold to whites, put on boats, and taken across the sea. No one knew what happened then.

Abd al-Rahman Ibrahima was born in 1762 in Fouta Djallon, a district of the present country of Guinea.[1] It is a beautiful land of green mountains rising majestically from grassy plains, a land rich with minerals, especially bauxite.

Ibrahima was a member of the powerful and 30 influential Fula people and a son of one of their chieftains. The religion of Islam had swept across

---

1. **Fouta Djallon** (füt′ə-jə-lōn′) . . . **Guinea** (gĭn′ē): Fouta Djallon is a small, mountainous region in Guinea, a small nation on the west coast of Africa.

Africa centuries before, and the young Ibrahima was raised in the tradition of the Moslems.[2]

The Fula were taller and lighter in complexion than the other <u>inhabitants</u> of Africa's west coast; they had silky hair, which they often wore long. A pastoral[3] people, the Fula had a complex system of government, with the state divided into nine provinces and each province divided again into smaller districts. Each
40 province had its chief and its subchiefs.

As the son of a chief, Ibrahima was expected to assume a role of political leadership when he came of age. He would also be expected to set a moral example and to be well versed in his religion. When he reached twelve he was sent to Timbuktu[4] to study.

Under the Songhai[5] <u>dynasty</u> leader Askia the Great, Timbuktu had become a center of learning and one of the largest cities in the Songhai Empire. The young Ibrahima knew he was privileged to attend the best-
50 known school in West Africa. Large and sophisticated, with wide, tree-lined streets, the city attracted scholars from Africa, Europe, and Asia. Islamic law, medicine, and mathematics were taught to the young men destined to become the leaders of their nations. It was a good place for a young man to be. The city was well guarded, too. It had to be, to prevent the <u>chaos</u> that, more and more, dominated African life nearer the coast.

---

2. **Islam** (ĭs-läm′) . . . **Moslems** (mŏz′ləmz): refers to the Arab conquests of the territory in North Africa, and the later spread of their religion beginning in the seventh century. (A Moslem is a believer in the religion of Islam.)

3. **pastoral** (păs′tər-əl): having a way of life based on raising livestock.

4. **Timbuktu** (tĭm′bŭk-tōō′): also known as Tombouctou, a city in the part of Africa now known as Mali.

5. **Songhai** (sông′hī′): a West African empire that thrived in the 1400s and 1500s.

WORDS TO KNOW
inhabitant (ĭn-hăb′ĭ-tənt) *n.* someone living in a particular place
dynasty (dī′nə-stē) *n.* a series of rulers who are members of the same family
chaos (kā′ŏs) *n.* a state of great disorder

Pause & Reflect

1. In the list below, mark a "T" beside each true statement and an "F" beside each false one. **(Evaluate)**

___ Ibrahima studied the Koran.

___ Timbuktu was a small city and not a center of learning.

___ Neighboring African states were on the brink of war.

___ Some Africans kidnapped innocent people.

2. Circle three words below that describe Ibrahima. **(Infer)**

playful   poor

educated   royal

long haired   short

NOTES

_____

_____

_____

_____

_____

_____

_____

Ibrahima learned first to recite from the Koran, the Moslem holy book, and then to read it in Arabic. From
60 the Koran, it was felt, came all other knowledge. After Ibrahima had finished his studies in Timbuktu, he returned to Fouta Djallon to continue to prepare himself to be a chief.

Pause & Reflect

FOCUS

Ibrahima and an Irish doctor become friends.

MARK IT UP As you read, underline details that tell you about their relationship.

The Fula had little contact with whites, and what little contact they did have was filled with danger. So when, in 1781, a white man claiming to be a ship's surgeon stumbled
70 into one of their villages, they were greatly surprised.

John Coates Cox hardly appeared to be a threat. A slight man, blind in one eye, he had been lost for days in the forested regions bordering the mountains. He had injured his leg, and it had become badly infected as he tried to find help. By the time he was found and brought to the Fula chiefs, he was more dead than alive.

Dr. Cox, an Irishman, told of being separated from a hunting party that had left from a ship on which he had
80 sailed as ship's surgeon. The Fula chief decided that he would help Cox. He was taken into a hut, and a healer was assigned the task of curing his infected leg.

During the months Dr. Cox stayed with the Fula, he met Ibrahima, now a tall, brown-skinned youth who had reached manhood. His bearing reflected his <u>status</u> as the son of a major chief. Dr. Cox had learned some Fulani, the Fula language, and the two men spoke.

WORDS TO KNOW
status (stā'təs) *n.* one's position in society; rank

Ibrahima was doubtless curious about the white man's world, and Dr. Cox was as impressed by Ibrahima's
90 education as he had been by the kindness of his people.

When Dr. Cox was well enough to leave, he was provided with a guard; but before he left, he warned the Fula about the danger of venturing too near the ships that docked off the coast of Guinea. The white doctor knew that the ships were there to take captives.

Cox and Ibrahima embraced fondly and said their good-byes, thinking they would never meet again.

Pause & Reflect

FOCUS

Ibrahima leads his people into battle. Read to find out what he is like as a leader.

Ibrahima married and became the father of several
100 children. He was in his mid-twenties when he found himself leading the Fula cavalry[6] in their war with the Mandingo.[7]

The first battles went well, with the enemy retreating before the advancing Fula. The foot warriors attacked first, breaking the enemy's ranks and making them easy prey for the well-trained Fula cavalry. With the enemy in full rout[8] the infantry[9] returned to their towns while the horsemen, led by Ibrahima, chased the remaining
110 stragglers. The Fula fought their enemies with spears, bows, slings, swords, and courage.

The path of pursuit led along a path that narrowed sharply as the forests thickened. The fleeing warriors disappeared into the forest that covered a sharply rising

---

6. **cavalry** (kăv′əl-rē): troops trained to ride on horseback.

7. **Mandingo** (măn-dĭng′gō): a member of any of various peoples of West Africa.

8. **in full rout:** in complete retreat.

9. **infantry** (ĭn′fən-trē): The branch of an army made up of units trained to fight on foot.

Pause & Reflect

1. Check the sentence below that describes the relationship between Ibrahima and Dr. Cox. **(Infer)**

   ❏ Ibrahima and Dr. Cox learned a lot from each other.

   ❏ Ibrahima had little to teach Dr. Cox.

   ❏ Dr. Cox had little to teach Ibrahima.

2. **REREAD** the boxed passage on page 120. How did the Fula help Dr. Cox? **(Cause and Effect)**

NOTES

Pause & Reflect

1. Write the numbers 1, 2, 3, or 4 to show the order in which the events below occurred. (Chronological Order)

___ European weapons defeated Ibrahima's soldiers.

___ Ibrahima was taken prisoner.

___ Ibrahima led his people into war.

___ Ibrahima's army fell into a trap.

2. How would you rate Ibrahima as a leader? (Evaluate)

mountain. Thinking the enemy had gone for good, Ibrahima felt it would be useless to chase them further.

"We could not see them," he would write later.

But against his better judgment, he decided to look for them. The horsemen dismounted at the foot of a hill and began the steep climb on foot. Halfway up the hill the Fula realized they had been lured into a trap! Ibrahima heard the rifles firing, saw the smoke from the powder and the men about him falling to the ground, screaming in agony. Some died instantly. Many horses, hit by the gunfire, thrashed about in pain and panic. The firing was coming from both sides, and Ibrahima ordered his men to the top of the hill, where they could, if time and Allah permitted it, try a charge using the speed and momentum of their remaining horses.

Ibrahima was among the first to mount, and urged his animal onward. The enemy warriors came out of the forests, some with bows and arrows, others with muskets that he knew they had obtained from the Europeans. The courage of the Fula could not match the fury of the guns. Ibrahima called out to his men to save themselves, to flee as they could. Many tried to escape, rushing madly past the guns. Few survived.

Those who did clustered about their young leader, determined to make one last, desperate stand. Ibrahima was hit in the back by an arrow, but the aim was not true and the arrow merely cut his broad shoulder. Then something smashed against his head from the rear.

The next thing Ibrahima knew was that he was choking. Then he felt himself being lifted from water. He tried to move his arms, but they had been fastened securely behind his back. He had been captured.

Pause & Reflect

FOCUS

Ibrahima has been captured by enemy warriors. Read to find out what happens to him.

|||MARK IT UP ⟩⟩ As you read, circle details that tell you about his sufferings.

When he came to his full senses, he looked around him. Those of his noble cavalry
150 who had not been captured were already dead. Ibrahima was unsteady on his legs as his clothes and sandals were stripped from him. The victorious Mandingo warriors now pushed him roughly into file with his men. They began the long <u>trek</u> that would lead them to the sea.

In Fouta Djallon being captured by the enemy meant being forced to do someone else's bidding,[10] sometimes
160 for years. If you could get a message to your people, you could, perhaps, buy your freedom. Otherwise, it was only if you were well liked, or if you married one of your captor's women, that you would be allowed to go free or to live like a free person.

Ibrahima sensed that things would not go well for him.

The journey to the sea took weeks. Ibrahima was tied to other men, with ropes around their necks. Each day they walked from dawn to dusk. Those who were slow were knocked brutally to the ground. Some of
170 those who could no longer walk were speared and left to die in agony. It was the lucky ones who were killed outright if they fell.

When they reached the sea, they remained bound hand and foot. There were men and women tied together. Small children clung to their mothers as they waited for the boats to come and the bargaining to begin.

Ibrahima, listening to the conversations of the men who held him captive, could understand those who spoke Arabic. These Africans were a low class of men, made
180 powerful by the guns they had been given, made evil by

10. **do someone else's bidding:** follow another's orders.

WORDS TO KNOW
trek (trĕk) *n.* a slow, difficult journey

NOTES

the white man's goods. But it didn't matter who was evil and who was good. It only mattered who held the gun.

Ibrahima was inspected on the shore, then put into irons and herded into a small boat that took him out to a ship that was larger than any he had ever seen.

The ship onto which Ibrahima was taken was already crowded with black captives. Some shook in fear; others, still tied, fought by hurling their bodies at their captors. The beating and the killing continued until the
190 ones who were left knew that their lot was hopeless.

On board the ship there were more whites with guns, who shoved them toward the open hatch. Some of the Africans hesitated at the hatch, and were clubbed down and pushed belowdecks.

It was dark beneath the deck, and difficult to breathe. Bodies were pressed close against other bodies. In the section of the ship he was in, men prayed to various gods in various languages. It seemed that the whites would never stop pushing men into the already
200 crowded space. Two sailors pushed the Africans into position so that each would lie in the smallest space possible. The sailors panted and sweated as they untied the men and then chained them to a railing that ran the length of the ship.

The ship rolled against its mooring as the anchor was lifted, and the journey began. The boards of the ship creaked and moaned as it lifted and fell in the sea. Some of the men got sick, vomiting upon themselves in the wretched darkness. They lay cramped, muscles aching,
210 irons cutting into their legs and wrists, gasping for air.

Once a day they would be brought out on deck and made to jump about for exercise. They were each given a handful of either beans or rice cooked with yams, and water from a cask. The white sailors looked hardly better than the Africans, but it was they who held the guns.

Illness and the stifling conditions on the ships caused many deaths. How many depended largely on how fast the ships could be loaded with Africans and how long the voyage from Africa took. It was not unusual for 10
220 percent of the Africans to die if the trip took longer than the usual twenty-five to thirty-five days.

Pause & Reflect

FOCUS

Ibrahima is sold into slavery in America.

MARK IT UP As you read, underline details that help you understand his hardships.

Ibrahima, now twenty-six years old, reached Mississippi in 1788. As the ship approached land, the Africans were brought onto the deck and fed. Some had oil put on their skins so they would look better; their sores were treated or covered with pitch. Then they were
230 given garments to wear in an obvious effort to improve their appearance.

Although Ibrahima could not speak English, he understood he was being bargained for. The white man who stood on the platform with him made him turn around, and several other white men neared him, touched his limbs, examined his teeth, looked into his eyes, and made him move about.

Thomas Foster, a tobacco grower and a hard-working man, had come from South Carolina with his
240 family and had settled on the rich lands that took their minerals from the Mississippi River. He already held one captive, a young boy. In August 1788 he bought two more. One of them was named Sambo, which means "second son." The other was Ibrahima.

Foster agreed to pay $930 for the two Africans. He paid $150 down and signed an agreement to pay

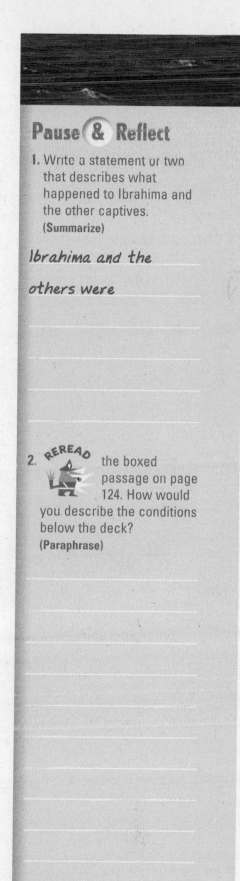

Pause & Reflect

1. Write a statement or two that describes what happened to Ibrahima and the other captives.
   (Summarize)

   Ibrahima and the

   others were

2. **REREAD** the boxed passage on page 124. How would you describe the conditions below the deck?
   (Paraphrase)

READING TIP The author uses **chronological order** to help keep track of important events in the story. As you read:

• Ask **questions** about what happened first, next, last.

NOTES

_____

_____

_____

_____

_____

_____

_____

READ ALOUD the boxed passage. What can you **infer** about how Ibrahima felt?

_____

_____

_____

_____

_____

_____

_____

_____

_____

_____

another $250 the following January and the remaining $530 in January of the following year.

250　　When Ibrahima arrived at Foster's farm, he tried to find someone who could explain to the white man who he was—the son of a chief. He wanted to offer a ransom for his own release, but Foster wasn't interested. He understood, perhaps from the boy whom he had purchased previously, that this new African was claiming to be an important person. Foster had probably never heard of the Fula or their culture; he had paid good money for the African, and wasn't about to give him up. Foster gave Ibrahima a new name: He called him Prince.

260　　For Ibrahima there was confusion and pain. What was he to do? A few months before, he had been a learned man and a leader among his people. Now he was a captive in a strange land where he neither spoke the language nor understood the customs. Was he never to see his family again? Were his sons forever lost to him?

As a Fula, Ibrahima wore his hair long; Foster insisted that it be cut. Ibrahima's clothing had been taken from him, and his sandals. Now the last remaining symbol of his people, his long hair, had been 270 taken as well.

He was told to work in the fields. He refused, and he was tied and whipped. The sting of the whip across his naked flesh was terribly painful, but it was nothing like the pain he felt within. The whippings forced him to work.

For Ibrahima this was not life, but a mockery of life. There was the waking in the morning and the sleeping at night; he worked, he ate, but this was not life. What was more, he could not see an end to it. It was this feeling that made him attempt to escape.

280　Ibrahima escaped to the backwoods regions of Natchez.[11] He hid there, eating wild berries and fruit, not daring to show his face to any man, white or black. There was no telling who could be trusted. Sometimes he saw men with dogs and knew they were searching for runaways, perhaps him.

　　Where was he to run? What was he to do? He didn't know the country, he didn't know how far it was from Fouta Djallon or how to get back to his homeland. He could tell that this place was ruled by white men who

290　held him in captivity. The other blacks he had seen were from all parts of Africa. Some he recognized by their tribal markings, some he did not. None were allowed to speak their native tongues around the white men. Some already knew nothing of the languages of their people.

　　As time passed, Ibrahima's despair deepened. His choices were simple. He could stay in the woods and probably die, or he could submit his body back into <u>bondage</u>. There is no place in Islamic law for a man to take his own life. Ibrahima returned to Thomas Foster.

300　Foster still owed money to the man from whom he had purchased Ibrahima. The debt would remain whether he still possessed the African or not. Foster was undoubtedly glad to see that the African had returned. Thin, nearly starving, Ibrahima was put to work.

Pause **&** Reflect

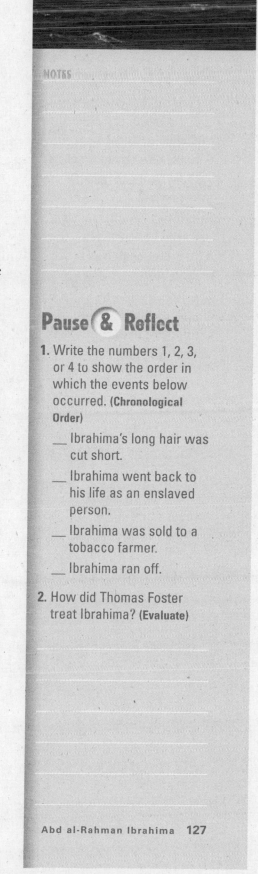

NOTES

Pause **&** Reflect

1. Write the numbers 1, 2, 3, or 4 to show the order in which the events below occurred. (**Chronological Order**)

___ Ibrahima's long hair was cut short.

___ Ibrahima went back to his life as an enslaved person.

___ Ibrahima was sold to a tobacco farmer.

___ Ibrahima ran off.

2. How did Thomas Foster treat Ibrahima? (**Evaluate**)

---

11. **Natchez** (năch′ĭz): an early settlement in what is now the state of Mississippi.

WORDS TO KNOW
　bondage (bŏn′dĭj) *n.* slavery

Pause & Reflect

1. Check three phrases below that are true of Ibrahima. **(Clarify)**

   ❏ kept his religious beliefs

   ❏ married and raised a family

   ❏ forgot his African name and traditions

   ❏ grew vegetables to sell in town

2. Do you think Dr. Cox will help Ibrahima get his freedom? **(Predict)**

   YES / NO, because

   _____

   _____

   _____

   _____

   _____

   _____

   _____

   _____

   _____

   _____

   _____

   _____

FOCUS
Read to find out about Ibrahima's later years as an enslaved person.

Ibrahima submitted himself to the will of Thomas Foster. He was a captive, held in bondage not only by Foster but by the society in
310 which he found himself. Ibrahima maintained his beliefs in the religion of Islam and kept its rituals as best he could. He was determined to be the same person he had always been: Abd al-Rahman Ibrahima of Fouta Djallon and of the proud Fula people.

By 1807 the area had become the Mississippi Territory. Ibrahima was forty-five and had been in bondage for twenty years. During those years he met and married a woman whom Foster had purchased, and they began to raise a family. Fouta Djallon was
320 more and more distant, and he had become resigned to the idea that he would never see it or his family again.

Thomas Foster had grown wealthy and had become an important man in the territory. At forty-five Ibrahima was considered old. He was less useful to Foster, who now let the tall African grow a few vegetables on a side plot and sell them in town, since there was nowhere in the territory that the black man could go where he would not be captured by some other white man and returned.

330 It was during one of these visits to town that Ibrahima saw a white man who looked familiar. The smallish man walked slowly and with a limp. Ibrahima cautiously approached the man and spoke to him. The man looked closely at Ibrahima, then spoke his name. It was Dr. Cox.

Pause & Reflect

FOCUS

Dr. Cox and others work to set Ibrahima free.

MARK IT UP As you read, circle key words or phrases that tell you about what happens to Ibrahima.

The two men shook hands, and Dr. Cox, who now lived in the territory, took Ibrahima to his home. John Cox had not <u>prospered</u> over the years, 340 but he was still hopeful. He listened carefully as Ibrahima told his story—the battle near Fouta Djallon, the defeat, the long journey across the Atlantic Ocean, and, finally, his sale to Thomas Foster and the years of labor.

Dr. Cox and Ibrahima went to the Foster plantation. Meeting with Foster, he explained how he had met the tall black man. Surely, he reasoned, knowing that Ibrahima was of royal blood, Foster would free him? 350 The answer was a firm, but polite, no. No amount of pleading would make Foster change his mind. It didn't matter that Dr. Cox had supported what Ibrahima had told Foster so many years before, that he was a prince. To Foster the man was merely his property.

Dr. Cox had to leave the man whose people had saved his life, but he told Ibrahima that he would never stop working for his freedom.

Andrew Marschalk, the son of a Dutch baker, was a printer, a pioneer in his field, and a man of great 360 curiosity. By the time Marschalk heard about it, Cox had told a great many people in the Natchez district the story of African royalty being held in slavery in America. Marschalk was fascinated. He suggested that Ibrahima write a letter to his people, telling them of his whereabouts and asking them to ransom him. But Ibrahima had not been to his homeland in twenty years. The people there were still being captured by slave traders. He would have to send a messenger who

---

WORDS TO KNOW
prosper (prŏs′pər) v. to be successful; thrive

knew the countryside, and who knew the Fula. Where
370 would he find such a man?

For a long time Ibrahima did nothing. Finally, some
time after the death of Dr. Cox in 1816, Ibrahima
wrote the letter that Marschalk suggested. He had little
faith in the <u>procedure</u> but felt he had nothing to lose.
Marschalk was surprised when Ibrahima appeared with
the letter written neatly in Arabic. Since one place in
Africa was the same as the next to Marschalk, he sent
the letter not to Fouta Djallon but to Morocco.

The government of Morocco did not know Ibrahima
380 but understood from his letter that he was a Moslem.
Moroccan officials, in a letter to President James
Monroe, pleaded for the release of Ibrahima. The letter
reached Henry Clay, the American secretary of state.

The United States had recently ended a bitter war with
Tripoli in North Africa and welcomed the idea of
establishing good relations with Morocco, another North
African country. Clay wrote to Foster about Ibrahima.

Foster resented the idea of releasing Ibrahima. The
very idea that the government of Morocco had written
390 to Clay and discussed a religion that Ibrahima shared
with other Africans gave Ibrahima a past that Foster
had long denied, a past as honorable as Foster's. This
idea challenged a basic <u>premise</u> of slavery—a premise
that Foster must have believed without <u>reservation</u>:
that the Africans had been nothing but savages, with
no humanity or human feelings, and therefore it was
all right to enslave them. But after more letters and
pressure from the State Department, Foster agreed to
release Ibrahima if he could be assured that Ibrahima
400 would leave the country and return to Fouta Djallon.

WORDS TO KNOW
procedure (prə-sē′jər) *n.* a course of action
premise (prĕm′ĭs) *n.* an idea that forms the basis of an argument
reservation (rĕz′ər-vā′shən) *n.* a doubt; an exception

Many people who believed that slavery was wrong also believed that Africans could not live among white Americans. The American Colonization Society had been formed expressly to send freed Africans back to Africa. The society bought land, and a colony called Liberia was established on the west coast of Africa. Foster was assured that Ibrahima would be sent there.

By then Ibrahima's cause had been taken up by a number of abolitionist[12] groups in the North as well as
410 by many free Africans. They raised money to buy his wife's freedom as well.

On February 7, 1829, Ibrahima and his wife sailed on the ship *Harriet* for Africa. The ship reached Liberia, and Ibrahima now had to find a way to reach his people again. He never found that way. Abd al-Rahman Ibrahima died in Liberia in July 1829.

> Who was Ibrahima? He was one of millions of Africans taken by force from their native lands. He was the son of a chief, a warrior, and a scholar. But to
> 420 Ibrahima the only thing that mattered was that he had lost his freedom. If he had been a herder in Fouta Djallon, or an artist in Benin, or a farmer along the Gambia, it would have been the same. Ibrahima was an African who loved freedom no less than other beings on earth. And he was denied that freedom. ❖

Pause & Reflect

Pause & Reflect

1. Write the numbers 1, 2, 3, or 4 to show the order in which the events below occurred. **(Chronological Order)**

___ Ibrahima died in Liberia.

___ Foster agreed to free Ibrahima.

___ Henry Clay wrote to Foster about Ibrahima.

___ Dr. Cox died before finding a way to help Ibrahima.

2. REREAD the boxed passage. Which of the following statements expresses the author's views? Circle it. **(Draw Conclusions)**

No human being should be denied freedom.

Bad things in the past should not be questioned.

 CHALLENGE What did you learn about the horrors of slavery from reading about Ibrahima? Mark passages in the biography to support your ideas. **(Analyze)**

_____

_____

_____

---

12. **abolitionist** (ăb′ə-lĭsh′ə-nĭst): favoring the end of slavery.

MARK IT UP > A **fact** is a statement that can be proved. An **opinion** is a statement that expresses a person's beliefs or feelings. Look back at "Abd al-Rahman Ibrahima." Circle at least three facts and three opinions that you find in the story. Then list them here.

FACTS	OPINIONS
1. Timbuktu had become a center of learning.	1. It was a good place for a young man to be.
2.	2.
3.	3.

Active Reading SkillBuilder

Chronological Order

Chronological order is the order in which events happen in time. This type of organization allows biographers to follow their subjects from birth to death and show the significant events of their lives in sequence.

Ibrahima's life spanned two continents and almost seven decades. Label the vertical lines on the time line with the important **dates** and **events** in Ibrahima's life. Place events without exact dates on the horizontal lines, near other events that occurred at about the same time.

birth of
Ibrahima

death of
Ibrahima in
Liberia

1762

1829

Literary Analysis SkillBuilder

Sources of Information

A biographer draws from many different **sources of information** to put together his or her version of a person's life. **Primary sources,** such as journals or letters written by the actual person, and **secondary sources,** such as history books or newspaper articles, help writers portray the life and times of biography subjects. List primary and secondary sources that would be useful to someone writing about you. Circle the sources that would provide facts about you. Then underline those sources that might provide insight into your feelings and ideas.

Primary Sources	Secondary Sources
photographs	school newspaper

Words to Know SkillBuilder

Words to Know

bondage	dynasty	premise	prosper	status
chaos	inhabitant	procedure	reservation	trek

A. Fill in each set of blanks with one of the Words to Know. The boxed letters will spell out the name of the people who captured Ibrahima and sold him into slavery.

1. This could be a long hike with a heavy backpack. ☐ __ __ __

2. Leaving a kindergarten class alone with no teacher could quickly result in this. __ ☐ __ __ __

3. This keeps you from being 100 percent sure or completely confident. __ __ __ ☐ __ __ __ __ __

4. If this thought or statement is not true, you may come to a false conclusion. __ __ __ ☐ __ __ __

5. This is higher for a general than for a private and lower for a commoner than for a king. __ __ ☐ __ __ __

6. This is what continues when a queen passes the crown on to her son or daughter. __ __ ☐ __ __ __ __

7. This is the sequence to be followed in doing something. __ __ __ __ __ ☐ __ __ __

8. If you're just passing through, then you are not this. __ __ __ __ __ ☐ __ __ ☐ __

9. This is the opposite of freedom. __ __ __ __ __ ☐ __

10. This is what parents hope their children will do. __ __ ☐ __ __ __

Who captured Ibrahima? _____

B. What did you learn from the story of Abd al-Rahman Ibrahima about what happened to enslaved people before they reached America? Use at least **four** of the Words to Know. Write your answer on a separate sheet of paper.

Connect to Your Life

Helen Keller was blind and deaf. She got to know her world mainly by using her senses of touch, smell, and taste. What things do you enjoy by using these three senses? Add at least two items to the lists below.

Sense of Touch	Sense of Smell	Sense of Taste
furry puppy	baking cookies	eating pizza

Key to the Autobiography

WHAT DO YOU THINK? Helen Keller wrote the following statement about herself. Think about what it means, and why she felt this way.

In the still, dark world in which I lived there was no strong sentiment or tenderness.

What would you say to her? Write your response on the lines below.

_____

_____

_____

_____

from

The
Story
of My
Life

by Helen Keller

PREVIEW In the selection you are about to read, Helen Keller describes some of her childhood experiences. Helen was a bright and active toddler. But, before she turned two, an illness left her blind and deaf and cut off from the world. Then someone came into her life and changed it forever.

READING TIP Imagine, or **visualize,** what Helen Keller describes. Don't let the difficult words slow you down. Try to focus on the strongest images and feelings.

NOTES

MARK IT UP **KEEP TRACK**
Remember to use these marks to keep track of your reading.

* This is important.

? I have a question about this.

! This is a surprise.

FOCUS

In this part, you'll get to know six-year-old Helen Keller. Read to find out what she was like before she met her teacher.

MARK IT UP Circle details that help you understand what Helen was like. An example is highlighted.

The most important day I remember in all my life is the one on which my teacher, Anne Mansfield Sullivan, came to me. I am filled with wonder when I consider the immeasurable contrasts between the two lives which it connects. It was the third of
10 March, 1887, three months before I was seven years old.

On the afternoon of that eventful day, I stood on the porch, dumb, expectant. I guessed vaguely[1] from my mother's signs and from the hurrying to and fro in the house that something unusual was about to happen, so I went to the door and waited on the steps. The afternoon sun penetrated the mass of honeysuckle that covered the porch, and fell on my upturned face. My fingers lingered almost unconsciously on the familiar
20 leaves and blossoms which had just come forth to greet the sweet southern spring. I did not know what the future held of marvel or surprise for me. Anger and bitterness had preyed upon me continually for weeks and a deep languor[2] had succeeded this passionate struggle.

Have you ever been at sea in a dense fog, when it seemed as if a tangible white darkness shut you in, and the great ship, tense and anxious, groped her way toward the shore with plummet and sounding-line,[3] and

---

1. **vaguely** (vāg′ lē): not clearly expressed; lacking clarity.
2. **languor** (lăng′ ər): lack of energy; tiredness; listlessness.
3. **plummet** (plŭm′ĭt) **and sounding-line:** a metal weight tied to the end of a rope that is used to determine water depth.

WORDS TO KNOW
bitterness (bĭt′ər-nĭs) *n.* a feeling of disgust or resentment
prey (prā) *v.* to have a harmful effect
succeed (sək-sēd′) *v.* to come after; follow
tangible (tăn′jə-bəl) *adj.* able to be touched or grasped

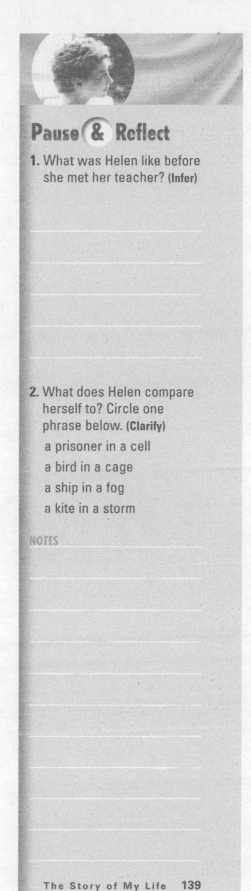

30 you waited with beating heart for something to happen? I was like that ship before my education began, only I was without compass or sounding-line, and had no way of knowing how near the harbor was. "Light! Give me light!" was the wordless cry of my soul, and the light of love shone on me in that very hour.

I felt approaching footsteps. I stretched out my hand as I supposed to my mother. Someone took it, and I was caught up and held close in the arms of her who had come to <u>reveal</u> all things to me, and, more than all
40 things else, to love me.

Pause & Reflect

FOCUS

Read to find out how Miss Sullivan tries to teach Helen.

MARK IT UP >> As you read, underline the details that help you understand Miss Sullivan's methods.

The morning after my teacher came she led me into her room and gave me a doll. The little blind children at the Perkins Institution had sent it and Laura Bridgman had dressed it; but I did not know this until afterward. When I had played with it a little
50 while, Miss Sullivan slowly spelled into my hand the word "d-o-l-l." I was at once interested in this finger play and tried to imitate it. When I finally succeeded in making the letters correctly I was flushed with childish pleasure and pride. Running downstairs to my

WORDS TO KNOW
reveal (rĭ-vēl') v. to bring to view; to show

Pause & Reflect

1. What was Helen like before she met her teacher? (Infer)

2. What does Helen compare herself to? Circle one phrase below. (Clarify)

   a prisoner in a cell

   a bird in a cage

   a ship in a fog

   a kite in a storm

NOTES

mother I held up my hand and made the letters for *doll*. I did not know that I was spelling a word or even that words existed; I was simply making my fingers go in monkey-like imitation. In the days that followed I learned to spell in this uncomprehending[4] way a great
60 many words, among them *pin, hat, cup* and a few verbs like *sit, stand,* and *walk*. But my teacher had been with me several weeks before I understood that everything has a name.

One day, while I was playing with my new doll, Miss Sullivan put my big rag doll into my lap also, spelled "d-o-l-l" and tried to make me understand that "d-o-l-l" applied to both. Earlier in the day we had had a tussle[5] over the words "m-u-g" and "w-a-t-e-r." Miss Sullivan had tried to <u>impress</u> upon me that
70 "m-u-g" is *mug* and that "w-a-t-e-r" is *water,* but I <u>persisted</u> in confounding[6] the two. In despair she had dropped the subject for the time, only to renew it at the first opportunity. I became impatient at her repeated attempts and, seizing the new doll, I dashed it upon the floor. I was keenly delighted when I felt the fragments of the broken doll at my feet. Neither sorrow nor regret followed my passionate outburst. I had not loved the doll. In the still, dark world in which I lived there was no strong <u>sentiment</u> or
80 tenderness. I felt my teacher sweep the fragments to one side of the hearth and I had a sense of satisfaction that the cause of my discomfort was removed. She brought me my hat, and I knew I was going out into

---

4. **uncomprehending** (ŭn kŏm-prĭ-hĕn′ dĭng): not understanding.
5. **tussle** (tŭs′əl): a rough struggle.
6. **confounding** (kən-found′ĭng): confusing.

WORDS TO KNOW
 impress (ĭm-prĕs′) *v.* to implant firmly in the mind; convey vividly
 persist (pər-sĭst′) *v.* to continue stubbornly
 sentiment (sĕn′tə-mənt) *n.* emotion

the warm sunshine. This thought, if a wordless sensation[7] may be called a thought, made me hop and skip with pleasure.

Pause & Reflect

FOCUS

Read to find out about Helen's new discovery.

We walked down the path to the well-house, attracted by the fragrance of the
90 honeysuckle with which it was covered. Someone was drawing water and my teacher placed my hand under the spout. As the cool stream gushed over one hand she spelled into the other the word *water,* first slowly, then rapidly. I stood still, my whole attention fixed upon the motions of her fingers. Suddenly I felt a misty consciousness as of something forgotten—a thrill of returning thought; and somehow the mystery of language was revealed to me. I knew then that "w-a-t-e-r" meant the wonderful
100 cool something that was flowing over my hand. That living word awakened my soul, gave it light, hope, joy, set it free! There were barriers[8] still, it is true, but barriers that could in time be swept away.

I left the well-house eager to learn. Everything had a name, and each name gave birth to a new thought. As we returned to the house every object which I touched seemed to quiver with life. That was because I saw everything with the strange, new sight that had come

---

7. **sensation** (sĕn-sā′shən): a feeling; a state of unusually strong interest or emotion.
8. **barriers** (băr′ē-ərs): things that obstruct; obstacles.

Pause & Reflect

1. How does Miss Sullivan try to teach Helen? Check one phrase below. **(Clarify)**
   ❏ spells words in Helen's hand
   ❏ sings the names of things
   ❏ punishes Helen often

2. What does Helen do because she is upset and angry? Check one phrase below. **(Cause and Effect)**
   ❏ runs away to the woods
   ❏ locks herself in her room
   ❏ breaks her doll

NOTES

Pause & Reflect

1. How did Helen learn that everything has a name? **(Cause and Effect)**

_____

_____

_____

_____

_____

_____

2. Helen says that for the first time she "longed for a new day to come." How do you imagine her life will be different from now on? **(Draw Conclusions)**

_____

_____

_____

_____

_____

_____

_____

_____

_____

CHALLENGE How does this selection help you understand what it is like to be deaf and blind? Mark passages in the selection to support your views. **(Analyze)**

110 to me. On entering the door I remembered the doll I had broken. I felt my way to the hearth and picked up the pieces. I tried <u>vainly</u> to put them together. Then my eyes filled with tears; for I realized what I had done, and for the first time I felt <u>repentance</u> and sorrow.

I learned a great many new words that day. I do not remember what they all were; but I do know that _mother, father, sister, teacher_ were among them— words that were to make the world blossom for me, "like Aaron's rod, with flowers."⁹ It would have been difficult to find a happier child than I was as I lay in 120 my crib at the close of that eventful day and lived over the joys it had brought me, and for the first time longed for a new day to come. ❖

Pause & Reflect

9. **"like Aaron's rod, with flowers":** a reference to a passage of the Bible in which a wooden rod miraculously bears flowers and fruit (Numbers 17:8).

WORDS TO KNOW
vainly (vān′lē) _adv._ without success
repentance (rǐ-pĕn′təns) _n._ a regret for past behavior

Active Reading SkillBuilder

Clarifying

When you pause to think about ideas in a story, to look up an unfamiliar word, or to connect new details with previous information, you are **clarifying.** Clarifying leads to a more complete understanding of what you read. Pause during your reading of the excerpt from Helen Keller's autobiography to note the important ideas and events. Also record questions that you have as well as the answers you find.

Important Events	Questions / Answers
Teacher Anne Sullivan arrives.	Why is the arrival of Miss Sullivan "the most important day"?
	She changes Helen's life by teaching her to communicate.

Literary Analysis SkillBuilder

Sensory Details

Images that appeal to the senses are called **sensory details.** Sensory details communicate vividly what a character hears, sees, touches, smells, or tastes. To describe her life before and after Anne Sullivan's arrival, Helen Keller uses sensory details that create strong mental images. Chart the sensory details and the senses to which they appeal.

Sensory Details	
Smell	
Touch	sun . . . fell on my upturned face
Taste	
Sight	
Hearing	

Words to Know SkillBuilder

Words to Know

bitterness	persist	repentance	sentiment	tangible
impress	prey	reveal	succeed	vainly

Write the Word to Know that best completes each sentence.

1. Miss Sullivan knew that once Helen understood one word, others would

   _____ .

2. Helen wanted to _____ upon Miss Sullivan her

   excitement at her new discovery.

3. Her frustration and _____ were expressed in bad behavior.

4. Anne Sullivan's teaching methods would _____

   Helen's natural intelligence, long hidden by Helen's disabilities.

5. Sometimes, Miss Sullivan must have been discouraged about Helen's

   progress and been tempted not to _____ in her efforts.

6. Helen was overcome by a feeling of _____ and tried

   to put the doll back together.

7. Because Helen could not see or hear, language had to be communicated

   in a _____ way that she could feel.

8. Doctors tried _____ to help the Kellers cope with

   Helen's frustration.

9. Miss Sullivan did not allow any _____ or pity to stop her.

10. Helen's mother felt worry about the future _____ on

   her mind and spirits.

Before You Read

Connect to Your Life

Have you ever seen a pet helping its owner in a special way?
Use the word web below to list ways that pets, such as dogs,
can help people.

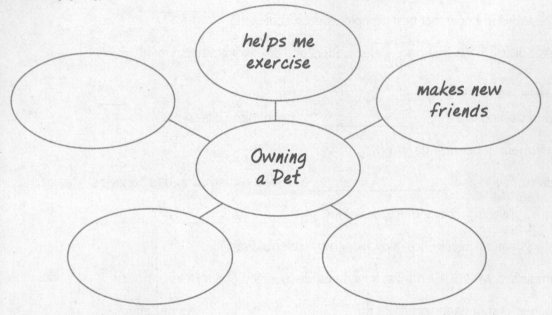

helps me
exercise

makes new
friends

Owning
a Pet

Key to the Story

WHAT YOU NEED TO KNOW Cornwall,
England is the setting of this story. Shade
the coastal areas of Southwest England,
where Cornwall is located. Then find
Liverpool—some 400 miles away to the
north. Lob, the hero of this story, finds
his way back to Cornwall from Liverpool
twice, and both times on foot.

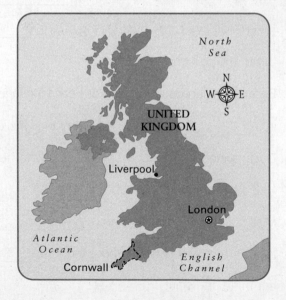

North
Sea

N
W E
S

UNITED
KINGDOM

Liverpool

London

Atlantic
Ocean

Cornwall

English
Channel

Lob's Girl

BY JOAN AIKEN

PREVIEW The opening sentence, "Some people choose their dogs, and some dogs choose their people," introduces you to Sandy and her beloved dog, Lob. Lob stands by Sandy to the end—and perhaps beyond.

READING TIP In this short
story, the author
uses some
British words. Don't worry if
you don't understand all of
them. Try reading aloud the
more difficult passages.

NOTES

FOCUS

As the story begins, you
meet Sandy Pengelly, a
girl in a close-knit family.

⫞ **MARK IT UP** ⟩ As you
read, underline key
details that tell about
Sandy and her family. An
example is highlighted.

S ome people choose their
 dogs, and some dogs
choose their people.

The Pengelly family had no
say in the choosing of Lob; he
came to them in the second
way, and very decisively.

It began on the beach, the
summer when Sandy was five,

10 Don, her older brother, twelve, and the twins were
three. Sandy was really Alexandra, because her
grandmother had a beautiful picture of a queen in a
diamond tiara and high collar of pearls. It hung by
Granny Pearce's kitchen sink and was as familiar as
the doormat. When Sandy was born everyone agreed
that she was the living spit[1] of the picture, and so she
was called Alexandra and Sandy for short.

On this summer day she was lying peacefully
reading a comic and not keeping an eye on the twins,

20 who didn't need it because they were occupied in
seeing which of them could wrap the most seaweed
around the other one's legs. Father—Bert Pengelly—
and Don were up on the Hard[2] painting the bottom
boards of the boat in which Father went fishing for
pilchards.[3] And Mother—Jean Pengelly—was getting
ahead with making the Christmas puddings because
she never felt easy in her mind if they weren't made
and safely put away by the end of August. As usual,
each member of the family was happily getting on

30 with his or her own affairs. Little did they guess how
soon this state of things would be changed by the large
new member who was going to erupt into their midst.

---

1. **the living spit:** an exact likeness.
2. **Hard:** *British*, a landing place for boats.
3. **pilchards** (pĭl′chərds): small fish, similar to sardines.

Sandy rolled onto her back to make sure that the twins were not climbing on slippery rocks or getting cut off by the tide. At the same moment a large body struck her forcibly in the midriff, and she was covered by flying sand. Instinctively she shut her eyes and felt the sand being wiped off her face by something that seemed like a warm, rough, damp flannel.[4] She opened
40 her eyes and looked. It was a tongue. Its owner was a large and bouncy young Alsatian, or German shepherd, with topaz eyes, black-tipped prick ears, a thick, soft coat, and a bushy, black-tipped tail.

Pause & Reflect

FOCUS

Read to find out how Sandy and Lob get to know each other.

|||MARK IT UP ⟩⟩ As you read, underline details that tell you how Sandy and Lob feel about each other.

"*Lob!*" shouted a man farther up the beach. "Lob, come here!"

But Lob, as if trying to <u>atone</u> for the surprise he had given her, went on licking the
50 sand off Sandy's face, wagging his tail so hard while he kept on knocking up more clouds of sand. His owner, a gray-haired man with a limp, walked over as quickly as he could and seized him by the collar.

"I hope he didn't give you a fright?" the man said to Sandy. "He meant it in play—he's only young."

"Oh, no, I think he's *beautiful,*" said Sandy truly. She picked up a bit of driftwood and threw it. Lob, whisking easily out of his master's grip, was after it
60 like a sand-colored bullet. He came back with the

---

4. **flannel:** *British,* a washcloth

WORDS TO KNOW
atone (ə-tōn´) *v.* to make amends

Pause & Reflect

1. What did you find out about Sandy? Check two phrases below. (Clarify)

❏ older than the twins

❏ named after a queen

❏ goes fishing with her father

❏ helps her mother make Christmas puddings

2. How does Sandy meet the German shepherd? (Summarize)

NOTES

stick, beaming, and gave it to Sandy. At the same time he gave himself, though no one else was aware of this at the time. But with Sandy, too, it was love at first sight, and when, after a lot more stick-throwing, she and the twins joined Father and Don to go home for tea, they cast many a backward glance at Lob being led firmly away by his master.

"I wish we could play with him every day," Tess sighed.

70 "Why can't we?" said Tim.

Sandy explained. "Because Mr. Dodsworth, who owns him, is from Liverpool, and he is only staying at the Fisherman's Arms till Saturday."

"Is Liverpool a long way off?"

"Right at the other end of England from Cornwall, I'm afraid."

It was a Cornish fishing village where the Pengelly family lived, with rocks and cliffs and a strip of beach and a little round harbor, and palm trees growing in 80 the gardens of the little whitewashed stone houses. The village was approached by a narrow, steep, twisting hillroad and guarded by a notice that said LOW GEAR FOR 1½ MILES, DANGEROUS TO CYCLISTS.

The Pengelly children went home to scones with Cornish cream and jam, thinking they had seen the last of Lob. But they were much mistaken. The whole family was playing cards by the fire in the front room after supper when there was a loud thump and a crash of china in the kitchen.

90 "My Christmas puddings!" exclaimed Jean, and ran out.

"Did you put TNT[5] in them, then?" her husband said.

---

5. **TNT:** trinitrotoluene, a powerful explosive.

But it was Lob, who, finding the front door shut, had gone around to the back and bounced in through the open kitchen window, where the puddings were cooling on the sill.

Luckily only the smallest was knocked down and broken.

100　Lob stood on his hind legs and plastered Sandy's face with licks. Then he did the same for the twins, who shrieked with joy.

"Where does this friend of yours come from?" inquired Mr. Pengelly.

"He's staying at the Fisherman's Arms—I mean his owner is."

"Then he must go back there. Find a bit of string, Sandy, to tie to his collar."

"I wonder how he found his way here," Mrs. 110　Pengelly said, when the reluctant Lob had been led whining away and Sandy had explained about their afternoon's game on the beach. "Fisherman's Arms is right round the other side of the harbor."

Lob's owner scolded him and thanked Mr. Pengelly for bringing him back. Jean Pengelly warned the children that they had better not encourage Lob any more if they met him on the beach, or it would only lead to more trouble. So they dutifully took no notice of him the next day until he spoiled their good 120　resolutions by dashing up to them with joyful barks, wagging his tail so hard that he winded[6] Tess and knocked Tim's legs from under him.

Pause & Reflect

---

6. **winded:** to cause to be out of or short of breath.

WORDS TO KNOW
inquire (ĭn-kwīr′) v. to question; ask

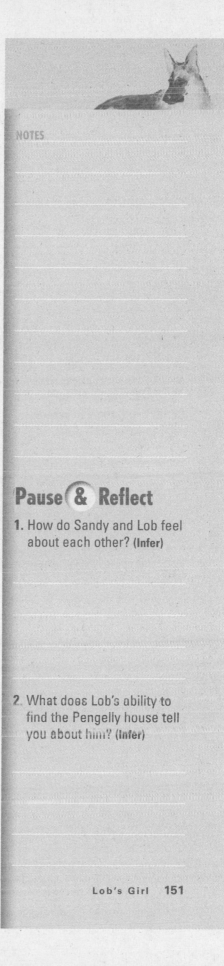

Pause & Reflect

1. How do Sandy and Lob feel about each other? (Infer)

2. What does Lob's ability to find the Pengelly house tell you about him? (Infer)

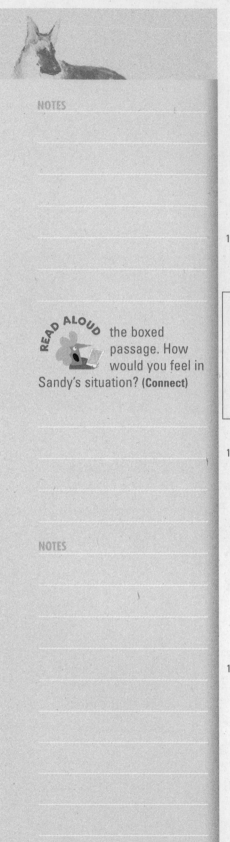

NOTES

READ ALOUD the boxed passage. How would you feel in Sandy's situation? (Connect)

NOTES

FOCUS

Read to find out about Lob's departure from Cornwall and what happens one week later.

They had a happy day, playing on the sand.

The next day was Saturday. Sandy had found out that Mr. Dodsworth was to catch the half-past-nine train. She went out secretly, down to the station, nodded to Mr.
130 Hoskins, the stationmaster, who wouldn't dream of charging any local for a platform ticket, and climbed up on the footbridge that led over the tracks.

She didn't want to be seen, but she did want to see. She saw Mr. Dodsworth get on the train, accompanied by an unhappy-looking Lob with drooping ears and tail. Then she saw the train slide away out of sight around the next headland, with a <u>melancholy</u> wail that sounded like Lob's last good-bye.

Sandy wished she hadn't had the idea of coming to
140 the station. She walked home miserably, with her shoulders hunched and her hands in her pockets. For the rest of the day, she was so cross and unlike herself that Tess and Tim were quite surprised, and her mother gave her a dose of senna.[7]

A week passed. Then, one evening, Mrs. Pengelly and the younger children were in the front room playing snakes and ladders.[8] Mr. Pengelly and Don had gone fishing on the evening tide. If your father is a fisherman, he will never be home at the same time
150 from one week to the next.

Suddenly, history repeating itself, there was a crash from the kitchen. Jean Pengelly leaped up, crying, "My blackberry jelly!" She and the children had spent the morning picking and the afternoon boiling fruit.

---

7. **senna:** a medicine made from senna leaves.

8. **snakes and ladders:** *British,* a board game, similar to an American game called Chutes and Ladders.

WORDS TO KNOW
melancholy (mĕl′ən-kŏl′ē) *adj.* sad; gloomy

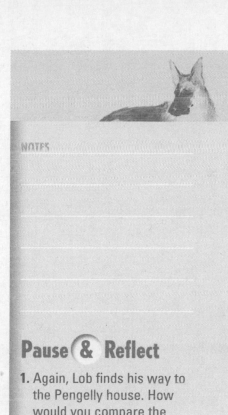

But Sandy was ahead of her mother. With flushed cheeks and eyes like stars she had darted into the kitchen, where she and Lob were hugging one another in a frenzy of joy. About a yard of his tongue was out, and he was licking every part of her that he could reach.

160 "Good heavens!" exclaimed Jean. "How in the world did *he* get here?"

"He must have walked," said Sandy. "Look at his feet."

They were worn, dusty, and tarry. One had a cut on the pad.

"They ought to be bathed," said Jean Pengelly. "Sandy, run a bowl of warm water while I get the disinfectant."

"What'll we do about him, Mother?" said Sandy
170 anxiously.

Mrs. Pengelly looked at her daughter's pleading eyes and sighed.

"He must go back to his owner, of course," she said, making her voice firm. "Your dad can get the address from the Fisherman's tomorrow, and phone him or send a telegram. In the meantime he'd better have a long drink and a good meal."

Lob was very grateful for the drink and the meal, and made no objection to having his feet washed.
180 Then he flopped down on the hearth rug and slept in front of the fire they had lit because it was a cold, wet evening, with his head on Sandy's feet. He was a very tired dog. He had walked all the way from Liverpool to Cornwall, which is more than four hundred miles.

Pause & Reflect

NOTES

Pause & Reflect

1. Again, Lob finds his way to the Pengelly house. How would you compare the two times he returns to the Pengellys? **(Compare and Contrast)**

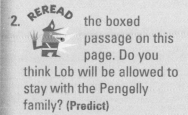

2. **REREAD** the boxed passage on this page. Do you think Lob will be allowed to stay with the Pengelly family? **(Predict)**

YES / NO, because

NOTES

|||| **MARK IT UP** ⟩ In the boxed paragraph, circle the words and phrases that show that Lob is determined to see Sandy again. **(Infer)**

NOTES

FOCUS

Read to find out more about how Lob feels about Sandy and her family.

The next day Mr. Pengelly phoned Lob's owner, and the following morning Mr. Dodsworth arrived off the night train, decidedly put out, 190 to take his pet home. That parting was worse than the first. Lob whined, Don walked out of the house, the twins burst out crying, and Sandy crept up to her bedroom afterward and lay with her face pressed into the quilt, feeling as if she were bruised all over.

Jean Pengelly took them all into Plymouth to see the circus on the next day and the twins cheered up a little, but even the hour's ride in the train each way and the Liberty horses and performing seals could not cure Sandy's sore heart.

200 She need not have bothered, though. In ten days' time Lob was back—limping this time, with a torn ear and a patch missing out of his furry coat, as if he had met and tangled with an enemy or two in the course of his four-hundred-mile walk.

Bert Pengelly rang up Liverpool again. Mr. Dodsworth, when he answered, sounded weary. He said, "That dog has already cost me two days that I can't spare away from my work—plus endless time in police stations and drafting newspaper advertisements. 210 I'm too old for these ups and downs. I think we'd better face the fact, Mr. Pengelly, that it's your family he wants to stay with—that is, if you want to have him."

Bert Pengelly gulped. He was not a rich man, and Lob was a pedigreed dog. He said cautiously, "How much would you be asking for him?"

"Good heavens, man, I'm not suggesting I'd *sell* him to you. You must have him as a gift. Think of the train fares I'll be saving. You'll be doing me a good turn."

"Is he a big eater?" Bert asked doubtfully.

WORDS TO KNOW
drafting (drăf'tĭng) *n.* putting into words and writing down; composing
draft *v.*

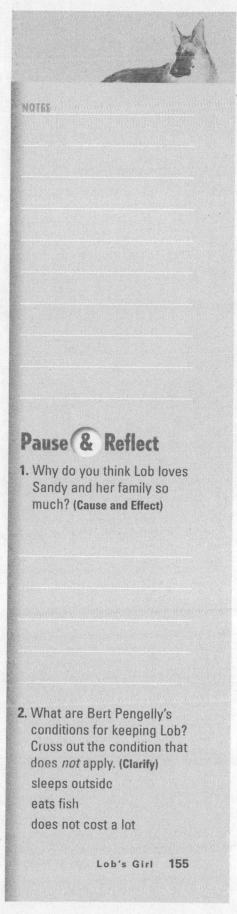

220　By this time the children, breathless in the background listening to one side of this conversation, had realized what was in the wind and were dancing up and down with their hands clasped beseechingly.

"Oh, not for his size," Lob's owner <u>assured</u> Bert. "Two or three pounds of meat a day and some vegetables and gravy and biscuits—he does very well on that."

Alexandra's father looked over the telephone at his daughter's swimming eyes and trembling lips. He reached a decision. "Well, then, Mr. Dodsworth," he
230　said briskly, "we'll accept your offer and thank you very much. The children will be overjoyed and you can be sure Lob has come to a good home. They'll look after him and see he gets enough exercise. But I can tell you," he ended firmly, "if he wants to settle in with us, he'll have to learn to eat a lot of fish."

So that was how Lob came to live with the Pengelly family. Everybody loved him and he loved them all. But there was never any question who came first with him. He was Sandy's dog. He slept by her bed and
240　followed her everywhere he was allowed.

Nine years went by, and each summer Mr. Dodsworth came back to stay at the Fisherman's Arms and call on his erstwhile dog. Lob always met him with recognition and dignified pleasure, accompanied him for a walk or two—but showed no signs of wishing to return to Liverpool. His place, he intimated, was definitely with the Pengellys.

In the course of nine years Lob changed less than Sandy. As she went into her teens he became a little
250　slower, a little stiffer, there was a touch of gray on his nose, but he was still a handsome dog. He and Sandy still loved one another devotedly.

Pause & Reflect

1. Why do you think Lob loves Sandy and her family so much? **(Cause and Effect)**

2. What are Bert Pengelly's conditions for keeping Lob? Cross out the condition that does *not* apply. **(Clarify)**

sleeps outside

eats fish

does not cost a lot

NOTES

FOCUS

Sandy and Lob leave the house on a rainy night. Read to find out what a doctor and his wife discover while driving through Cornwall.

One evening in October all the summer visitors had left, and the little fishing town looked empty and secretive. It was a wet, windy dusk. When the children came home from school—even the twins were 260 at high school[9] now, and Don was a full-fledged fisherman—Jean Pengelly said, "Sandy, your Aunt Rebecca says she's lonesome because Uncle Will Hoskins has gone out trawling,[10] and she wants one of you to go and spend the evening with her. You go, dear; you can take your homework with you."

Sandy looked far from enthusiastic.

"Can I take Lob with me?"

"You know Aunt Becky doesn't really like dogs— Oh, very well." Mrs. Pengelly sighed. "I suppose she'll 270 have to put up with him as well as you."

Reluctantly Sandy tidied herself, took her schoolbag, put on the damp raincoat she had just taken off, fastened Lob's lead to his collar, and set off to walk through the dusk to Aunt Becky's cottage, which was five minutes' climb up the steep hill.

The wind was howling through the shrouds[11] of boats drawn up on the Hard.

"Put some cheerful music on, do," said Jean Pengelly to the nearest twin. "Anything to drown that 280 wretched sound while I make your dad's supper." So Don, who had just come in, put on some rock music, loud. Which was why the Pengellys did not hear the truck hurtle down the hill and crash against the post office wall a few minutes later.

---

9. **high school:** In Great Britain, students leave elementary school and begin attending high school when they are about 11 years old.

10. **trawling:** fishing with a net pulled behind a boat.

11. **shrouds:** ropes or cables on a boat's mast.

Dr. Travers was driving through Cornwall with his wife, taking a late holiday before patients began coming down with winter colds and flu. He saw the sign that said STEEP HILL. LOW GEAR FOR 1½ MILES. Dutifully he changed into second gear.

290 "We must be nearly there," said his wife, looking out of her window. "I noticed a sign on the coast road that said the Fisherman's Arms was two miles. What a narrow, dangerous hill! But the cottages are very pretty—Oh, Frank, stop, *stop!* There's a child, I'm sure it's a child—by the wall over there!"

Dr. Travers jammed on his brakes and brought the car to a stop. A little stream ran down by the road in a shallow stone culvert,[12] and half in the water lay something that looked, in the dusk, like a pile of
300 clothes—or was it the body of a child? Mrs. Travers was out of the car in a flash, but her husband was quicker.

"Don't touch her, Emily!" he said sharply. "She's been hit. Can't be more than a few minutes. Remember that truck that overtook us half a mile back, speeding like the devil? Here, quick, go into that cottage and phone for an ambulance. The girl's in a bad way. I'll stay here and do what I can to stop the bleeding. Don't waste a minute."

Doctors are expert at stopping dangerous bleeding,
310 for they know the right places to press. This Dr. Travers was able to do, but he didn't dare do more; the girl was lying in a queerly crumpled heap, and he guessed she had a number of bones broken and that it would be highly dangerous to move her. He watched her with great concentration, wondering where the truck had got to and what other damage it had done.

Mrs. Travers was very quick. She had seen plenty of accident cases and knew the importance of speed. The first cottage she tried had a phone; in four minutes she

---

12. **culvert:** a gutter or tunnel that runs along or under a road.

READ ALOUD the boxed passage. Who do you think the injured girl might turn out to be? **(Predict)**

Pause & Reflect

1. Write the numbers, 1, 2, 3, or 4 to show the order in which the events below occur. **(Sequence)**

___ Dr. Travers and his wife leave for a holiday.

___ The injured girl is rushed to a hospital in Plymouth.

___ Dr. Travers and his wife find a badly-injured girl.

___ Sandy and Lob set out for Aunty Becky Hoskins's house.

2. Do you think the injured girl will live? **(Predict)**

YES / NO, because

_____

_____

_____

_____

_____

NOTES

_____

_____

_____

_____

_____

_____

_____

_____

_____

320 was back, and in six an ambulance was wailing down the hill.

Its attendants lifted the child onto a stretcher as carefully as if she were made of fine thistledown. The ambulance sped off to Plymouth—for the local cottage hospital did not take serious accident cases—and Dr. Travers went down to the police station to report what he had done.

He found that the police already knew about the speeding truck—which had suffered from loss of 330 brakes and ended up with its radiator halfway through the post-office wall. The driver was concussed[13] and shocked, but the police thought he was the only person injured—until Dr. Travers told his tale.

Pause & Reflect

FOCUS

Aunt Rebecca hears about the accident. Read to find out about Sandy's fight for life.

MARK IT UP > As you read, circle details that tell you about Sandy's condition.

At half-past nine that night Aunt Rebecca Hoskins was sitting by her fire thinking aggrieved thoughts about the inconsiderateness of nieces who were asked to supper 340 and never turned up, when she was startled by a neighbor, who burst in, exclaiming, "Have you heard about Sandy Pengelly, then, Mrs. Hoskins? Terrible thing, poor little soul, and they don't know if she's likely to live. Police have got the truck driver that hit her—ah, it didn't ought to be allowed, speeding through the place like that at umpty miles an hour, they ought to jail him for life— not that that'd be any comfort to poor Bert and Jean."

---

13. **concussed:** suffering from a concussion, an injury that results from being struck in the head.

350   Horrified, Aunt Rebecca put on a coat and went down to her brother's house. She found the family with white shocked faces; Bert and Jean were about to drive off to the hospital where Sandy had been taken, and the twins were crying bitterly. Lob was nowhere to be seen. But Aunt Rebecca was not interested in dogs; she did not inquire about him.

>   "Thank the Lord you've come, Beck," said her brother. "Will you stay the night with Don and the twins? Don's out looking for Lob and heaven knows
> 360 when we'll be back; we may get a bed with Jean's mother in Plymouth."

    "Oh, if only I'd never invited the poor child," wailed Mrs. Hoskins. But Bert and Jean hardly heard her.

    That night seemed to last forever. The twins cried themselves to sleep. Don came home very late and grim-faced. Bert and Jean sat in a waiting room of the Western Counties Hospital, but Sandy was unconscious, they were told, and she remained so. All that could be done for her was done. She was given
370 <u>transfusions</u> to replace all the blood she had lost. The broken bones were set and put in slings and cradles.

    "Is she a healthy girl? Has she a good constitution?"[14] the emergency doctor asked.

    "Aye, Doctor, she is that," Bert said hoarsely. The lump in Jean's throat prevented her from answering; she merely nodded.

    "Then she ought to have a chance. But I won't <u>conceal</u> from you that her condition is very serious, unless she shows signs of coming out from this <u>coma</u>."

---

14. **constitution:** physical makeup.

WORDS TO KNOW
  transfusion (trăns-fyōō′zhən) *n.* an injection of blood, usually to replace a loss due to bleeding
  conceal (kən-sēl′) *v.* to hide
  coma (kō′mə) *n.* a sleeplike state in which a person cannot sense or respond to light, sound, or touch

REREAD the boxed text. Do you think Don will find Lob? **(Predict)**

YES / NO, because

Pause & Reflect

1. Cross out the phrase below that does *not* apply to Sandy. **(Clarify)**

   tries to walk

   cannot move

   is in a coma

   has received transfusions

2. Suppose you were one of Sandy's parents. How would you feel about your daughter's condition? **(Connect)**

NOTES

380   But as hour succeeded hour, Sandy showed no signs of recovering consciousness. Her parents sat in the waiting room with haggard faces; sometimes one of them would go to telephone the family at home, or to try to get a little sleep at the home of Granny Pearce, not far away.

Pause & Reflect

FOCUS

Read to find out about the strange dog that is trying to get inside the hospital.

    At noon next day Dr. and Mrs. Travers went to the Pengelly cottage to inquire how Sandy was doing, but the 390 report was gloomy: "Still in a very serious condition." The twins were miserably unhappy. They forgot that they had sometimes called their elder sister bossy and only remembered how often she had shared her pocket money with them, how she read to them and took them for picnics and helped with their homework. Now there was no Sandy, no Mother and Dad, Don went around with a gray, shuttered face, and worse still, there was no Lob.

400   The Western Counties Hospital is a large one, with dozens of different departments and five or six connected buildings, each with three or four entrances. By that afternoon it became noticeable that a dog seemed to have taken up position outside the hospital, with the fixed intention of getting in. Patiently he would try first one entrance and then another, all the way around, and then begin again. Sometimes he would get a little way inside, following a visitor, but animals were, of course, forbidden, and he was always

410 kindly but firmly turned out again. Sometimes the guard at the main entrance gave him a pat or offered him a bit of sandwich —he looked so wet and beseeching and desperate. But he never ate the sandwich. No one seemed to own him or to know where he came from; Plymouth is a large city and he might have belonged to anybody.

At tea time Granny Pearce came through the pouring rain to bring a flask of hot tea to her daughter and son-in-law. Just as she reached the main entrance

420 the guard was gently but forcibly shoving out a large, <u>agitated</u>, soaking-wet Alsatian dog.

"No, old fellow, you can *not* come in. Hospitals are for people, not for dogs."

"Why, bless me," exclaimed old Mrs. Pearce. "That's Lob! Here, Lob, Lobby boy!"

Lob ran to her, whining. Mrs. Pearce walked up to the desk.

"I'm sorry, madam, you can't bring that dog in here," the guard said.

430 Mrs. Pearce was a very determined old lady. She looked the porter in the eye.

"Now, see here, young man. That dog has walked twenty miles from St. Killan to get to my granddaughter. Heaven knows how he knew she was here, but it's plain he knows. And he ought to have his rights! He ought to get to see her! Do you know," she went on, bristling, "that dog has walked the length of England—*twice*—to be with that girl? And you think you can keep him out with your fiddling rules and regulations?"

440 "I'll have to ask the medical officer," the guard said weakly.

"You do that, young man." Granny Pearce sat down in a determined manner, shutting her umbrella, and

WORDS TO KNOW
agitated (ăj′ĭ-tāt′ĭd) *adj.* disturbed; upset agitate *v.*

NOTES

READ ALOUD the boxed passage. As you read aloud Granny Pearce's words, try to express her determination.

NOTES

Pause & Reflect

Pause & Reflect

1. Check three phrases below that apply to Lob. **(Infer)**
   ❑ wants to see Sandy
   ❑ seems weighted down
   ❑ bites the porter
   ❑ looks very wet

2. How does Granny Pearce help Lob? **(Summarize)**

NOTES

Lob sat patiently dripping at her feet. Every now and then he shook his head, as if to dislodge something heavy that was tied around his neck.

Presently a tired, thin, intelligent-looking man in a white coat came downstairs, with an impressive, silver-haired man in a dark suit, and there was a low-voiced 450 discussion. Granny Pearce eyed them, biding her time.

"Frankly . . . not much to lose," said the older man. The man in the white coat approached Granny Pearce.

"It's strictly against every rule, but as it's such a serious case we are making an exception," he said to her quietly. "But only *outside* her bedroom door—and only for a moment or two."

Pause & Reflect

FOCUS

Granny Pearce and Lob head towards Sandy's room.

[|| **MARK IT UP** ⟩] As you read, underline details that show how Sandy responds to Lob's visit.

Without a word, Granny Pearce rose and stumped upstairs. Lob followed close 460 to her skirts, as if he knew his hope lay with her.

They waited in the green-floored corridor outside Sandy's room. The door was half-shut. Bert and Jean were inside. Everything was terribly quiet. A nurse came out. The white-coated man asked her something and she shook her head. She had left the door ajar and through it could now be seen a high, narrow bed with a lot of gadgets around 470 it. Sandy lay there, very flat under the covers, very still. Her head was turned away. All Lob's attention was <u>riveted</u> on the bed. He strained toward it, but Granny Pearce clasped his collar firmly.

WORDS TO KNOW
rivet (rĭv′ĭt) *v.* to fasten firmly

"I've done a lot for you, my boy, now you behave yourself," she whispered grimly. Lob let out a faint whine, anxious and pleading.

At the sound of that whine, Sandy stirred just a little. She sighed and moved her head the least fraction. Lob whined again. And then Sandy turned her head right 480 over. Her eyes opened, looking at the door.

"Lob?" she murmured—no more than a breath of sound. "Lobby, boy?"

The doctor by Granny Pearce drew a quick, sharp breath. Sandy moved her left arm—the one that was not broken—from below the covers and let her hand dangle down, feeling, as she always did in the mornings, for Lob's furry head. The doctor nodded slowly.

"All right," he whispered. "Let him go to the 490 bedside. But keep a hold of him."

Granny Pearce and Lob moved to the bedside. Now she could see Bert and Jean, white-faced and shocked, on the far side of the bed. But she didn't look at them. She looked at the smile on her granddaughter's face as the groping fingers found Lob's wet ears and gently pulled them. "Good boy," whispered Sandy, and fell asleep again.

Pause & Reflect

FOCUS

Read to find out what happens to Lob.

Granny Pearce led Lob out into the passage again. There 500 she let go of him, and he ran off swiftly down the stairs. She would have followed him, but Bert and Jean had come out into the passage, and she spoke to Bert fiercely.

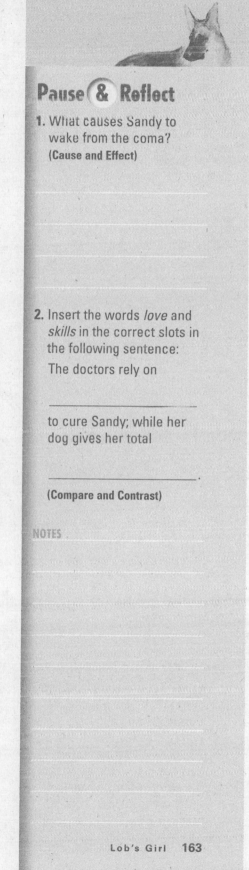

Pause & Reflect

1. What causes Sandy to wake from the coma? (Cause and Effect)

2. Insert the words *love* and *skills* in the correct slots in the following sentence:
The doctors rely on

_____

to cure Sandy; while her dog gives her total

_____.

(Compare and Contrast)

NOTES

Pause & Reflect

1. REREAD the boxed passage. What has happened to Lob? **(Summarize)**

_____

_____

_____

2. How did you feel about the ending of the story? **(Connect)**

_____

_____

_____

_____

_____

_____

CHALLENGE This story has several **settings:** the beaches at Cornwall, the Pengelly cottage, a steep road, and a hospital. What role do the settings play in the events of the story? Mark passages in the story to support your ideas. **(Analyze)**

"*I* don't know why you were so foolish as not to bring the dog before! Leaving him to find the way here himself—"

"But, Mother!" said Jean Pengelly. "That can't have been Lob. What a chance to take! Suppose Sandy
510 hadn't—" She stopped, with her handkerchief pressed to her mouth.

"Not Lob? I've known that dog nine years! I suppose I ought to know my own granddaughter's dog?"

"Listen, Mother," said Bert. "Lob was killed by the same truck that hit Sandy. Don found him—when he went to look for Sandy's schoolbag. He was—he was dead. Ribs all smashed. No question of that. Don told me on the phone—he and Will Hoskins rowed a half
520 mile out to sea and sank the dog with a lump of concrete tied to his collar. Poor old boy. Still—he was getting on. Couldn't have lasted forever."

"*Sank him at sea?* Then what—?"

Slowly old Mrs. Pearce, and then the other two, turned to look at the trail of dripping-wet footprints that led down the hospital stairs.

In the Pengellys' garden they have a stone, under the palm tree. It says: "Lob. Sandy's dog. Buried at sea." ❖

Pause & Reflect

Active Reading SkillBuilder

Cause and Effect

Two events are related as **cause and effect** if one brings about, or causes, the other.
The event that happens first is the cause; the one that follows is the effect. Sometimes
the first event may cause more than one thing to happen. Complete the chart below
with cause-and-effect relationships from the story.

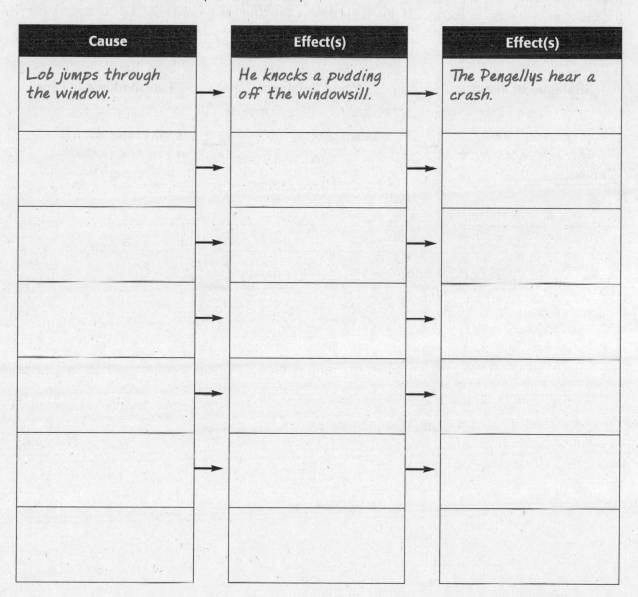

Cause	Effect(s)	Effect(s)
Lob jumps through the window.	He knocks a pudding off the windowsill.	The Pengellys hear a crash.

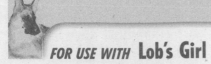

Literary Analysis SkillBuilder

Foreshadowing

A hint about an event that will occur later in a story is called **foreshadowing.** Authors often use vivid descriptions of events and characters to create suspense and to foreshadow future events. Writers carefully choose words and phrases to create **moods** like sadness, excitement, and anger. Complete the chart below by considering the dialogue or events in "Lob's Girl," the mood they create, and the events they foreshadow.

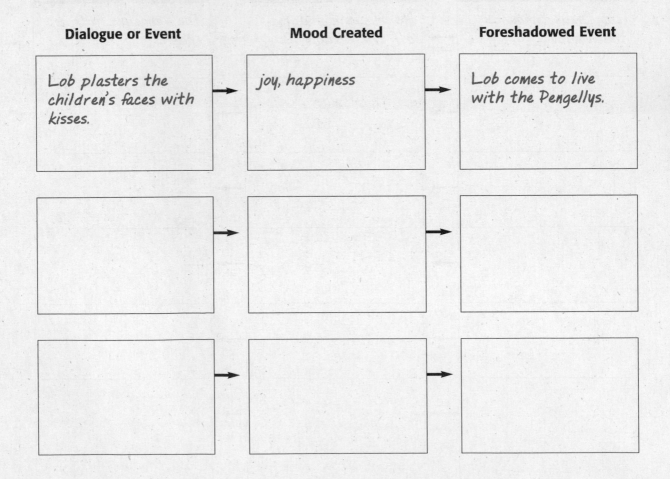

Dialogue or Event	Mood Created	Foreshadowed Event
Lob plasters the children's faces with kisses.	joy, happiness	Lob comes to live with the Pengellys.

Words to Know SkillBuilder

Words to Know

agitated	atone	conceal	inquire	rivet
assure	coma	draft	melancholy	transfusion

A. Fill in each set of blanks with one of the Words to Know. Then use the boxed letters to complete the sentence below the puzzle.

1. How you might feel on a rainy day. __ __ __ __ __ __ ☐ __ __ __

2. What you should do if you've done something mean to a friend. __ __ __ __ ☐

3. One of the early steps of the Writing Process. __ __ ☐ __ __

4. What you do when you don't understand. __ __ __ __ __ ☐ __

5. A welder might attach two pieces of metal with this. __ __ __ __ ☐

6. Sandy needed this because she'd lost so much blood. __ __ __ __ __ ☐ __ __ __ __

7. When you promise someone you'll do something, you do this. __ __ __ __ __ __ ☐

8. You might want to do this with a bad report card. __ __ __ __ __ __ __ ☐

9. Bad news might make you feel this way. __ __ __ __ __ ☐ __ __

Complete the following sentence with the word that the boxed letters spell out.

10. Lob and Sandy had a _____ friendship.

B. For each phrase in the first column, find the word or phrase in the second column that is closest in meaning. Write the letter of that word or phrase in the blank.

_____ 1. affirm positively   A. fully agitated

_____ 2. hid and harbored   B. deep melancholy

_____ 3. deep unconsciousness   C. readily assure

_____ 4. gloomy mood   D. in a coma

_____ 5. deeply disturbed   E. consciously concealed

Before You Read

Connect to Your Life

Some adventure stories involve a **quest**, a journey that a character makes to reach a certain goal. Think of characters in books, movies, or television shows that go on quests. List them in the chart below.

Character	From	Goal
Dorothy	The Wizard of Oz	to get home

Key to the Drama

WHAT DO YOU THINK? Much of the humor in *The Phantom Tollbooth* comes from **word play**—funny uses or mix-ups of words. Read the following lines from the drama.

> **Milo.** I thought you were the Weather Man.
>
> **Whether Man.** Oh, no, I'm the Whether Man, not the weather man.

Weather and *whether* are **homophones**—words that sound alike but have different spellings and meanings. Think of three pairs of homophones and write them on the lines. As you read the play, you will find many more.

_____ board, bored _____

1. _____ , _____

2. _____ , _____

3. _____ , _____

from THE PHANTOM TOLLBOOTH

PREVIEW Milo is always bored—until a mysterious tollbooth transports him to a land full of amazing characters and places. There, Milo goes on a dangerous quest.

NOVEL BY
NORTON JUSTER

DRAMATIZED BY
SUSAN NANUS

READING TIP Many of the places and characters have made-up names. The "roots" of these made-up words are real words that tell about the character or place. For example, the word *math* in the Mathemagician's name tells you that this character has something to do with numbers. The footnotes for the invented words will also help you with their meanings.

NOTES

_____

_____

_____

_____

_____

_____

_____

_____

_____

_____

_____

_____

_____

_____

_____

_____

_____

FOCUS

Read the names of the characters you will meet and the places you will visit in the play.

MARK IT UP > As you read, circle the characters that you are most curious about.

CAST (in order of appearance)

The Clock

Milo, a boy

The Whether Man

Six Lethargarians

Tock, the Watchdog
(same as The Clock)

Azaz the Unabridged,
King of Dictionopolis

The Mathemagician,
King of Digitopolis

Princess Sweet Rhyme

Princess Pure Reason

Gatekeeper of Dictionopolis

Three Word Merchants

The Letterman
(Fourth Word Merchant)

Spelling Bee

The Humbug

The Duke of Definition

The Minister of Meaning

The Earl of Essence

The Count of Connotation

The Undersecretary of
Understanding

A Page

Kakafonous A. Dischord,
Doctor of Dissonance

The Awful Dynne

The Dodecahedron

Miners of the Numbers Mine

The Everpresent Wordsnatcher

The Terrible Trivium

The Demon of Insincerity

Senses Taker

THE SETS

1. Milo's bedroom

With shelves, pennants, pictures on the wall, as well as suggestions of the characters of the Land of Wisdom.

2. The road to the Land of Wisdom

A forest, from which the Whether Man and the Lethargarians emerge.

3. Dictionopolis

A marketplace full of open-air stalls as well as little shops. Letters and signs should abound. There may be street signs and lampposts in the shapes of large letters (large O's and Q's) and all windows and doors can be in the shape of H's and A's.

4. Digitopolis

A dark, glittering place without trees or greenery, but full of shining rocks and cliffs, with hundreds of numbers shining everywhere. When the scene change is made to the Mathemagician's room, set pieces are simply carried in from the wings.

5. The Land of Ignorance

A gray, gloomy place full of cliffs and caves, with frightening faces. Different levels and heights should be suggested through one or two platforms or risers, with a set of stairs that lead to the castle in the air.

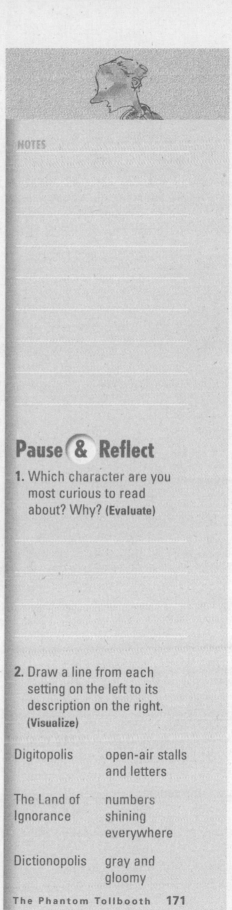

NOTES

Pause & Reflect

1. Which character are you most curious to read about? Why? (Evaluate)

2. Draw a line from each setting on the left to its description on the right. (Visualize)

Digitopolis	open-air stalls and letters
The Land of Ignorance	numbers shining everywhere
Dictionopolis	gray and gloomy

READING TIP The words shown in italics and parentheses are the **stage directions**. They are instructions for the actors and stage crew.

NOTES

MARK IT UP **KEEP TRACK**
Remember to use these marks to keep track of your reading.

* This is important.

? I have a question about this.

! This is a surprise.

FOCUS

In this section, you will meet two characters, Clock and the main character, Milo.

MARK IT UP As you read, underline details that help you get to know Milo. An example is shown in line 49.

Act One
Scene 1

The stage is completely dark and silent. Suddenly the sound of someone winding an alarm clock is heard, and after that, the sound of loud ticking is heard.

Lights up on the Clock, a huge alarm clock. The Clock reads 4:00. The lighting should make it appear that the Clock is suspended in
10 *mid-air (if possible). The Clock ticks for 30 seconds.*

Clock. See that! Half a minute gone by. Seems like a long time when you're waiting for something to happen, doesn't it? Funny thing is, time can pass very slowly or very fast, and sometimes even both at once. The time now? Oh, a little after four, but what that means should depend on you. Too often, we do something simply because time tells us to. Time for school, time for bed, whoops, 12:00, time to be hungry. It can get a little silly, don't you
20 think? Time is important, but it's what you do with it that makes it so. So my advice to you is to use it. Keep your eyes open and your ears perked. Otherwise it will pass before you know it, and you'll certainly have missed something!

Things have a habit of doing that, you know.

Being here one minute and gone the next.

In the twinkling of an eye.

In a jiffy.

In a flash!

30 I know a girl who yawned and missed a whole

summer vacation. And what about that caveman who took a nap one afternoon, and woke up to find himself completely alone. You see, while he was sleeping, someone had invented the wheel and everyone had moved to the suburbs. And then of course, there is Milo. (*Lights up to reveal Milo's bedroom. The Clock appears to be on a shelf in the room of a young boy—a room filled with books, toys, games, maps, papers, pencils, a bed, a desk.*

40 *There is a dartboard with numbers and the face of the Mathemagician, a bedspread made from King Azaz's cloak, a kite looking like the Spelling Bee, a punching bag with the Humbug's face, as well as records, a television, a toy car, and a large box that is wrapped and has an envelope taped to the top. The sound of footsteps is heard, and then enter Milo* dejectedly. *He throws down his books and coat, flops into a chair, and sighs loudly.*) Who never knows what to do with himself—not just

50 sometimes, but always. When he's in school, he wants to be out, and when he's out, he wants to be in. (*During the following speech, Milo examines the various toys, tools, and other possessions in the room, trying them out and rejecting them.*) Wherever he is, he wants to be somewhere else— and when he gets there, so what. Everything is too much trouble or a waste of time. Books—he's already read them. Games—boring. T.V.—dumb. So what's left? Another long, boring afternoon. Unless

60 he bothers to notice a very large package that happened to arrive today.

WORDS TO KNOW
dejectedly (dĭ-jĕk'tĭd-lē) *adv.* in a depressed manner

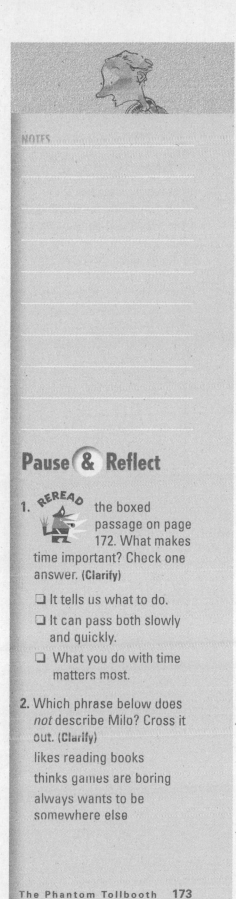

Pause & Reflect

1. REREAD the boxed passage on page 172. What makes time important? Check one answer. (Clarify)

❑ It tells us what to do.

❑ It can pass both slowly and quickly.

❑ What you do with time matters most.

2. Which phrase below does *not* describe Milo? Cross it out. (Clarify)

likes reading books

thinks games are boring

always wants to be somewhere else

NOTES

Milo. (*Suddenly notices the package. He drags himself over to it, and disinterestedly reads the label.*) "For Milo, who has plenty of time." Well, that's true. (*Sighs and looks at it.*) No. (*Walks away.*) Well . . . (*Comes back. Rips open envelope and reads.*)

70 **Voice.** "One genuine turnpike tollbooth,[1] easily assembled at home for use by those who have never traveled in lands beyond."

Milo. Beyond what? (*Continues reading.*)

Voice. "This package contains the following items:" (*Milo pulls the items out of the box and sets them up as they are mentioned.*) "One (1) genuine turnpike tollbooth to be erected according to directions. Three (3) precautionary signs to be used in a precautionary fashion. Assorted coins for paying tolls. One (1) map,

80 strictly up to date, showing how to get from here to there. One (1) book of rules and traffic regulations which may not be bent or broken. Warning! Results are not guaranteed. If not perfectly satisfied, your wasted time will be refunded."

Milo. (*Skeptically.*) Come off it, who do you think you're kidding? (*Walks around and examines tollbooth.*) What am I supposed to do with this? (*The ticking of the Clock grows loud and impatient.*) Well . . . what else do I have to do.

90 (*Milo gets into his toy car and drives up to the first sign. NOTE: The car may be an actual toy propelled by pedals or a small motor, or simply a cardboard imitation that Milo can fit into, and move by walking.*)

---

1. **turnpike tollbooth** (tûrn′pīk′ tōl′bŏŏth′): a booth where the fee for using a toll road is collected.

Voice. "Have your <u>destination</u> in mind."

Milo. (*Pulls out the map.*) Now, let's see. That's funny. I never heard of any of those places. Well, it doesn't matter anyway. Dictionopolis.[2] That's a weird name. I might as well go there. (*Begins to*
100 *move, following map. Drives off.*)

Clock. See what I mean? You never know how things are going to get started. But when you're bored, what you need more than anything is a rude awakening.

(*The alarm goes off very loudly as the stage darkens. The sound of the alarm is transformed into the honking of a car horn, and then is joined by the blasts, bleeps, roars and growls of heavy highway traffic. When the lights come up, Milo's bedroom is gone and we see a lonely road in the middle of nowhere.*)

Pause & Reflect

FOCUS

Milo meets a strange character in the Land of Expectations. Read to find out what this character is like.

Scene 2

110 The Road to Dictionopolis
Enter Milo in his car.

Milo. This is weird! I don't recognize any of this scenery at all. (*A sign is held up before Milo, startling him.*) Huh? (*Reads.*) Welcome to Expectations.[3] Information, predictions and advice cheerfully offered. Park here and blow horn. (*Milo blows horn.*)

---

2. **Dictionopolis** (dĭk′shə-nŏp′ə-lĭs): an imaginary place name, formed from *dictionary* and the root *–polis*, meaning "city or state."

3. **Expectations** (ĕk′spĕk-tā′shəns): predictions of success or gain; here, referring to an imaginary place.

WORDS TO KNOW
destination (dĕs′tə-nā′shən) *n.* the place to which one intends to go

Pause & Reflect

1. What does the package in Milo's room contain? Circle three things below. **(Clarify)**

   a map

   coins

   a flashlight

   keys

   a turnpike tollbooth

2. ▥ **MARK IT UP** ⟩ Where does Milo decide to go after he gets in the car? Find and circle the answer on this page. **(Clarify)**

3. Put yourself in Milo's place. What do you hope will happen on your car trip? **(Connect)**

NOTES

Whether Man. (*A little man wearing a long coat and*
120 *carrying an umbrella pops up from behind the sign
that he was holding. He speaks very fast and
excitedly.*) My, my, my, my, my, welcome, welcome,
welcome, welcome to the Land of Expectations,
Expectations, Expectations! We don't get many
travelers these days; we certainly don't get many
travelers. Now what can I do for you? I'm the
Whether Man.

Milo. (*Referring to map.*) Uh . . . is this the right road
to Dictionopolis?

130 **Whether Man.** Well now, well now, well now, I don't
know of any wrong road to Dictionopolis, so if this
road goes to Dictionopolis at all, it must be the
right road, and if it doesn't, it must be the right
road to somewhere else, because there are no wrong
roads to anywhere. Do you think it will rain?

Milo. I thought you were the Weather Man.

Whether Man. Oh, no, I'm the Whether Man, not
the weather man. (*Pulls out a sign or opens a flap
of his coat, which reads: "Whether."*) After all, it's
140 more important to know whether there will be
weather than what the weather will be.

Milo. What kind of place is Expectations?

Whether Man. Good question, good question!
Expectations is the place you must always go to
before you get where you are going. Of course, some
people never go beyond Expectations, but my job is
to hurry them along whether they like it or not. Now
what else can I do for you? (*Opens his umbrella.*)

Milo. I think I can find my own way.

150 **Whether Man.** Splendid, splendid, splendid! Whether
or not you find your own way, you're bound to
find some way. If you happen to find my way,

REREAD the boxed passage. What does the Whether Man mean when he says that "some people never go beyond Expectations"? Do you think Milo will "go beyond Expectations"? **(Predict)**

please return it. I lost it years ago. I imagine by now it must be quite rusty. You did say it was going to rain, didn't you? (*Escorts Milo to the car under the open umbrella.*) I'm glad you made your own decision. I do so hate to make up my mind about anything, whether it's good or bad, up or down, rain or shine. Expect everything, I always say, and the unexpected never happens. Goodbye, goodbye, goodbye, good . . . (*A loud clap of thunder is heard.*) Oh dear! (*He looks up at the sky, puts out his hand to feel for rain and runs away. Milo watches puzzledly, and drives on.*)

Milo. I'd better get out of Expectations, but fast. Talking to a guy like that all day would get me nowhere for sure. (*He tries to speed up, but finds instead that he is moving slower and slower.*) Oh, oh, now what? (*He can barely move. Behind Milo, the Lethargarians[4] begin to enter from all parts of the stage. They are dressed to blend in with the scenery and carry small pillows that look like rocks. Whenever they fall asleep, they rest on the pillows.*) Now I really am getting nowhere. I hope I didn't take a wrong turn. (*The car stops. He tries to start it. It won't move. He gets out and begins to tinker with it.*) I wonder where I am.

Pause & Reflect

Pause & Reflect

1. 〔ⅢMARK IT UP〕> What does the Whether Man hate to do? Circle the answer on this page. **(Clarify)**

2. Insert the words *weather* and *whether* in the following sentence. **(Clarify)**

I do not know _____

the _____ will be sunny or rainy.

NOTES

---

4. **Lethargarians** (lĕth´ər-jâr´ē-anz): a made-up name based on the word *lethargy*. A *Lethargarian* would thus be dull, inactive, or uncaring.

Legal Terms The Lethargarians tell Milo to read the rule book. The "local ordinances" are laws. In the Doldrums, it is illegal to think and to laugh.

FOCUS

Milo gets trapped in a place called the Doldrums. Read to find out what the people there do.

MARK IT UP As you read, circle details that tell you about their activities.

Lethargarian 1. You're . . . in . . . the . . . Dol . . . drums[5] . . . 180 (*Milo looks around.*)

Lethargarian 2. Yes . . . in . . . the . . . Dol . . . drums . . . (*A yawn is heard.*)

Milo. (*Yelling.*) What are the Doldrums?

Lethargarian 3. The Doldrums, my friend, are where nothing ever happens and nothing ever changes. (*Parts of the scenery stand up or six people come out of the* 190 *scenery colored in the same colors of the trees or the road. They move very slowly and as soon as they move, they stop to rest again.*) Allow me to introduce all of us. We are the Lethargarians at your service.

Milo. (*Uncertainly.*) Very pleased to meet you. I think I'm lost. Can you help me?

Lethargarian 4. Don't say think. (*He yawns.*) It's against the law.

Lethargarian 1. No one's allowed to think in the 200 Doldrums. (*He falls asleep.*)

Lethargarian 2. Don't you have a rule book? It's local ordinance 175389-J. (*He falls asleep.*)

Milo. (*Pulls out rule book and reads.*) Ordinance 175389-J: "It shall be unlawful, illegal and unethical to think, think of thinking, surmise, presume, reason, meditate or speculate while in the Doldrums. Anyone breaking this law shall be severely punished." That's a ridiculous law! Everybody thinks.

All the Lethargarians. We don't!

---

5. **in the Doldrums** (dōl′drəmz′): the condition of being depressed or without energy; here, *the Doldrums* refers to an imaginary land.

Lethargarian 2. And the most of the time, you don't, that's why you're here. You weren't thinking and you weren't paying attention either. People who don't pay attention often get stuck in the Doldrums. Face it, most of the time, you're just like us. (*Falls, snoring, to the ground. Milo laughs.*)

Lethargarian 5. Stop that at once. Laughing is against the law. Don't you have a rule book? It's local ordinance 574381-W.

Milo. (*Opens the rule book and reads.*) "In the Doldrums, laughter is frowned upon and smiling is permitted only on alternate Thursdays." Well, if you can't laugh or think, what can you do?

Lethargarian 6. Anything as long as it's nothing, and everything as long as it isn't anything. There's lots to do. We have a very busy schedule . . .

Lethargarian 1. At 8:00 we get up and then we spend from 8 to 9 daydreaming.

Lethargarian 2. From 9:00 to 9:30 we take our early midmorning nap . . .

Lethargarian 3. From 9:30 to 10:30 we dawdle and delay . . .

Lethargarian 4. From 10:30 to 11:30 we take our late early morning nap . . .

Lethargarian 5. From 11:30 to 12:00 we bide our time and then we eat our lunch.

Lethargarian 6. From 1:00 to 2:00 we linger and loiter . . .

Lethargarian 1. From 2:00 to 2:30 we take our early afternoon nap . . .

Lethargarian 2. From 2:30 to 3:30 we put off for tomorrow what we could have done today . . .

Lethargarian 3. From 3:30 to 4:00 we take our early late afternoon nap . . .

Lethargarian 4. From 4:00 to 5:00 we loaf and lounge until dinner . . .

Lethargarian 5. From 6:00 to 7:00 we dilly-dally . . .

Lethargarian 6. From 7:00 to 8:00 we take our early evening nap and then for an hour before we go to bed, we waste time.

250 **Lethargarian 1.** (*Yawning.*) You see, it's really quite strenuous[6] doing nothing all day long, and so once a week, we take a holiday and go nowhere.

Lethargarian 5. Which is just where we were going when you came along. Would you care to join us?

Milo. (*Yawning.*) That's where I seem to be going, anyway. (*Stretching.*) Tell me, does everyone here do nothing?

Lethargarian 3. Everyone but the terrible Watchdog. He's always sniffing around to see that nobody

260 wastes time. A most unpleasant character.

Milo. The Watchdog?

Lethargarian 6. The Watchdog!

All the Lethargarians. (*Yelling at once.*) Run! Wake up! Run! Here he comes! The Watchdog! (*They all run off. Enter a large dog with the head, feet, and tail of a dog, and the body of a clock, having the same face as the character The Clock.*)

Pause & Reflect

---

6. **strenuous** (strĕn′yo͞o-əs): requiring great effort or energy.

Pause & Reflect

1. Review the details you circled as you read. How do the Lethargarians spend their time? Check three things. **(Clarify)**

   ❏ take the Watchdog for walks

   ❏ linger and loiter

   ❏ run laps

   ❏ daydream

   ❏ waste time

2. Why do you think the Lethargarians dislike the Watchdog? **(Infer)**

FOCUS

Read to find out how the Watchdog helps Milo.

Watchdog. What are you doing here?

270 **Milo.** Nothing much. Just killing time. You see . . .

Watchdog. Killing time! (*His alarm rings in fury.*) It's bad enough wasting time without killing it. What are you doing in the Doldrums, anyway? Don't you have anywhere to go?

Milo. I think I was on my way to Dictionopolis when I got stuck here. Can you help me?

Watchdog. Help you! You've got to help yourself. I suppose you know why you got stuck.

280 **Milo.** I guess I just wasn't thinking.

Watchdog. Precisely. Now you're on your way.

Milo. I am?

Watchdog. Of course. Since you got here by not thinking, it seems reasonable that in order to get out, you must start thinking. Do you mind if I get in? I love automobile rides. (*He gets in. They wait.*) Well?

Milo. All right. I'll try. (*Screws up his face and thinks.*) Are we moving?

290 **Watchdog.** Not yet. Think harder.

Milo. I'm thinking as hard as I can.

Watchdog. Well, think just a little harder than that. Come on, you can do it.

Milo. All right, all right. . . . I'm thinking of all the planets in the solar system, and why water expands when it turns to ice, and all the words that begin with "q," and . . . (*The wheels begin to move.*) We're moving! We're moving!

Watchdog. Keep thinking.

READ ALOUD the boxed passage. Work with a partner. One person should take the role of Milo and the other the Watchdog. Practice your lines several times. Then, with your partner, use your voice to express the character's feelings.

NOTES

Pause & Reflect

1. What is the secret to escaping from the Doldrums? **(Clarify)**

2. Name something you would think about if you had to escape from the Doldrums. **(Connect)**

NOTES

300 **Milo.** (*Thinking.*) How a steam engine works and how to bake a pie and the difference between Fahrenheit and centigrade[7] . . .

Watchdog. Dictionopolis, here we come.

Milo. Hey, Watchdog, are you coming along?

Watchdog. You can call me Tock, and keep your eyes on the road.

Pause & Reflect

FOCUS

In this section you find out about a disagreement between King Azaz and the Mathemagician.

▐▐▌ **MARK IT UP** > As you read, underline the details that help you understand the conflict between the two rulers.

Milo. What kind of place is Dictionopolis, anyway?

Tock. It's where all the words 310 in the world come from. It used to be a marvelous place, but ever since Rhyme and Reason[8] left, it hasn't been the same.

Milo. Rhyme and Reason?

Tock. The two princesses. They used to settle all the arguments between their two brothers who rule over the Land of Wisdom. You see, Azaz is the king of Dictionopolis and the Mathemagician is the king 320 of Digitopolis[9] and they almost never see eye to eye on anything. It was the job of the Princesses Sweet Rhyme and Pure Reason to solve the differences between the two kings, and they always did so well

---

7. **Fahrenheit** (făr′ən-hīt′) **and centigrade** (sĕn′tĭ-grād′): *Fahrenheit* is a temperature scale on which water freezes at 32 and boils at 212 degrees. On the centigrade (Celsius) scale, water freezes at 0 and boils at 100 degrees.

8. **Rhyme and Reason:** sense or explanation. In this play, they are the names of two princesses who try to establish order. When they disappear, there is "neither Rhyme nor Reason in this kingdom."

9. **Digitopolis** (dĭj′ə-tŏp′ə-lĭs): another made-up place name, this uses *digit* (any of the numbers 0–9) and the root *–polis* ("city or state") to describe a land of numbers.

that both sides usually went home feeling very satisfied. But then, one day, the kings had an argument to end all arguments. . . .

(The lights dim on Tock and Milo, and come up on King Azaz of Dictionopolis on another part of the stage. Azaz has a great stomach, a gray beard
330 *reaching to his waist, a small crown and a long robe with the letters of the alphabet written all over it.)*

Azaz. Of course, I'll abide by the decision of Rhyme and Reason, though I have no doubt as to what it will be. They will choose words, of course. Everyone knows that words are more important than numbers any day of the week.

(The Mathemagician appears opposite Azaz. The Mathemagician wears a long flowing robe covered entirely with complex mathematical equations, and a
340 *tall pointed hat. He carries a long staff with a pencil point at one end and a large rubber eraser at the other.)*

Mathemagician. That's what you think, Azaz. People wouldn't even know what day of the week it is without numbers. Haven't you ever looked at a calendar? Face it, Azaz. It's numbers that count.

Azaz. Don't be ridiculous. *(To audience, as if leading a cheer.)* Let's hear it for words!

Mathemagician. *(To audience, in the same manner.)* Cast your vote for numbers!

350 **Azaz.** A, B, C's!

Mathemagician. 1, 2, 3's! *(A fanfare is heard.)*

Azaz and Mathemagician. *(To each other.)* Quiet! Rhyme and Reason are about to announce their decision.

(Rhyme and Reason appear.)

WORDS TO KNOW
fanfare (făn'fâr') *n.* a loud blast of trumpets

READING TIP The passage that tells about the argument between Azaz and the Mathemagician is a **flashback**. A flashback shows something that happened before the beginning of a story.

NOTES

Rhyme. Ladies and gentlemen, letters and numerals, fractions and punctuation marks—may we have your attention, please. After careful consideration of the problem set before us by King Azaz of

360   Dictionopolis (*Azaz bows.*) and the Mathemagician of Digitopolis (*Mathemagician raises his hands in a victory salute.*) we have come to the following conclusion:

Reason. Words and numbers are of equal value, for in the cloak of knowledge, one is the warp and the other is the woof.[10]

Rhyme. It is no more important to count the sands than it is to name the stars.

Rhyme and Reason. Therefore, let both kingdoms,

370   Dictionopolis and Digitopolis, live in peace.

(*The sound of cheering is heard.*)

Azaz. Boo! is what I say. Boo and Bah and Hiss!

Mathemagician. What good are these girls if they can't even settle an argument in anyone's favor? I think I have come to a decision of my own.

Azaz. So have I.

Azaz and Mathemagician. (*To the Princesses.*) You are hereby banished from this land to the Castle-in-the-Air. (*To each other.*) And as for you, keep out

380   of my way! (*They stalk off in opposite directions.*)

(*During this time, the set has been changed to the Market Square of Dictionopolis. Lights come up on a deserted square.*)

Tock. And ever since then, there has been neither Rhyme nor Reason in this kingdom. Words are misused and numbers mismanaged. The argument between the two kings has divided everyone and

---

10. **warp and . . . woof:** in weaving, the *warp* is made of parallel threads stretched on a loom. The *woof* is made of threads that wind between the warp to make cloth.

the real value of both words and numbers has been forgotten. What a waste!

390 **Milo.** Why doesn't somebody rescue the princesses and set everything straight again?

Tock. That is easier said than done. The Castle-in-the-Air is very far from here, and the one path which leads to it is guarded by ferocious demons. But hold on, here we are. (*A man appears, carrying a gate and a small tollbooth.*)

Pause & Reflect

FOCUS

Milo and Tock arrive in Dictionopolis, the kingdom of words and letters, on Market Day.

MARK IT UP Underline the different words for sale at the Word Market.

Gatekeeper.
AHHHHREMMMM! This is Dictionopolis, a happy
400 kingdom, advantageously located in the foothills of Confusion and caressed by gentle breezes from the Sea of Knowledge. Today, by royal proclamation, is Market Day. Have you come to buy or sell?

Milo. I beg your pardon?

Gatekeeper. Buy or sell, buy or sell. Which is it? You must have come here for a reason.

410 **Milo.** Well, I . . .

Gatekeeper. Come now, if you don't have a reason, you must at least have an explanation or certainly an excuse.

Milo. (*Meekly.*) Uh . . . no.

Gatekeeper. (*Shaking his head.*) Very serious. You can't get in without a reason. (*Thoughtfully.*) Wait

Pause & Reflect

1. Look back at the details you underlined as you read. What is the basic disagreement between Azaz and the Mathemagician? (**Summarize**)

2. Before the princesses were banished, what was their job in the Land of Wisdom? (**Clarify**)

3. What questions do you have about the play so far? (**Question**)

a minute. Maybe I have an old one you can use. (*Pulls out an old suitcase from the tollbooth and rummages through it.*) No . . . no . . . no . . . this

420 won't do . . . hmmm . . .

Milo. (*To Tock.*) What's he looking for? (*Tock shrugs.*)

Gatekeeper. Ah! This is fine. (*Pulls out a medallion on a chain. Engraved in the medallion is: "Why not?"*) Why not. That's a good reason for almost anything . . . a bit used, perhaps, but still quite serviceable.[11] There you are, sir. Now I can truly say: Welcome to Dictionopolis.

(*He opens the gate and walks off. Citizens and merchants appear on all levels of the stage, and Milo*

430 *and Tock find themselves in the middle of a noisy marketplace. As some people buy and sell their wares, others hang a large banner which reads: Welcome to the Word Market.*)

Milo. Tock! Look!

Merchant 1. Hey-ya, hey-ya, hey-ya, step right up and take your pick. Juicy tempting words for sale. Get your fresh-picked "if's," "and's" and "but's"! Just take a look at these nice ripe "where's" and "when's."

440 **Merchant 2.** Step right up, step right up, fancy, best-quality words here for sale. Enrich your vocabulary and expand your speech with such elegant items as "quagmire," "flabbergast," or "upholstery."

Merchant 3. Words by the bag, buy them over here. Words by the bag for the more talkative customer. A pound of "happy's" at a very reasonable price . . . very useful for "Happy Birthday," "Happy New Year," "happy days," or "happy-go-lucky." Or how about a package of "good's," always handy for

---

11. **serviceable** (sûr′vĭ-sə-bəl): ready for service, usable.

450   "good morning," "good afternoon," "good evening," and "goodbye."

Milo. I can't believe it. Did you ever see so many words?

Tock. They're fine if you have something to say. (*They come to a Do-It-Yourself Bin.*)

Milo. (*To Merchant 4 at the bin.*) Excuse me, but what are these?

Merchant 4. These are for people who like to make up their own words. You can pick any assortment
460   you like or buy a special box complete with all the letters and a book of instructions. Here, taste an "A." They're very good. (*He pops one into Milo's mouth.*)

Milo. (*Tastes it hesitantly.*) It's sweet! (*He eats it.*)

Merchant 4. I knew you'd like it. "A" is one of our best-sellers. All of them aren't that good, you know. The "Z," for instance—very dry and sawdusty. And the "X?" Tastes like a trunkful of stale air. But most of the others aren't bad at all. Here, try the "I."

470 **Milo.** (*Tasting.*) Cool! It tastes icy.

Merchant 4. (*To Tock.*) How about the "C" for you? It's as crunchy as a bone. Most people are just too lazy to make their own words, but take it from me, not only is it more fun, but it's also *de*-lightful, (*Holds up a "D."*) *e*-lating, (*Holds up an "E."*) and extremely *useful*! (*Holds up a "U."*)

Milo. But isn't it difficult? I'm not very good at making words.

Pause & Reflect

NOTES

Pause & Reflect

1. Look back at the words you circled as you read. What word or words for sale at the Word Market would you find most useful? **(Connect)**

Why?

2. **MARK IT UP** What does the Word Market look like? Underline words and phrases that help you picture it. **(Visualize)**

FOCUS

In this section, Milo meets two new characters, the Spelling Bee and the Humbug. Read to find out how these characters live up to their names.

480 (*The Spelling Bee, a large colorful bee, comes up from behind.*)

Spelling Bee. Perhaps I can be of some assistance . . . a-s-s-i-s-t-a-n-c-e. (*The Three turn around and see him.*) Don't be alarmed . . . a-l-a-r-m-e-d. I am the Spelling Bee. I can spell anything. Anything. A-n-y-t-h-i-n-g. Try me. Try me.

Milo. (*Backing off, Tock on his guard.*) Can you spell
490   goodbye?

Spelling Bee. Perhaps you are under the misapprehension[12] . . . m-i-s-a-p-p-r-e-h-e-n-s-i-o-n that I am dangerous. Let me assure you that I am quite peaceful. Now, think of the most difficult word you can, and I'll spell it.

Milo. Uh . . . o.k. (*At this point, Milo may turn to the audience and ask them to help him choose a word or he may think of one on his own.*) How about . . . "Curiosity"?

500 **Spelling Bee.** (*Winking.*) Let's see now . . . uh . . . how much time do I have?

Milo. Just ten seconds. Count them off, Tock.

Spelling Bee. (*As Tock counts.*) Oh dear, oh dear. (*Just at the last moment, quickly.*) C-u-r-i-o-s-i-t-y.

Merchant 4. Correct! (*All cheer.*)

Milo. Can you spell anything?

Spelling Bee. (*Proudly.*) Just about. You see, years ago, I was an ordinary bee minding my own business, smelling flowers all day, occasionally
510   picking up part-time work in people's bonnets. Then

---

12. **misapprehension** (mĭs-ăp′rĭ-hĕn′shən): the misunderstanding of something.

one day, I realized that I'd never amount to anything without an education, so I decided that . . .

> **Humbug.**[13] (*Coming up in a booming voice.*) Balderdash! (*He wears a lavish coat, striped pants, checked vest, spats and a derby hat.*) Let me repeat . . . Balderdash! (*Swings his cane and clicks his heels in the air.*) Well, well, what have we here? Isn't someone going to introduce me to the little boy?

Spelling Bee. (*Disdainfully.*) This is the Humbug. You
520   can't trust a word he says.

Humbug. Nonsense! Everyone can trust a Humbug. As I was saying to the king just the other day . . .

Spelling Bee. You've never met the king. (*To Milo.*) Don't believe a thing he tells you.

Humbug. Bosh, my boy, pure bosh. The Humbugs are an old and noble family, honorable to the core. Why, we fought in the Crusades with Richard the Lionhearted,[14] crossed the Atlantic with Columbus, blazed trails with the pioneers. History is full of
530   Humbugs.

Spelling Bee. A very pretty speech . . . s-p-e-e-c-h. Now, why don't you go away? I was just advising the lad of the importance of proper spelling.

Humbug. Bah! As soon as you learn to spell one word, they ask you to spell another. You can never catch up, so why bother? (*Puts his arm around Milo.*) Take my advice, boy, and forget about it. As my great-great-great-grandfather George Washington Humbug used to say . . .

---

13. **Humbug** (hŭm′bŭg′): a person who pretends to be something he or she is not.

14. **fought in the Crusades with Richard the Lionhearted:** the Crusades were journeys undertaken by European Christians in the eleventh through thirteenth centuries to fight the Muslims for control of the Holy Land. Richard the Lionhearted was an English king (1190–1192) who led the Third Crusade.

 the boxed passage. **Visualize** the Humbug. Think about the way he speaks and how he is described. Draw a picture of the Humbug in the space below.

NOTES

540 **Spelling Bee.** You, sir, are an impostor[15] i-m-p-o-s-t-o-r who can't even spell his own name!

Humbug. What? You dare to doubt my word? The word of a Humbug? The word of a Humbug who has direct access to the ear of a king? And the king shall hear of this, I promise you . . .

Voice 1. Did someone call for the king?

Voice 2. Did you mention the monarch?

Voice 3. Speak of the sovereign?

Voice 4. Entreat the emperor?

550 **Voice 5.** Hail his highness?

(*Five tall, thin gentlemen regally dressed in silks and satins, plumed hats and buckled shoes appear as they speak.*)

Milo. Who are they?

Spelling Bee. The king's advisors. Or in more formal terms, his cabinet.

Minister 1. Greetings!

Minister 2. Salutations!

Minister 3. Welcome!

560 **Minister 4.** Good afternoon!

Minister 5. Hello!

Milo. Uh . . . Hi.

(*All the Ministers, from here on called by their numbers, unfold their scrolls and read in order.*)

Minister 1. By the order of Azaz the Unabridged . . .

Minister 2. King of Dictionopolis . . .

Minister 3. Monarch of letters . . .

Minister 4. Emperor of phrases, sentences, and miscellaneous figures of speech . . .

---

15. **impostor** (ĭm-pŏs′tər): one who takes on a different name or identity in order to deceive.

570 **Minister 5.** We offer you the hospitality of our
   kingdom . . .

Minister 1. Country

Minister 2. Nation

Minister 3. State

Minister 4. Commonwealth

Minister 5. Realm

Minister 1. Empire

Minister 2. Palatinate

Minister 3. Principality.

580 **Milo.** Do all those words mean the same thing?

Minister 1. Of course.

Minister 2. Certainly.

Minister 3. Precisely.

Minister 4. Exactly.

Minister 5. Yes.

Milo. Then why don't you just use one? Wouldn't
   that make a lot more sense?

Minister 1. Nonsense!

Minister 2. Ridiculous!

590 **Minister 3.** Fantastic!

Minister 4. Absurd!

Minister 5. Bosh!

Minister 1. We're not interested in making sense. It's
   not our job.

Minister 2. Besides, one word is as good as another,
   so why not use them all?

Minister 3. Then you don't have to choose which one
   is right.

Minister 4. Besides, if one is right, then ten are ten
600 times as right.

REREAD the boxed passage. How are these words related? Circle one. **(Clarify)**

They are antonyms.
They are homophones.
They are synonyms.

NOTES

Pause & Reflect

1. Why is the name "Humbug" appropriate for this character? Use footnote 13 on page 189 to help you. **(Evaluate)**

2. [MARK IT UP] What message do the king's advisors have for Milo? Find and circle the answer on this page. **(Clarify)**

Minister 5. Obviously, you don't know who we are. (*Each presents himself and Milo* <u>acknowledges</u> *the introduction.*)

Minister 1. The Duke of Definition.

Minister 2. The Minister of Meaning.

Minister 3. The Earl of Essence.

Minister 4. The Count of Connotation.

Minister 5. The Undersecretary of Understanding.

All Five. And we have come to invite you to the
610   Royal Banquet.

Spelling Bee. The banquet! That's quite an honor, my boy. A real h-o-n-o-r.

Humbug. Don't be ridiculous! Everybody goes to the Royal Banquet these days.

Spelling Bee. (*To the Humbug.*) True, everybody does go. But some people are invited and others simply push their way in where they aren't wanted.

Humbug. How dare you? You buzzing little upstart, I'll show you who's not wanted . . . (*Raises his cane*
620   *threateningly.*)

Spelling Bee. You just watch it! I'm warning w-a-r-n-i-n-g you! (*At that moment, an ear-shattering blast of trumpets, entirely off-key, is heard, and a Page appears.*)

Pause & Reflect

WORDS TO KNOW
acknowledge (ăk-nŏl′ĭj) *v.* to admit or to value the existence of

FOCUS

Milo attends a fancy dinner given by King Azaz. Read to find out what "foods" are served and why.

▌**MARK IT UP** ⟩ As you read, underline descriptions of the items served.

Page. King Azaz the Unabridged is about to begin the Royal Banquet. All guests who do not appear promptly at the table will automatically 630 lose their place. (*A huge table is carried out with King Azaz sitting in a large chair, carried out at the head of the table.*)

Azaz. Places. Everyone take your places. (*All the characters, including the Humbug and the Spelling Bee, who forget their quarrel, rush to take their places at the table. Milo and Tock sit near the King. Azaz looks at Milo.*) And just who is this?

Milo. Your Highness, my name is Milo and this is 640 Tock. Thank you very much for inviting us to your banquet, and I think your palace is beautiful!

Minister 1. Exquisite.

Minister 2. Lovely.

Minister 3. Handsome.

Minister 4. Pretty.

Minister 5. Charming.

Azaz. Silence! Now tell me, young man, what can you do to entertain us? Sing songs? Tell stories? Juggle plates? Do tumbling tricks? Which is it?

650 **Milo.** I can't do any of those things.

Azaz. What an ordinary little boy. Can't you do anything at all?

Milo. Well . . . I can count to a thousand.

Azaz. AARGH, numbers! Never mention numbers here. Only use them when we absolutely have to. Now, why don't we change the subject and have

REREAD the boxed passage. Why do the waiters serve rays of light when Milo requests a "light snack" and squares when he asks for a "square meal"? **(Question)**

NOTES

_____

_____

_____

_____

_____

_____

_____

_____

_____

_____

_____

_____

_____

_____

||| **MARK IT UP** > Why do the banquet guests recite lists of foods when they are asked to make speeches? Circle the answer on page 195. **(Clarify)**

some dinner? Since you are the guest of honor, you may pick the menu.

Milo. Me? Well, uh . . . I'm not very hungry. Can we
660   just have a light snack?

Azaz. A light snack it shall be!

(*Azaz claps his hands. Waiters rush in with covered trays. When they are uncovered, shafts of light pour out. The light may be created through the use of battery-operated flashlights which are secured in the trays and covered with a false bottom. The guests help themselves.*)

Humbug. Not a very substantial meal. Maybe you can suggest something a little more filling.

670   **Milo.** Well, in that case, I think we ought to have a square meal . . .

Azaz. (*Claps his hands.*) A square meal it is! (*Waiters serve trays of colored squares of all sizes. People serve themselves.*)

Spelling Bee. These are awful. (*Humbug coughs and all the guests do not care for the food.*)

Azaz. (*Claps his hands and the trays are removed.*) Time for speeches. (*To Milo.*) You first.

Milo. (*Hesitantly.*) Your Majesty, ladies and gentlemen,
680   I would like to take this opportunity to say that . . .

Azaz. That's quite enough. Musn't talk all day.

Milo. But I just started to . . .

Azaz. Next!

Humbug. (*Quickly.*) Roast turkey, mashed potatoes, vanilla ice cream.

Spelling Bee. Hamburgers, corn on the cob, chocolate pudding p-u-d-d-i-n-g. (*Each guest names two dishes and a dessert.*)

Azaz. (*The last.*) Pâté de fois gras, soupe a l'oignon,
690   salade endives, fromage et fruits et demitasse.[16]
(*He claps his hands. Waiters serve each guest his
words.*) Dig on. (*To Milo.*) Though I can't say I
think much of your choice.

Milo. I didn't know I was going to have to eat my
words.

Azaz. Of course, of course, everybody here does.
Your speech should have been in better taste.

Minister 1. Here, try some somersault. It improves
the flavor.

700   **Minister 2.** Have a rigamarole. (*Offers breadbasket.*)

Minister 3. Or a ragamuffin.

Minister 4. Perhaps you'd care for a synonym bun.

Minister 5. Why not wait for your just desserts?

Azaz. Ah yes, the dessert. We're having a special treat
today . . . freshly made at the half-bakery.

Milo. The half-bakery?

Azaz. Of course, the half-bakery! Where do you
think half-baked ideas[17] come from? Now, please
don't interrupt. By royal command, the pastry chefs
710   have . . .

Milo. What's a half-baked idea?

(*Azaz gives up the idea of speaking as a cart is
wheeled in and the guests help themselves.*)

Humbug. They're very tasty, but they don't always
agree with you. Here's a good one. (*Humbug hands
one to Milo.*)

Milo. (*Reads.*) "The earth is flat."

READ ALOUD the boxed
passage. Notice
the plays on
words. Then draw a line from
each banquet dish on the left
to the food it sounds like on
the right. **(Word Play)**

synonym bun	salt
somersault	muffin
rigamarole	cinnamon bun
ragamuffin	dinner roll

---

16. **pâté de foie gras . . . demitasse** *French:* *pâté de foie gras* (pä-tä′ də fwä grä): a
paste made from goose liver; *soupe a l'oignon* (sōōp a lô′nyôn): onion soup;
salade endives (sä′läd än′dēv): lettuce salad; *fromage et fruits* (frô′mäzh ā frwē):
cheese and fruit; *demitasse* (děm′ē′täs): a small cup of strong, black coffee.

17. **half-baked ideas:** ideas that are not well thought out or that lack common sense.

Spelling Bee. People swallowed that one for years. (*Picks up one and reads.*) "The moon is made of

720 green cheese." Now, there's a half-baked idea.

(*Everyone chooses one and eats. They include: "It Never Rains but Pours," "Night Air Is Bad Air," "Everything Happens for the Best," "Coffee Stunts Your Growth."*)

Azaz. And now for a few closing words. Attention! Let me have your attention! (*Everyone leaps up and exits, except for Milo, Tock and the Humbug.*) Loyal subjects and friends, once again on this gala occasion, we have . . .

730 **Milo.** Excuse me, but everybody left.

Azaz. (*Sadly.*) I was hoping no one would notice. It happens every time.

Humbug. They've gone to dinner, and as soon as I finish this last bite, I shall join them.

Milo. That's ridiculous. How can they eat dinner right after a banquet?

Azaz. Scandalous! We'll put a stop to it at once. From now on, by royal command, everyone must eat dinner before the banquet.

740 **Milo.** But that's just as bad.

Humbug. Or just as good. Things which are equally bad are also equally good. Try to look at the bright side of things.

Milo. I don't know which side of anything to look at. Everything is so confusing, and all your words only make things worse.

Azaz. How true. There must be something we can do about it.

Humbug. Pass a law.

750 **Azaz.** We have almost as many laws as words.

Humbug. Offer a reward. (*Azaz shakes his head and looks madder at each suggestion.*) Send for help? Drive a bargain? Pull the switch? Lower the boom? Toe the line? (*As Azaz continues to scowl, the Humbug loses confidence and finally gives up.*)

Pause & Reflect

FOCUS

Read to find out why it is so difficult to rescue the princesses.

MARK IT UP Underline the obstacles or dangers involved.

Milo. Maybe you should let Rhyme and Reason return.

Azaz. How nice that would be. Even if they were a 760 bother at times, things always went so well when they were here. But I'm afraid it can't be done.

Humbug. Certainly not. Can't be done.

Milo. Why not?

Humbug. (*Now siding with Milo.*) Why not, indeed?

Azaz. Much too difficult.

Humbug. Of course, much too difficult.

Milo. You could, if you really wanted to.

Humbug. By all means, if you really wanted to, you 770 could.

Azaz. (*To Humbug.*) How?

Milo. (*Also to Humbug.*) Yeah, how?

Humbug. Why . . . uh, it's a simple task for a brave boy with a stout heart, a steadfast dog and a serviceable small automobile.

Azaz. Go on.

Humbug. Well, all that he would have to do is cross the dangerous, unknown countryside between here

Pause & Reflect

1. "The earth is flat" is said to be a half-baked idea. Explain why. **(Analyze)**

_____

_____

_____

_____

_____

_____

_____

2. **MARK IT UP** Why do most of the guests leave the banquet during the closing words? Find and circle the answer on page 196. **(Clarify)**

NOTES

_____

_____

_____

_____

_____

_____

_____

_____

_____

_____

_____

_____

_____

780 and Digitopolis, where he would have to persuade the Mathemagician to release the princesses, which we know to be impossible because the Mathemagician will never agree with Azaz about anything. Once achieving that, it's a simple matter of entering the Mountains of <u>Ignorance</u> from where no one has ever returned alive, an effortless climb up a two-thousand-foot stairway without railings in a high wind at night to the Castle-in-the-Air. After a pleasant chat with the princesses, all that remains is a <u>leisurely</u> ride back through those

790 chaotic crags where the frightening fiends have sworn to tear any intruder from limb to limb and devour him down to his belt buckle. And finally after doing all that, a triumphal parade! If, of course, there is anything left to parade . . . followed by hot chocolate and cookies for everyone.

Azaz. I never realized it would be so simple.

Milo. It sounds dangerous to me.

Tock. And just who is supposed to make that journey?

800 **Azaz.** A very good question. But there is one far more serious problem.

Milo. What's that?

Azaz. I'm afraid I can't tell you that until you return.

Milo. But wait a minute, I didn't . . .

Azaz. Dictionopolis will always be grateful to you, my boy and your dog. (*Azaz pats Tock and Milo.*)

Tock. Now, just one moment, sire . . .

Azaz. You will face many dangers on your journey, but fear not, for I can give you something for your

810 protection. (*Azaz gives Milo a box.*) In this box are

WORDS TO KNOW
ignorance (ĭg′nər-əns) *n.* the state of being uneducated or unaware
leisurely (lē′zhər-lē) *adj.* unhurried

the letters of the alphabet. With them you can form all the words you will ever need to help you overcome the obstacles that may stand in your path. All you must do is use them well and in the right places.

Milo. (*Miserably.*) Thanks a lot.

Azaz. You will need a guide, of course, and since he knows the obstacles so well, the Humbug has cheerfully volunteered to accompany you.

820 **Humbug.** Now, see here . . . !

Azaz. You will find him dependable, brave, resourceful and loyal.

Humbug. (*Flattered.*) Oh, Your Majesty.

Milo. I'm sure he'll be a great help. (*They approach the car.*)

Tock. I hope so. It looks like we're going to need it.

(*The lights darken and the King fades from view.*)

Azaz. Good luck! Drive carefully! (*The three get into the car and begin to move. Suddenly a thunderously* 830 *loud noise is heard. They slow down the car.*)

Milo. What was that?

Tock. It came from up ahead.

Humbug. It's something terrible. I just know it. Oh, no. Something dreadful is going to happen to us. I can feel it in my bones. (*The noise is repeated. They all look at each other fearfully as the lights fade.*)

END of ACT ONE

Pause & Reflect

Pause & Reflect

1. [MARK IT UP] Review the details you underlined as you read. Which of these obstacles sounds the scariest? Put an exclamation point beside it. **(Evaluate)**

2. Do you think Milo and his friends will rescue Rhyme and Reason? **(Predict)**

YES / NO, because

_____

_____

CHALLENGE Compare Milo at the beginning and at the end of Act One. Is he the same or different? What makes you think so? **(Compare and Contrast)**

_____

_____

_____

Moving On

If you would like to check the prediction you made above, you can read the rest of the play. If you have a copy of *The Language of Literature,* turn to page 533 for Act Two, Scene 1. You might also enjoy the novel *The Phantom Tollbooth,* available in most libraries.

MARK IT UP What was your favorite scene or event in the drama? Draw a picture of it in the space below. **(Visualize)**

This picture is from Act 1, Scene _____ of *The Phantom Tollbooth*.

The characters are _____

_____

_____.

Active Reading SkillBuilder

Visualizing

Writers of fantasy include descriptions to help readers **visualize,** or form mental pictures of, settings and characters. *The Phantom Tollbooth* has imaginary settings and fantastic characters. Can you picture them? Fill out the chart below with descriptions from the drama and describe the mental pictures that you see. An example has been done.

Setting	Details from Text	Mental Picture
Dictionopolis	"located in the foothills of Confusion and caressed by gentle breezes from the Sea of Knowledge"	a city snuggled in gentle, rolling hills above a sparkling sea

Character	Details from Text	Mental Picture

Literary Analysis SkillBuilder

Fantasy

Fantasy is fiction that contains unrealistic elements. The setting or characters might have magical or extraordinary qualities. Keep track of the realistic and the fantastic details of characters and settings in *The Phantom Tollbooth* by jotting them down in the chart below.

Setting or Character	Fantastic Details	Realistic Details
Milo's bedroom	talking clock, mysterious voice, disappearance of room as Milo drives off in toy car	bed, desk, toys, books, and other possessions scattered around room

Words to Know SkillBuilder

Words to Know

acknowledge	destination	ignorance
dejectedly	fanfare	leisurely

A. For each Word to Know in the first column, find the definition in the second column. Write the letter of the definition in the blank.

_____ 1. fanfare   A. unhurried

_____ 2. dejectedly   B. the place one means to go

_____ 3. leisurely   C. as if depressed

_____ 4. acknowledge   D. the state of being unaware

_____ 5. destination   E. to admit the existence of

_____ 6. ignorance   F. a blast of trumpets

B. Fill in each set of blanks with the correct Word to Know. The boxed letters spell the name of a character in *The Phantom Tollbooth*.

1. So the saying goes, "This is bliss!" __ __ __ __ ☐ __ __ __ __

2. My ears and tail droop, and I stare at my empty bowl this way.

    __ __ __ ☐ __ __ __ __ __ __

3. The entrance of the celebrity had enough of this to please any fan.

    __ __ __ __ ☐ __ __

4. You might take this kind of stroll on a lazy afternoon. __ __ __ ☐ __ __ __ __

5. It takes courage to do this to your mistakes. __ __ __ __ ☐ __ __ __ __ __

6. This is where you plan to go. __ __ __ __ __ __ __ __ __ ☐

C. On a separate sheet of paper, write a paragraph telling about something that happens to Milo and his friends on their way to rescue the princesses. Use at least **three** Words to Know.

Before You Read

Connect to Your Life

Think of ways that advances in technology have made your life different from the lives of your grandparents. Fill in the word web below.

cellular phones

Advances in Technology

Key to the Story

WHAT DO YOU THINK? This story describes what school might be like far into the future:

> *Margie went into the schoolroom. It was right next to her bedroom, and the mechanical teacher was on and waiting for her.*

Do you think school might be more fun or less fun in the future?

More fun/Less fun, because _____

_____

_____

THE Fun They Had

BY ISAAC ASIMOV

PREVIEW Eleven-year-old Margie sees her friend Tommy reading an old-fashioned book—one made out of paper. Why does Margie find the book and its contents so strange?

FOCUS

Margie's friend Tommy finds "a real book" in his attic. Read to find out what has taken the place of books and teachers in the future.

Margie even wrote about it that night in her diary. On the page headed May 17, 2157, she wrote, "Today Tommy found a real book!"

It was a very old book. Margie's grandfather once said that when he was a little boy, his grandfather told him that there was a time when all stories were
10 printed on paper.

They turned the pages, which were yellow and crinkly, and it was awfully funny to read words that stood still instead of moving the way they were supposed to—on a screen, you know. And then, when they turned back to the page before, it had the same words on it that it had when they read it the first time.

"Gee," said Tommy, "what a waste. When you're through with the book, you just throw it away, I guess. Our television screen must have had a million
20 books on it and it's good for plenty more. I wouldn't throw it away."

"Same with mine," said Margie. She was eleven and hadn't seen as many telebooks[1] as Tommy had. He was thirteen.

She said, "Where did you find it?"

"In my house." He pointed without looking, because he was busy reading. "In the attic."

"What's it about?"

"School."

30 Margie was <u>scornful</u>. "School? What's there to write about school? I hate school." Margie always hated school, but now she hated it more than ever. The

---

1. **telebooks** (tĕl′ə-bŏŏks): books presented on a television screen.

WORDS TO KNOW
scornful (skôrn′fəl) *adj.* having an attitude of contempt; disdainful

mechanical teacher[2] had been giving her test after test in geography, and she had been doing worse and worse until her mother had shaken her head sorrowfully and sent for the county inspector.

He was a round little man with a red face and a whole box of tools with dials and wires. He smiled at her and gave her an apple, then took the teacher apart.
40 Margie had hoped he wouldn't know how to put it together again, but he knew how all right, and after an hour or so, there it was again, large and ugly, with a big screen on which all the lessons were shown and the questions were asked. That wasn't so bad. The part she hated most was the slot where she had to put homework and test papers. She always had to write them out in a punch code they made her learn when she was six years old, and the mechanical teacher calculated the mark in no time.

50 The inspector had smiled after he was finished and patted her head. He said to her mother, "It's not the little girl's fault, Mrs. Jones. I think the geography <u>sector</u> was geared a little too quick. Those things happen sometimes. I've slowed it up to an average ten-year level. Actually, the overall pattern of her progress is quite satisfactory." And he patted Margie's head again.

Margie was disappointed. She had been hoping they would take the teacher away altogether. They had
60 once taken Tommy's teacher away for nearly a month because the history sector had blanked out completely.

Pause & Reflect

---

2. **mechanical teacher:** a machine or computer that serves as a teacher.

WORDS TO KNOW
  sector (sĕk′tər) *n.* a part or division

NOTES

FOCUS

Read to find out more about how Margie's school differs from schools of the past.

⬛**MARK IT UP** ⬎ As you read, underline details that help you understand the contrast. An example is highlighted.

So she said to Tommy, "Why would anyone write about school?"

Tommy looked at her with very superior eyes, "Because it's not our kind of school, stupid. This is the old kind of school that they had hundreds
70 and hundreds of years ago."

He added <u>loftily</u>, pronouncing the word carefully, "*Centuries* ago."

Margie was hurt. "Well, I don't know what kind of school they had all that time ago." She read the book over his shoulder for a while, then said, "Anyway, they had a teacher."

"Sure they had a teacher, but it wasn't a regular teacher. It was a man."

"A man? How could a man be a teacher?"

80 "Well, he just told the boys and girls things and gave them homework and asked them questions."

"A man isn't smart enough."

"Sure he is. My father knows as much as my teacher."

"He can't. A man can't know as much as a teacher."

"He knows almost as much I betcha."

Margie wasn't prepared to <u>dispute</u> that. She said, "I wouldn't want a strange man in my house to teach me."

90 Tommy screamed with laughter. "You don't know much, Margie. The teachers didn't live in the house. They had a special building and all the kids went there."

"And all the kids learned the same thing?"

"Sure, if they were all the same age."

WORDS TO KNOW
loftily (lôf′tĭ-lē) *adv.* in a grand or pompous way
dispute (dĭ-spyōōt′) *v.* to argue about; debate

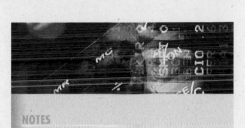

"But my mother says a teacher has to be adjusted to fit the mind of each boy and girl it teaches and that each kid has to be taught differently."

"Just the same, they didn't do it that way then. If
100 you don't like it, you don't have to read the book."

"I didn't say I didn't like it," Margie said quickly. She wanted to read about those funny schools.

They weren't even half finished when Margie's mother called, "Margie! School!"

Margie looked up. "Not yet, Mamma."

"Now," said Mrs. Jones. "And it's probably time for Tommy, too."

Margie said to Tommy, "Can I read the book some more with you after school?"

110 "Maybe," he said, <u>nonchalantly</u>. He walked away whistling, the dusty old book tucked beneath his arm.

Margie went into the schoolroom. It was right next to her bedroom, and the mechanical teacher was on and waiting for her. It was always on at the same time every day except Saturday and Sunday, because her mother said little girls learned better if they learned at regular hours.

The screen was lit up, and it said: "Today's arithmetic lesson is on the addition of proper
120 fractions. Please insert yesterday's homework in the proper slot."

Margie did so with a sigh. She was thinking about the old schools they had when her grandfather's grandfather was a little boy. All the kids from the whole neighborhood came, laughing and shouting in the schoolyard, sitting together in the schoolroom, going home together at the end of the day. They learned the same things so they could help one another on the homework and talk about it.

130 And the teachers were people. . . .

WORDS TO KNOW
nonchalantly (nŏn'shə-länt'lē) *adv.* in a casual, unconcerned way

REREAD the boxed passage. What do you think Margie's feelings are toward the schools of the past? **(Infer)**

NOTES

1. List two differences between Margie's school and schools of the past. **(Compare and Contrast)**

_____

_____

_____

_____

_____

_____

2. How does Margie feel at the end of the story? Circle the answer below. **(Infer)**

She is glad she has a mechanical teacher.

She likes going to school at home.

She thinks kids had more fun in school in the old days.

A **theme** is a message about life or human nature that is conveyed by a work of literature. A science-fiction writer may set a story in the future to raise questions about something in today's world. What warning does Asimov give in this story? Mark passages to support your views. **(Analyze)**

The mechanical teacher was flashing on the screen: "When we add the fractions ½ and ¼—"

Margie was thinking about how the kids must have loved it in the old days. She was thinking about the fun they had. ❖

Pause & Reflect

Active Reading SkillBuilder

Making Inferences

An **inference** is a logical conclusion based on evidence. Readers make inferences based on information given in the story and their own experience. You can make inferences about characters, plot, setting, theme, and other aspects of a story. In the chart below, practice making inferences about "The Fun They Had."

Clue from Text	Inference
"Today Tommy found a real book!"	People in the future don't have the kind of books that we have today.
. . . there was a time when all stories were printed on paper.	

Literary Analysis SkillBuilder

Setting

The **setting** is the time and place in which the action of a story happens. Setting may influence the plot, characters, and theme of a work. Science-fiction writers often set their stories in the future. To appreciate the author's vision of the future, compare and contrast the setting of "The Fun They Had" with the present time in which you live. Write down differences and similarities in the Venn diagram below.

Present   **Future—May of 2157**

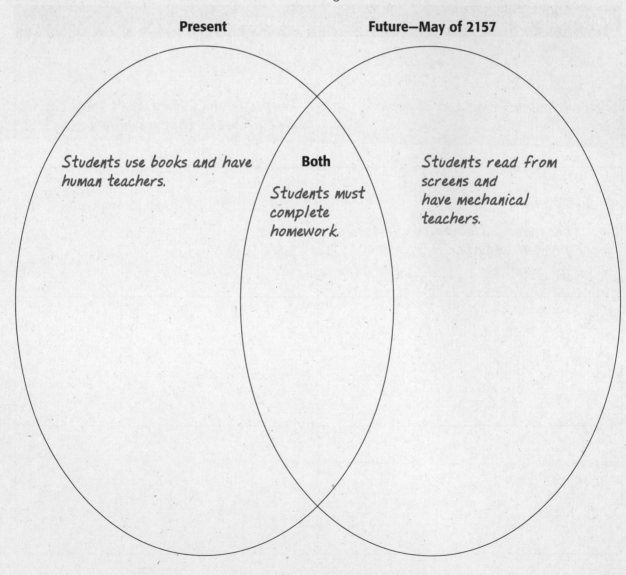

Students use books and have human teachers.

Both

Students must complete homework.

Students read from screens and have mechanical teachers.

Words to Know SkillBuilder

Words to Know

dispute	loftily	nonchalantly	scornful	sector

A. Write the Word to Know that has a similar meaning to the underlined word(s).

_____ 1. Tommy <u>casually</u> mentioned that he had found an old-fashioned book.

_____ 2. Margie wanted to <u>argue against</u> her mother's idea that she should have school at the same time every day.

_____ 3. The one advantage of a machine was that it wouldn't notice if the student gave it a <u>contemptuous</u> look.

_____ 4. The computer had a different <u>section or area</u> for each subject.

_____ 5. Sometimes people speak <u>grandly</u> to try to impress others.

B. Complete each analogy with one of the Words to Know. In an **analogy,** the last two words must be related in the same way the first two are related.

1. PIE : WEDGE : : city : _____

2. DECLINE : INCREASE : : settle : _____

3. LAUGH : MERRILY : : stroll : _____

4. ENERGETIC : LAZY : : humbly : _____

5. ACADEMIC : SCHOLARLY : : disdainful : _____

C. Finish Margie's diary entry (May 17, 2157). Use **three** of the Words to Know.

<u>Today Tommy found a real book!</u> _____

_____

_____

Before You Read

Connect to Your Life

How might you compensate—make up for—the loss of sight? Try standing or sitting in a busy room and closing your eyes. What can you "see" with your ears and your nose?

I can smell	I can hear
popcorn	

Key to the Story

WHAT'S THE BIG IDEA? What would you like to know about the ancient city of Pompeii? In the chart, record what you already know about this city, and what you would like to learn. Fill in the third column when you have finished the story.

What I Know	What I Want to Learn	What I Learned
It was buried by a volcanic eruption.		

THE DOG OF POMPEII

BY LOUIS UNTERMEYER

PREVIEW In the Roman Empire, in the city of Pompeii, the blind boy Tito and his dog Bimbo live on the streets. Together they roam the city, exploring its smells and sounds. What will happen to them when a nearby volcano erupts?

FOCUS

Tito and his beloved dog, Bimbo, live in the ancient city of Pompeii.

MARK IT UP ▷ As you read, underline details that tell you about the boy and his dog. An example is highlighted.

Tito and his dog Bimbo lived (if you could call it living) under the wall where it joined the inner gate. They really didn't live there; they just slept there. They lived anywhere. Pompeii was one of the gayest of the old Latin towns, but although Tito was

10 never an unhappy boy, he was not exactly a merry one. The streets were always lively with shining chariots and bright red trappings; the open-air theaters rocked with laughing crowds; sham battles and athletic sports were free for the asking in the great stadium. Once a year the Caesar[1] visited the pleasure city, and the fireworks lasted for days; the sacrifices[2] in the forum were better than a show. But Tito saw none of these things. He was blind—had been blind from birth. He was known to everyone in the poorer quarters. But

20 no one could say how old he was; no one remembered his parents; no one could tell where he came from. Bimbo was another mystery. As long as people could remember seeing Tito—about twelve or thirteen years—they had seen Bimbo. Bimbo had never left his side. He was not only dog but nurse, pillow, playmate, mother, and father to Tito.

Did I say Bimbo never left his master? (Perhaps I had better say comrade, for if anyone was the master, it was Bimbo.) I was wrong. Bimbo did trust Tito alone

30 exactly three times a day. It was a fixed routine, a custom understood between boy and dog since the beginning of their friendship, and the way it worked was this: Early in the morning, shortly after dawn, while Tito was still dreaming, Bimbo would disappear.

---

1. **the Caesar** (sē′zər): the Roman emperor.
2. **sacrifices:** offerings of animals or objects to the gods.

When Tito woke, Bimbo would be sitting quietly at his side, his ears cocked, his stump of a tail tapping the ground, and a fresh baked bread—more like a large round roll—at his feet. Tito would stretch himself; Bimbo would yawn; then they would breakfast. At noon, no matter where they happened to be, Bimbo would put his paw on Tito's knee, and the two of them would return to the inner gate. Tito would curl up in the corner (almost like a dog) and go to sleep, while Bimbo, looking quite important (almost like a boy), would disappear again. In half an hour he'd be back with their lunch. Sometimes it would be a piece of fruit or a scrap of meat; often it was nothing but a dry crust. But sometimes there would be one of those flat, rich cakes, sprinkled with raisins and sugar, that Tito liked so much. At suppertime the same thing happened, although there was a little less of everything, for things were hard to snatch in the evening with the streets full of people. Besides, Bimbo didn't approve of too much food before going to sleep. A heavy supper made boys too restless and dogs too stodgy—and it was the business of a dog to sleep lightly with one ear open and muscles ready for action.

But whether there was much or little, hot or cold, fresh or dry, food was always there. Tito never asked where it came from, and Bimbo never told him. There was plenty of rainwater in the hollows of soft stones; the old egg-woman at the corner sometimes gave him a cupful of strong goat's milk; in the grape season the fat winemaker let him have drippings of the mild juice. So there was no danger of going hungry or thirsty. There was plenty of everything in Pompeii if you knew where to find it—and if you had a dog like Bimbo.

Pause & Reflect

NOTES

Pause & Reflect

1. Cross out the phrase below that is *not* true of Tito. **(Clarify)**

   sleeps outside

   is blind

   is accompanied by Bimbo

   has wealthy parents

2. Do you think Tito could survive without Bimbo? **(Evaluate)**

   YES / NO, because

FOCUS

Tito and Bimbo set out to explore Pompeii. Read to find out what Tito "sees" on their walks.

MARK IT UP As you read, circle details that help you form impressions of daily life in Pompeii.

As I said before, Tito was not the merriest boy in
70 Pompeii. He could not romp with the other youngsters and play hare and hounds and I spy and follow-your-master and ball-against-the-building and jackstones and kings and robbers with them. But that did not make him sorry for himself. If he could not see the sights that delighted the lads of Pompeii, he could hear and smell things
80 they never noticed. He could really see more with his ears and nose than they could with their eyes. When he and Bimbo went out walking, he knew just where they were going and exactly what was happening.

"Ah," he'd sniff and say as they passed a handsome villa, "Glaucus Pansa is giving a grand dinner tonight. They're going to have three kinds of bread, and roast pigling, and stuffed goose, and a great stew—I think bear stew—and a fig pie." And Bimbo would note that this would be a good place to visit tomorrow.

90 Or, "H'm," Tito would murmur, half through his lips, half through his nostrils. "The wife of Marcus Lucretius is expecting her mother. She's shaking out every piece of goods in the house; she's going to use the best clothes—the ones she's been keeping in pine needles and camphor[3]—and there's an extra girl in the kitchen. Come, Bimbo, let's get out of the dust!"

Or, as they passed a small but elegant dwelling opposite the public baths, "Too bad! The tragic poet is ill again. It must be a bad fever this time, for they're
100 trying smoke fumes instead of medicine. Whew! I'm glad I'm not a tragic poet!"

---

3. **camphor** (kăm′fər): a strong-smelling substance used as a moth repellent.

Or, as they neared the forum, "Mm-m! What good things they have in the macellum[4] today!" (It really was a sort of butcher-grocer-marketplace, but Tito didn't know any better. He called it the macellum.) "Dates from Africa, and salt oysters from sea caves, and cuttlefish, and new honey, and sweet onions, and—ugh!—water-buffalo steaks. Come, let's see what's what in the forum." And Bimbo, just as curious
110 as his comrade, hurried on. Being a dog, he trusted his ears and nose (like Tito) more than his eyes. And so the two of them entered the center of Pompeii.

Pause & Reflect

FOCUS

The people of Pompeii go to the forum to discuss the latest news. Read to find out about this place and what Tito hears there about earthquakes.

The forum was the part of the town to which everybody came at least once during each day. It was the central square, and everything happened here. There were no private houses; all was public—the chief
120 temples, the gold and red bazaars, the silk shops, the town hall, the booths belonging to the weavers and jewel merchants, the wealthy woolen market, the shrine of the household gods. Everything glittered here. The buildings looked as if they were new—which, in a sense, they were. The earthquake of twelve years ago had brought down all the old structures, and since the citizens of Pompeii were ambitious to rival Naples and even Rome, they had seized the opportunity to rebuild the whole town. And they had done it all within a dozen years. There was
130 scarcely a building that was older than Tito.

---

4. **macellum** (mü-kĕl' əm): *Latin,* a provision market or grocery store.

WORDS TO KNOW
shrine (shrīn) *n.* a place of worship

1. **READ ALOUD** the boxed text on page 218. How well do you think Tito copes with his blindness? **(Evaluate)**

2. What does Tito experience on his walks around Pompeii? Check three phrases below. **(Clarify)**
   ❑ street theater
   ❑ food cooking
   ❑ spring cleaning
   ❑ fresh fish market

NOTES

Pause & Reflect

1. [MARK IT UP] What details help you picture the forum? Circle these details on the previous page. (Visualize)

2. Today, the forum would most likely be called which one of the following? (Compare and Contrast)

   city center

   sports stadium

   place of worship

3. Tito hears different opinions about the causes of earthquakes. Cross out the sentence below that is *not* mentioned as a cause of earthquakes. (Cause and Effect)

   The gods are angry.

   People are greedy and uncaring.

   Priests get too many offerings.

   Foreign goods bring bad luck.

NOTES

Tito had heard a great deal about the earthquake, though being about a year old at the time, he could scarcely remember it. This particular quake had been a light one—as earthquakes go. The weaker houses had been shaken down; parts of the outworn wall had been wrecked; but there was little loss of life, and the brilliant new Pompeii had taken the place of the old. No one knew what caused these earthquakes. Records showed they had happened in the neighborhood since 140 the beginning of time. Sailors said that it was to teach the lazy city folk a lesson and make them appreciate those who risked the dangers of the sea to bring them luxuries and protect their town from invaders. The priests said that the gods took this way of showing their anger to those who refused to worship properly and who failed to bring enough sacrifices to the altars and (though they didn't say it in so many words) presents to the priests. The tradesmen said that the foreign merchants had corrupted the ground and it was 150 no longer safe to traffic in imported goods that came from strange places and carried a curse with them. Everyone had a different explanation—and everyone's explanation was louder and sillier than his neighbor's.

Pause & Reflect

FOCUS

In the forum, Tito listens to a stranger who warns the people.

[MARK IT UP] As you read, circle details about the stranger's warning.

They were talking about it this afternoon as Tito and Bimbo came out of the side street into the public square. The forum was the favorite promenade[5] for rich and poor. 160 What with the priests arguing

---

5. promenade (prŏm´ə-nād´): a public place for leisurely walking.

with the politicians, servants doing the day's shopping, tradesmen crying their wares, women displaying the latest fashions from Greece and Egypt, children playing hide-and-seek among the marble columns, knots of soldiers, sailors, peasants from the provinces[6]—to say nothing of those who merely came to lounge and look on—the square was crowded to its last inch. His ears even more than his nose guided Tito to the place where the talk was loudest. It was in front
170 of the shrine of the household gods that, naturally enough, the householders were arguing.

"I tell you," rumbled a voice which Tito recognized as bath master Rufus's, "there won't be another earthquake in my lifetime or yours. There may be a tremble or two, but earthquakes, like lightnings, never strike twice in the same place."

"Do they not?" asked a thin voice Tito had never heard. It had a high, sharp ring to it, and Tito knew it as the accent of a stranger. "How about the two towns
180 of Sicily that have been ruined three times within fifteen years by the <u>eruptions</u> of Mount Etna? And were they not warned? And does that column of smoke above Vesuvius mean nothing?"

"That?" Tito could hear the grunt with which one question answered another. "That's always there. We use it for our weather guide. When the smoke stands up straight, we know we'll have fair weather; when it flattens out, it's sure to be foggy; when it drifts to the east—"

190 "Yes, yes," cut in the edged voice. "I've heard about your mountain barometer. But the column of smoke seems hundreds of feet higher than usual, and it's

---

6. **provinces:** areas of a country that are far from the capital.

WORDS TO KNOW
    eruption (ĭ-rŭp′shən) *n.* an outburst or throwing forth of lava, water, steam, and other materials

NOTES

1. **READ ALOUD** the boxed passage. In your own words, tell what the stranger warns the people about. **(Paraphrase)**

_____

_____

_____

_____

_____

2. For what purpose do the people of Pompeii use the smoke from Mount Vesuvius? Check one. **(Clarify)**

❏ to forecast weather

❏ to contact their gods

❏ to scare their children

NOTES

_____

_____

_____

_____

_____

_____

_____

_____

thickening and spreading like a shadowy tree. They say in Naples—"

"Oh, Naples!" Tito knew this voice by the little squeak that went with it. It was Attilio, the cameo[7] cutter. "They talk while we suffer. Little help we got from them last time. Naples commits the crimes, and Pompeii pays the price. It's become a proverb with us.
200 Let them mind their own business."

"Yes," grumbled Rufus, "and others, too."

"Very well, my confident friends," responded the thin voice, which now sounded curiously flat. "We also have a proverb—and it is this: Those who will not listen to men must be taught by the gods. I say no more. But I leave a last warning. Remember the holy ones. Look to your temples. And when the smoke tree above Vesuvius grows to the shape of an umbrella pine, look to your lives."

Pause & Reflect

FOCUS

Tito and Bimbo celebrate Caesar's birthday. Read to find out how the people of Pompeii make merry.

210 Tito could hear the air whistle as the speaker drew his toga[8] about him, and the quick shuffle of feet told him the stranger had gone.

"Now what," said the cameo cutter, "did he mean by that?"

"I wonder," grunted Rufus. "I wonder."

Tito wondered, too. And Bimbo, his head at a thoughtful angle, looked as if he had been doing a

---

7. **cameo** (kăm′ē-ō′): a gem or shell with a picture carved on it.

8. **toga:** a loose one-piece outer garment worn by citizens of ancient Rome.

220 heavy piece of pondering. By nightfall the argument
had been forgotten. If the smoke had increased, no
one saw it in the dark. Besides, it was Caesar's
birthday, and the town was in holiday mood. Tito
and Bimbo were among the merrymakers, dodging
the charioteers who shouted at them. A dozen times
they almost upset baskets of sweets and jars of
Vesuvian wine, said to be as fiery as the streams
inside the volcano, and a dozen times they were
cursed and cuffed. But Tito never missed his footing.
230 He was thankful for his keen ears and quick
instinct—most thankful of all for Bimbo.

They visited the uncovered theater, and though
Tito could not see the faces of the actors, he could
follow the play better than most of the audience, for
their attention wandered—they were distracted by
the scenery, the costumes, the by-play, even by
themselves—while Tito's whole attention was
centered in what he heard. Then to the city walls,
where the people of Pompeii watched a mock naval
240 battle in which the city was attacked by the sea and
saved after thousands of flaming arrows had been
exchanged and countless colored torches had been
burned. Though the thrill of flaring ships and lighted
skies was lost to Tito, the shouts and cheers excited
him as much as any, and he cried out with the
loudest of them.

Pause & Reflect

NOTES

Pause & Reflect

1. [||| MARK IT UP] Circle the
   words and phrases that
   describe the celebrations
   on Caesar's birthday.
   (Visualize)

2. What do you think will
   happen to the people of
   Pompeii the next day?
   (Predict)

FOCUS

The next day, there is a change in the air. Read to find out what Tito senses as he and Bimbo walk through the city.

MARK IT UP As you read, underline details that describe what Tito senses.

The next morning there were *two* of the beloved raisin and sugar cakes for his 250 breakfast. Bimbo was unusually active and thumped his bit of a tail until Tito was afraid he would wear it out. The boy could not imagine whether Bimbo was urging him to some sort of game or was trying to tell him something. After a while, he ceased to notice Bimbo. He felt drowsy. Last night's late hours had tired him. Besides, there was a heavy 260 mist in the air—no, a thick fog rather than a mist—a fog that got into his throat and scraped it and made him cough. He walked as far as the marine gate[9] to get a breath of the sea. But the blanket of haze had spread all over the bay, and even the salt air seemed smoky.

He went to bed before dusk and slept. But he did not sleep well. He had too many dreams—dreams of ships lurching in the forum, of losing his way in a screaming crowd, of armies marching across his chest, of being pulled over every rough pavement[10] of 270 Pompeii.

He woke early. Or, rather, he was pulled awake. Bimbo was doing the pulling. The dog had dragged Tito to his feet and was urging the boy along. Somewhere. Where, Tito did not know. His feet stumbled uncertainly; he was still half asleep. For a while he noticed nothing except the fact that it was hard to breathe. The air was hot. And heavy. So heavy that he could taste it. The air, it seemed, had turned to powder, a warm powder that stung his nostrils and 280 burned his sightless eyes.

---

9. **marine gate:** a gate in the city wall, leading to the sea.

10. **pavement:** a hard smooth surface of concrete, asphalt, brick, or a similar material, as for a road or sidewalk.

Then he began to hear sounds. Peculiar sounds. Like animals under the earth. Hissings and groanings and muffled cries that a dying creature might make dislodging the stones of his underground cave. There was no doubt of it now. The noises came from underneath. He not only heard them—he could feel them. The earth twitched; the twitching changed to an uneven shrugging of the soil. Then, as Bimbo half pulled, half coaxed him across, the ground jerked

290 away from his feet and he was thrown against a stone fountain.

Pause & Reflect

FOCUS

Bimbo leads Tito through a city in panic.

MARK IT UP As you read, circle words or phrases that describe the dangers that threaten Tito and Bimbo.

The water—hot water— splashing in his face revived him. He got to his feet, Bimbo steadying him, helping him on again. The noises grew louder; they came closer. The cries were even more animal-like than before, but

300 now they came from human throats. A few people, quicker of foot and more hurried by fear, began to rush by. A family or two—then a section—then, it seemed, an army broken out of bounds. Tito, bewildered though he was, could recognize Rufus as he bellowed[11] past him, like a water buffalo gone mad. Time was lost in a nightmare.

---

11. **bellowed:** roared as a bull does; shouted in a loud voice.

WORDS TO KNOW
dislodging (dĭs-lŏj'ĭng) adj. moving from a settled position **dislodge** v.

Pause & Reflect

1. **MARK IT UP** Review the details you underlined as you read. Put a star next to the ones that helped you the most to picture Tito's situation. (Evaluate)

2. At this point in the story, what **questions** do you have about Pompeii? Write one question in the space below.

NOTES

Pause & Reflect

1. Tito and Bimbo are trapped in the city. What would you do if you were in their situation? (Connect)

_____

_____

_____

_____

_____

2. Cross out the phrase below that does *not* apply to Tito's dangerous situation. (Infer)

flaming buildings

bitter cold

loss of direction

mass confusion

NOTES

_____

_____

_____

_____

_____

_____

_____

_____

_____

It was then the crashing began. First a sharp crackling, like a monstrous snapping of twigs; then a roar like the fall of a whole forest of trees; then an explosion that tore earth and sky. The heavens, though Tito could not see them, were shot through with continual flickerings of fire. Lightnings above were answered by thunders beneath. A house fell. Then another. By a miracle the two companions had escaped the dangerous side streets and were in a more open space. It was the forum. They rested here awhile—how long he did not know.

Tito had no idea of the time of day. He could *feel* it was black—an unnatural blackness. Something inside—perhaps the lack of breakfast and lunch—told him it was past noon. But it didn't matter. Nothing seemed to matter. He was getting drowsy, too drowsy to walk. But walk he must. He knew it. And Bimbo knew it; the sharp tugs told him so. Nor was it a moment too soon. The sacred ground of the forum was safe no longer. It was beginning to rock, then to pitch, then to split. As they stumbled out of the square, the earth wriggled like a caught snake, and all the columns of the temple of Jupiter[12] came down. It was the end of the world—or so it seemed.

Pause & Reflect

FOCUS

Bimbo takes drastic steps to try to save Tito.

MARK IT UP > Underline details that describe how Bimbo helps Tito.

To walk was not enough now. They must run. Tito was too frightened to know what to do or where to go. He had lost all sense of direction. He started to go back to the

12. **Jupiter:** the supreme god in Roman mythology.

inner gate; but Bimbo, straining his back to the last inch, almost pulled his clothes from him. What did the creature want? Had the dog gone mad?

340 Then, suddenly, he understood. Bimbo was telling him the way out—urging him there. The sea gate, of course. The sea gate—and then the sea. Far from falling buildings, heaving ground. He turned, Bimbo guiding him across open pits and dangerous pools of bubbling mud, away from buildings that had caught fire and were dropping their burning beams. Tito could no longer tell whether the noises were made by the shrieking sky or the agonized people. He and Bimbo ran on—the only silent beings in a howling 350 world.

New dangers threatened. All Pompeii seemed to be thronging toward the marine gate; and, squeezing among the crowds, there was the chance of being trampled to death. But the chance had to be taken. It was growing harder and harder to breathe. What air there was choked him. It was all dust now—dust and pebbles, pebbles as large as beans. They fell on his head, his hands—pumice[13] stones from the black heart of Vesuvius. The mountain was turning itself 360 inside out. Tito remembered a phrase that the stranger had said in the forum two days ago: "Those who will not listen to men must be taught by the gods." The people of Pompeii had refused to heed the warnings; they were being taught now—if it was not too late.

Suddenly it seemed too late for Tito. The red hot ashes blistered[14] his skin; the stinging vapors tore his

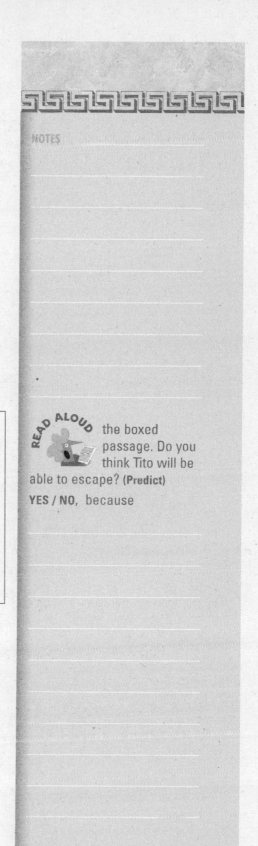

READ ALOUD the boxed passage. Do you think Tito will be able to escape? (Predict)

YES / NO, because

---

13. pumice (pŭm′ĭs): a light rock formed from lava.

14. blistered: caused a thin fluid-filled sac to form on the skin as a result of a burn.

WORDS TO KNOW
vapor (vā′pər) n. fumes, mist, or smoke

throat. He could not go on. He staggered toward a small tree at the side of the road and fell. In a moment 370 Bimbo was beside him. He coaxed.[15] But there was no answer. He licked Tito's hands, his feet, his face. The boy did not stir. Then Bimbo did the last thing he could—the last thing he wanted to do. He bit his comrade, bit him deep in the arm. With a cry of pain, Tito jumped to his feet, Bimbo after him. Tito was in despair, but Bimbo was determined. He drove the boy on, snapping at his heels, worrying his way through the crowd; barking, baring his teeth, heedless of kicks or falling stones. Sick with hunger, half dead with fear 380 and sulphur[16] fumes, Tito pounded on, pursued by Bimbo. How long he never knew. At last he staggered through the marine gate and felt soft sand under him. Then Tito fainted. . . .

Someone was dashing seawater over him. Someone was carrying him toward a boat.

"Bimbo," he called. And then louder, "Bimbo!" But Bimbo had disappeared.

Voices jarred against each other. "Hurry—hurry!" "To the boats!" "Can't you see the child's frightened 390 and starving!" "He keeps calling for someone!" "Poor boy, he's out of his mind." "Here, child—take this!"

They tucked him in among them. The oarlocks creaked; the oars splashed; the boat rode over toppling waves. Tito was safe. But he wept continually.

"Bimbo!" he wailed. "Bimbo! Bimbo!"

He could not be comforted.

Pause & Reflect

Pause & Reflect

1. How does Bimbo save Tito? (Cause and Effect)

2. MARK IT UP > What details help you imagine what Tito is going through when Bimbo disappears? Circle those details on this page. (Visualize)

228 The InterActive Reader PLUS

15. **coaxed:** persuaded or tried to persuade by gently urging.
16. **sulphur** (sŭl′fər): a pale yellow chemical element that produces a choking fume when burned.

FOCUS

Read to find out what scientists discover in Pompeii 1000 years later.

Eighteen hundred years passed. Scientists were <u>restoring</u> the ancient city; 400 excavators[17] were working their way through the stones and trash that had buried the entire town. Much had already been brought to light—statues, bronze instruments, bright mosaics,[18] household articles; even delicate paintings had been preserved by the fall of ashes that had taken over two thousand lives. Columns were dug up, and the forum was beginning to emerge.

It was at a place where the ruins lay deepest that the 410 director paused.

"Come here," he called to his assistant. "I think we've discovered the remains of a building in good shape. Here are four huge millstones that were most likely turned by slaves or mules—and here is a whole wall standing with shelves inside it. Why! It must have been a bakery. And here's a curious thing. What do you think I found under this heap where the ashes were thickest? The skeleton of a dog!"

"Amazing!" gasped his assistant. "You'd think a 420 dog would have had sense enough to run away at the time. And what is that flat thing he's holding between his teeth? It can't be a stone."

---

17. **excavators:** persons who expose or uncover by or as if by digging.

18. **mosaics** (mō-zā′ĭks): pictures or designs made by setting small colored stones or tiles into surfaces.

WORDS TO KNOW
  restore (rĭ-stôr′) v. to bring back to an original condition

NOTES

"No. It must have come from this bakery. You know it looks to me like some sort of cake hardened with the years. And, bless me, if those little black pebbles aren't raisins. A raisin cake almost two thousand years old! I wonder what made him want it at such a moment."

"I wonder," murmured the assistant. ❖

Pause & Reflect

Active Reading SkillBuilder

Distinguishing Fact from Nonfact

A **fact** is a statement that can be proven to be true. Historical fiction contains many facts. However, historical fiction also contains details about imaginary people, places, and events. As you read, think about which details are facts and which are not. Record your ideas in the chart below.

Fact	Nonfact
Once a year the Caesar visited the pleasure city.	Bimbo didn't approve of too much food before going to sleep.

Literary Analysis SkillBuilder

Historical Fiction

When fiction contains details about important people, places, and events from the past, it is called **historical fiction.** Even though this type of writing contains many facts, it is still considered fiction. With a group, discuss the author's use of fictional elements in "The Dog of Pompeii." Note the main ideas in the chart.

Discussion Results

Main Characters:	
Events Leading to Climax:	
Climax (turning point):	
How Setting is Important:	
Possible Theme:	

Follow Up: If you were writing a nonfiction history of the destruction of Pompeii, how would your account differ from this story? Write your answer on a sheet of paper.

Words to Know SkillBuilder

Words to Know

dislodging   eruption   restore   shrine   vapor

A. For each phrase in the first column, find the phrase in the second column that is closest in meaning. Write the letter of that phrase in the blank.

_____ 1. a splendid holy place   A. restore the floor

_____ 2. displacing car shelters   B. the worst outburst

_____ 3. lots of vapor   C. escape the vapor

_____ 4. repair the wood planks   D. dislodging garages

_____ 5. the most terrible eruption   E. extremely steamy

_____ 6. restore the sneakers   F. a fine shrine

_____ 7. flee the fog   G. renew the shoes

B. Fill in each blank with the correct Word to Know.

1. The sound of rocks _____ is one noise a mountain climber never wants to hear.

2. It can be difficult to _____ a painting that has been covered with layers of dirt and old varnish.

3. At natural hot springs, you can often see _____ over the water.

4. After the _____ of the volcano Mount St. Helens, it didn't take long for new plants and trees to begin to grow again.

5. An ancient Roman might have gone to a _____ to ask the gods for answers to questions.

C. Pretend you are one of the scientists who worked to uncover the city of Pompeii. On a sheet of paper, write a letter home telling your family about your work. Use at least **three** of the Words to Know in your letter.

Before You Read

Connect to Your Life

Suppose you were able to be part of an archaeological dig in the Valley of the Kings in Egypt. What would you most like to find? Add to the list below.

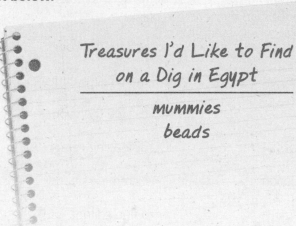

Treasures I'd Like to Find
on a Dig in Egypt

mummies

beads

Key to the Informative Article

WHAT YOU NEED TO KNOW For more than 1,000 years ancient Egyptians built great pyramids as tombs for their kings, or pharaohs. The treasures of these tombs were often stolen by grave robbers. By the 15th century B.C., pharaohs were no longer buried in pyramids. Instead, their tombs were hidden underground in what became known as the Valley of the Kings. Look at the map. Circle the area where an archaeologist—a person studying ancient remains—might dig to find out about Egyptian pharoahs.

TUTANKHAMEN
FROM LOST WORLDS
BY ANNE TERRY WHITE

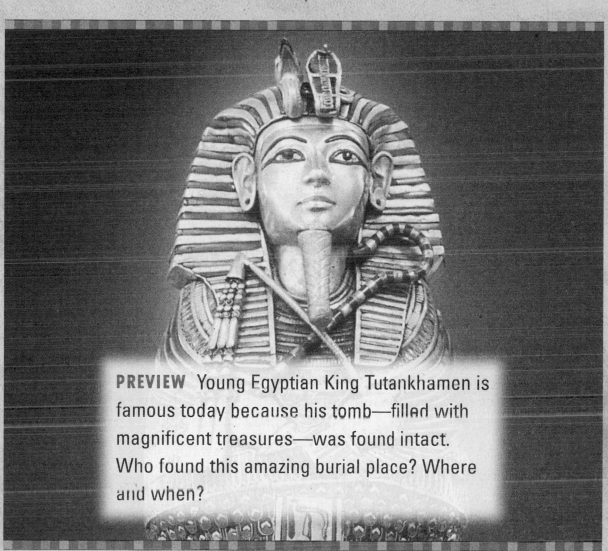

PREVIEW Young Egyptian King Tutankhamen is famous today because his tomb—filled with magnificent treasures—was found intact. Who found this amazing burial place? Where and when?

NOTES

Five seasons had passed and British archaeologist Howard Carter and his backer Lord Carnarvon had failed in their search for the 3,200-year-old tomb of Tutankhamen. Carter was sure that the tomb must lie in the center of the Valley of the Kings. In November 1922, Carter and crew began uncovering the only section of the valley that had not been dug up.

FOCUS

Carnarvon and Carter continue to search for the tomb. They have a theory about where to dig.

MARK IT UP ⟩ Circle details that help you understand how that theory guides their actions. An example is shown.

Now Carnarvon and Carter were not planning to dig at random in the Valley of the Tombs of the Kings. They were on the lookout for a particular tomb, the tomb of the Pharaoh Tutankhamen, and they believed they had worked out the location where
10 it lay. To the eyes of most people their undertaking seemed absurd. Nearly everybody was convinced that Tutankhamen's tomb had already been found. But Lord Carnarvon and Mr. Carter were not to be <u>dissuaded</u>, for they believed that the pit-tomb containing the fragments bearing the figures and names of Tutankhamen and his queen was far too small and insignificant for a king's burial. In their opinion the things had been placed there at some later time and did not indicate that the Pharaoh himself
20 had been buried on the spot. They were convinced that the tomb of Tutankhamen was still to be found, and that the place they had chosen—the center of the Valley—was the best place to look for it. In that vicinity had been unearthed something which they considered very good evidence—two jars containing broken bits of things that had been used at the funeral ceremonies of King Tutankhamen.

WORDS TO KNOW
dissuade (dĭ-swād′) *v.* to persuade someone not to do something

Nevertheless, when in the autumn of 1917 the excavators came out to look over the spot they had chosen and to begin their Valley campaign in earnest, even they thought it was a desperate undertaking. The site was piled high with refuse thrown out by former excavators. They would have to remove all that before they could begin excavating in virgin soil.[1] But they had made up their minds and meant to go through with it; even though it took many seasons, they would go systematically over every inch of ground.

In the years that followed, they did. They went over every inch, with the exception of a small area covered with the ruins of stone huts that had once sheltered workmen probably employed in building the tomb of Rameses VI.[2] These huts lay very near the tomb of the Pharaoh on a spot which Carter and Carnarvon had not touched for reasons of courtesy. The tomb of Rameses VI was a popular show place in the valley, and digging in the area of the huts would have cut off visitors to the tomb. They let it be, and turned instead to another site which they felt had possibilities.

The new ground proved, however, no better than the old, and now Lord Carnarvon began to wonder whether with so little to show for six seasons' work they were justified in going on. But Carter was firm. So long as a single area of unturned ground remained, he said, they ought to risk it. There was still the area of the huts. He insisted on going back to it. On November first, 1922, he had his diggers back in the old spot.

Pause & Reflect

---

1. **virgin soil:** ground that has not been dug up or explored.
2. **Rameses** (răm′ĭ-sēz′) **VI:** a Pharaoh whose tomb was built higher on the hill, above Tutankhamen's.

WORDS TO KNOW
systematically (sĭs′tə-măt′ĭk-lē) *adv.* In an orderly, thorough manner

Pause & Reflect

1. Why did Carter and Carnarvon think that King Tutankhamen's tomb was at the center of the Valley of the Kings? Check two sentences below. (**Text Structure**)

   ❑ A tomb containing figures of the king was too small.

   ❑ Two jars found at the center of the valley contained items from Tutankhamen's funeral.

   ❑ Kings were usually buried at the center of the valley.

   ❑ Most people thought Tutankhamen's tomb was at the center of the valley.

2. What can you **infer** about Howard Carter? Circle two words that describe him.

   careful   careless

   determined   unsure

FOCUS

The diggers make a thrilling discovery. Read to find out what it is and how Carter reacts.

And now things happened with such suddenness that Carter afterward declared 60 they left him in a dazed condition. Coming to work on the fourth day after the digging on the little area had started, he saw at once that something extraordinary had happened. Things were too quiet; nobody was digging and hardly anybody was talking. He hurried forward, and there before him was a shallow step cut in the rock beneath the very first hut attacked! He could hardly believe his eyes. After all the disappointments of the past six 70 seasons, was it possible that he was actually on the threshold[3] of a great discovery? He gave the command to dig, and the diggers fell to work with a will. By the next afternoon Carter was able to see the upper edges of a stairway on all its four sides, and before very long there stood revealed twelve steps, and at the level of the twelfth the upper part of a sealed and plastered doorway.

MARK IT UP Circle the words and phrases in the boxed text that describe what Carter sees. **(Clarify)**

NOTES

Carter's excitement was fast reaching fever pitch. Anything, literally anything, might lie beyond. It needed all his self-control to keep from breaking the 80 doorway down and satisfying his curiosity then and there. But was it fair to see what lay beyond that door alone? Although Lord Carnarvon was in England, was it not his discovery as much as Carter's? To the astonishment of the workmen, the excavator gave orders to fill the stairway in again, and then he sent the following cable off to Carnarvon: "At last have made wonderful discovery in Valley. A magnificent tomb with seals intact. Recovered same for your arrival. Congratulations."

---

3. **threshold** (thrĕsh′ōld): an entrance or beginning.

WORDS TO KNOW
intact (ĭn-tăkt′) *adj.* whole and undamaged

90 As he waited for Lord Carnarvon to come, Carter found it hard to persuade himself at times that the whole episode had not been a dream. The entrance to the tomb was only thirteen feet below the entrance to the tomb of Rameses VI. No one would have suspected the presence of a tomb so near the other. Had he actually found a flight of steps? Was it really there under the sand, waiting to conduct him to the great mystery?

Pause & Reflect

FOCUS

Carter and Carnarvon clear the stairway. Read to find out what Carter sees through a hole in the sealed door.

|||MARK IT UP > As you read, circle words and phrases that help you picture the things that Carter sees.

In two weeks' time Lord
100 Carnarvon and his daughter were on the spot. Carter now ordered his men to clear the stairway once more, and there on the lower part of the sealed doorway the explorers beheld what almost took their breath away—the seal of the Pharaoh Tutankhamen. Now they knew. Beyond this doorway lay either the
110 Pharaoh's secret treasure store or else the very tomb for which they were searching. Yet one thing made them uneasy. They noticed that part of the door was patched up and that in the patched-up part there stood out clearly the seal of the cemetery. It was evident that the door had been partly broken down—by robbers, of course—and then patched up again by cemetery officials. Had the robbers been caught in time? Did at least some of Tutankhamen's glory yet remain behind that twice-sealed doorway? Or would perhaps only
120 barren walls reward their years of <u>tedious</u> toil?

WORDS TO KNOW
tedious (tē'dō-əs) *adj.* long, tiring, and boring

Pause & Reflect

1. How did Carter react to what he saw? (Sequence of Events)

    First, Carter

    Next, he

    Then all he could do was wait.

2. If you were Carter, would you wait for Carnarvon? (Connect)

    YES / NO, because

NOTES

With pounding hearts they broke down the door. Beyond lay only another obstacle to their progress—a passage filled with stone. Had the robbers got beyond that? They began slowly to clear away the stone, and on the following day—"the day of days," Carter called it, "and one whose like I can never hope to see again"—they came upon a second sealed doorway, almost exactly like the first and also bearing distinct signs of opening and reclosing.

130 His hands trembling so that he could scarcely hold a tool, Carter managed to make a tiny hole in the door and to pass a candle through it. At first he could see nothing, but as his eyes grew accustomed to the light, "details of the room slowly emerged from the mist, strange animals, statues, and gold—everywhere the glint of gold."

"Can you see anything?" Carnarvon asked anxiously as Carter stood there dumb with amazement.

140 "Yes, wonderful things!" was all the explorer could get out.

And no wonder. What he saw was one of the most amazing sights anybody has ever been privileged to see. It seemed as if a whole museumful of objects was in that room. Three gilt[4] couches, their sides carved in the form of monstrous animals, and two statues of a king, facing each other like two <u>sentinels</u>, were the most prominent things in the room, but all around and between were hosts of other things—inlaid

150 caskets, alabaster vases, shrines, beds, chairs, a golden inlaid throne, a heap of white boxes (which they later found were filled with trussed ducks and other food offerings), and a glistening pile of overturned chariots.

READ ALOUD the boxed passage. Notice the descriptive details that help you **visualize**, or picture, the treasures.

NOTES

4. **gilt:** covered with a layer of gold.

WORDS TO KNOW
sentinel (sĕn′tə-nəl) *n.* one who keeps watch; guard

When Carter and Carnarvon got their senses together again, they realized all at once that there was no coffin in the room. Was this then merely a hiding place for treasure? They examined the room very intently once again, and now they saw that the two statues stood one on either side of a sealed doorway. Gradually the truth dawned on them. They were but on the threshold of their discovery. What they saw was just an antechamber.[5] Behind the guarded door there would be other rooms, perhaps a whole series of them, and in one of them, beyond any shadow of doubt they would find the Pharaoh lying.

But as they thought the thing over, the explorers were by no means certain that their first wild expectations would actually come to pass. Perhaps that sealed doorway, like the two before it, had also been re-opened. In that case there was no telling what lay behind it.

Pause & Reflect

FOCUS

The archaeologists enter the next chamber. Read to learn what they find there.

On the following day they took down the door through which they had been peeping, and just as soon as the electric connections had been made and they could see things clearly, they rushed over to the doubtful door between the royal sentinels. From a distance it had looked untouched, but when they examined it more closely, they saw that here again the robbers had been before them; near the bottom was distinct evidence that a small hole had been made and filled up and resealed. The robbers had indeed been stopped, but not before they had got into the inner chamber.

---

5. **antechamber** (ăn'tē-chām'bər): a small room leading to a larger one.

Pause & Reflect

1. Write the numbers 1, 2, 3, or 4 to show the order in which the events below occurred. **(Sequence of Events)**

___ Carter made a tiny hole in a second sealed doorway.

___ Treasures were seen in the antechamber.

___ Carnarvon rejoined Carter in Egypt.

___ Workers found a doorway with Tutankhamen's seal.

2. **MARK IT UP** Circle any clues in the boxed passage that told the archaeologists they might be close to finding Tutankhamen's body. Then check one clue below that does *not* apply. **(Infer)**

❏ many doorways in the room

❏ no coffin in the room

❏ two statues guarding sealed doorway

NOTES

1. Mark "T" beside each true statement and "F" beside each false one. (Clarify)

__ Carnarvon and Carter were disappointed in their findings.

__ They found evidence of plunderers before them.

__ Carnarvon and Carter were in this for money.

__ They were prepared to work to sort and label the treasures.

2. **REREAD** the last sentence. What was going to happen to the treasure? Do you think it should have been shipped to museums or left where it was found? (Make Judgments)

_____

_____

_____

_____

 CHALLENGE Some transitions for showing spatial relationships are: *behind, below, here, on the left, over,* and *on top.* Find and circle a passage that presents ideas in **spatial order.** How does this way of structuring text help you to visualize the scene?

It took almost as much self-command not to break down that door and see how much damage the robbers had done as to have filled in the staircase after it had once been cleared. But Carter and Carnarvon were not treasure-seekers; they were archaeologists, and they would not take the chance of injuring the objects within the antechamber just to satisfy their curiosity. For the moment they let that go and turned their attention to the things already before them.

There was enough there to leave them altogether bewildered. But while they were yet going crazily from one object to another and calling excitedly to each other, they stumbled on yet another discovery. In the wall, hidden behind one of the monstrous couches, was a small, irregular hole, unquestionably made by the plunderers[6] and never re-sealed. They dragged their powerful electric light to the hole and looked in. Another chamber, smaller than the one they were in, but even more crowded with objects! And everything was in the most amazing mess they had ever seen. The cemetery officials had made some attempt to clean up the antechamber after the robbers and to pile up the funeral furniture in some sort of order, but in the annex they had left things just as they were, and the robbers had done their work "about as thoroughly as an earthquake." Not a single inch of floor space remained unlittered.

Carter and Carnarvon drew a long breath and sobered down. They realized now that the job before them was going to take months and months. It would be a monumental task to photograph, label, mend, pack, and ship all this furniture, clothing, food, these chariots, weapons, walking sticks, jewels—this museumful of treasures. ❖

Pause & Reflect

---

6. **plunderers:** people who invade a place to rob and destroy it.

Active Reading SkillBuilder

Analyzing Text Structure

Writers of nonfiction present many details about their subjects and organize the information in various ways. Writers may use cause and effect, comparison and contrast, chronological order, or spatial order. When you **analyze the text structure** of nonfiction, look for one of these patterns.

Practice analyzing text structure by reading the first four paragraphs of "Tutankhamen." Then answer the questions in the chart below.

"Tutankhamen"	
What is the text structure of this section?	
What transitional words or other clues suggest the structure?	
What is the main idea of each paragraph?	
Paragraph 1:	
Paragraph 2:	
Paragraph 3:	
Paragraph 4:	
What is one detail that supports the first main idea?	
What information does it provide about the main idea?	

Literary Analysis SkillBuilder

Informative Nonfiction

Writers of **informative nonfiction** do a great deal of research to find the facts that they use in their articles. The author of an article such as "Tutankhamen" would probably use sources such as the following:

autobiographies	encyclopedias	letters/telegrams	newspaper articles
biographies	history books	logs or journals	photographs
diaries	interviews	museum catalogs	speeches

Some of these sources are **primary sources.** That is, they provide direct, firsthand reports on a subject or event. **Secondary sources** contain secondhand information by people who did not directly observe an event.

Read each item from "Tutankhamen" and decide which of the sources listed above Anne Terry White might have used to learn that detail. Write your answers in the chart.

Information from Article	Possible Source
1. He sent the following cable: "At last have made wonderful discovery in Valley. . . ."	
2. Lord Carnarvon and his daughter arrived two weeks after they received news of the discovery.	
3. Carter could not talk at first when he saw all the gold.	
4. The small, irregular hole in the wall was discovered behind a huge couch.	
5. The robbers had done their work "about as thoroughly as an earthquake."	

Follow Up: Which of the sources listed above the chart are primary sources? Circle them.

Words to Know SkillBuilder

Words to Know

dissuade   intact   sentinel   systematically   tedious

A. On each blank line, write the Word to Know that the rhyme describes.

To do this to a friend, you might say, "Please take my advice.
For if you do what you are planning, you will pay a price."

_____

This person has a job that's lonely, filled with many dangers,
And he or she must keep alert for signs of any strangers.

_____

If you do a thing carefully and keep working through it,
And don't stop until you're done, this is how you do it.

_____

Imagine you are faced with 40 cakes that all need frosting.
This describes a job like that one—boring and exhausting.

_____

To keep their property this way, some people
lose their senses.
Some hire guards, some fence their yards,
and some dig border trenches.

_____

B. Fill in each blank with the correct word from the word list.

1. Working on an assembly line can be _____ work.

2. You might need a password to get past a _____ .

3. Parents try to _____ their children from fighting.

4. It is easier to do something _____ if you have a plan.

5. If a glass remained _____ after you dropped it on a concrete
   floor, you would be surprised.

C. Imagine that a museum is going to display the objects from Tutankhamen's
tomb. On a separate sheet of paper, write a list of instructions for the museum
employees. Use at least **three** of the Words to Know.

Before You Read

Connect to Your Life

Just what is bravery? Is bravery simply a willingness to fight?
Consider acts of bravery you have heard about or seen.
Then write your own definition of bravery. Give an example
with your definition.

Definition: _____

Example: _____

Key to the Poem

WHAT TO LISTEN FOR "Barbara Frietchie" is a narrative poem—
a poem that tells a story. The poem is made up of pairs of rhymed
lines, or couplets. The rhythm—or beat—of the couplets allows
you to read them quickly. Note the brisk pace of this couplet:

> *"Who touches a hair of yon gray head*
> *Dies like a dog! March on!" he said.*

BARBARA FRIETCHIE

BY JOHN GREENLEAF WHITTIER

PREVIEW The Civil War was raging as Confederate Generals Robert E. Lee and "Stonewall" Jackson led almost 40,000 soldiers through Frederick, Maryland. Such times bring out the best and the worst in people. Barbara Frietchie, an elderly widow who lived in Frederick, greeted the Confederate army in her own daring way.

FOCUS

The speaker describes the town of Frederick on the morning when the rebels arrive.

MARK IT UP > As you read, circle words and phrases that help you **visualize** this town. An example is shown.

Up from the meadows rich with corn,
Clear in the cool September morn,

The clustered spires of Frederick stand
Green-walled by the hills of Maryland.

5   Round about them orchards sweep,
Apple and peach tree fruited deep,

Fair as the garden of the Lord
To the eyes of the famished rebel horde,

On that pleasant morn of the early fall
10   When Lee marched over the mountain-wall;

Over the mountains winding down,
Horse and foot, into Frederick town.

Forty flags with their silver stars,
Forty flags with their crimson bars,

15   Flapped in the morning wind; the sun
Of noon looked down and saw not one.

Pause & Reflect

Use this guide for help with unfamiliar
words and difficult passages.

READING TIP You may want to pause at the
end of every few couplets—
pairs of lines—to **clarify**
what you have just read.

• Read some lines aloud. Sometimes,
listening to the sound can help you
understand the meaning of a line.

• Jot down key events in the narrative,
using your own words.

3 clustered spires: groups of tall, pointed
towers.

7 garden of the Lord: Garden of Eden.

8 famished rebel horde: the hungry
Confederate troops.

10 Lee: Robert E. Lee, the Commander of
the Confederate Army of Northern Virginia.

**13–16 Forty flags with their silver stars . . .
and saw not one:** the Union flag of 1861,
used during the Civil War, had stars for 34
states, including the Southern states that had
left the Union. In the morning there were
forty Union flags flying. By noon there were
none.

Pause & Reflect

1. Cross out the one phrase that does *not*
relate to the town of Frederick. **(Clarify)**

    abundant crops

    houses of worship

    flat landscape

    apple and peach orchards

2. Why did the people of Frederick take
down the 40 flags? **(Infer)**

FOCUS

Barbara Frietchie defies the rebel army. Read to find out how she does that.

Up rose old Barbara Frietchie then,
Bowed with her fourscore years and ten;

Bravest of all in Frederick town,
20   She took up the flag the men hauled down;

In her attic window the staff she set,
To show that one heart was loyal yet.

Up the street came the rebel tread,
Stonewall Jackson riding ahead.

25   Under his slouched hat left and right
He glanced; the old flag met his sight.

"Halt!"—the dust-brown ranks stood fast.
"Fire!"—out blazed the rifle-blast.

It shivered the window, pane and sash;
30   It rent the banner with seam and gash.

Quick, as it fell, from the broken staff
Dame Barbara snatched the silken scarf.

Pause & Reflect

18 Bowed with her fourscore years and ten: a score is 20; fourscore years and ten would equal 90 years.

21 staff: a pole on which a flag is displayed.

25 slouched hat: a soft hat with a wide, flexible brim.

29 shivered: shattered; **sash:** window frame.
30 rent: tore or split apart.

32 silken scarf: refers to the flag torn down from the banner.

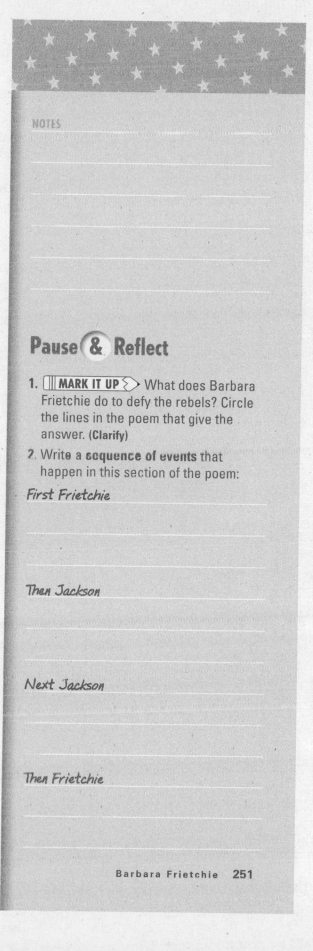

NOTES

Pause & Reflect

1. **MARK IT UP** What does Barbara Frietchie do to defy the rebels? Circle the lines in the poem that give the answer. **(Clarify)**

2. Write a **sequence of events** that happen in this section of the poem:

First Frietchie

Then Jackson

Next Jackson

Then Frietchie

FOCUS

Read to find out how Barbara
Frietchie challenges Stonewall
Jackson.

MARK IT UP As you read,
underline details that show you her
courage.

She leaned far out on the window-sill,
And shook it forth with a royal will.

35 "Shoot, if you must, this old gray head,
But spare your country's flag," she said.

A shade of sadness, a blush of shame,
Over the face of the leader came;

The nobler nature within him stirred
40 To life at that woman's deed and word:

"Who touches a hair of yon gray head
Dies like a dog! March on!" he said.

All day long through Frederick street
Sounded the tread of marching feet:

45 All day long that free flag tossed
Over the heads of the rebel host.

Pause & Reflect

34 a royal will: determination.

46 rebel host: the Confederate army.

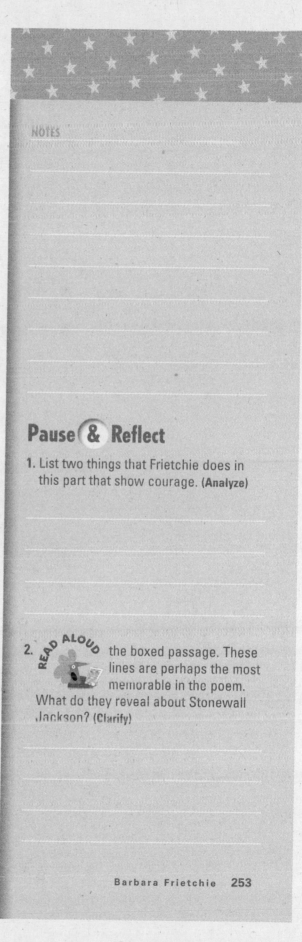

NOTES

Pause & Reflect

1. List two things that Frietchie does in this part that show courage. **(Analyze)**

2. READ ALOUD the boxed passage. These lines are perhaps the most memorable in the poem. What do they reveal about Stonewall Jackson? **(Clarify)**

Barbara Frietchie **253**

Ever its torn folds rose and fell
On the loyal winds that loved it well;

And through the hill-gaps sunset light
50 Shone over it with a warm good-night.

Barbara Frietchie's work is o'er,
And the Rebel rides on his raids no more.

Honor to her! and let a tear
Fall, for her sake, on Stonewall's bier.

55 Over Barbara Frietchie's grave,
Flag of Freedom and Union, wave!

Peace and order and beauty draw
Round that symbol of light and law;

And ever the stars above look down
60 On thy stars below in Frederick town!

Pause & Reflect

52 And the Rebel rides on his raids no more: the rebel, or Confederate, army lost to the Union.

54 bier (bîr): a coffin and its stand.

59–60 And ever the stars . . . below in Frederick town!: The stars in the heavens look down on the starred Union flag in Frederick.

Pause & Reflect

1. What happens to Frietchie's flag? Check the sentence that is *incorrect*. **(Clarify)**

   ❑ Frietchie's flag flies all day and night.

   ❑ Stonewall Jackson takes it down.

   ❑ It becomes a symbol of freedom and union.

2. List three vivid adjectives that you would use to tell a friend about Barbara Frietchie. **(Connect)**

 Review the **dialogue** that is spoken by Frietchie and by Jackson. How are these people alike and different? How do they each show courage? Mark details in the poem that support your ideas. **(Compare and Contrast)**

Active Reading SkillBuilder

Clarifying

The process of stopping while reading to quickly review what has happened and to look for answers to questions you may have is called **clarifying.** Complete the chart below by doing the following:

• Read 5–10 lines of the poem.
• Stop to clarify those lines.
• Paraphrase what the lines are about in one of the boxes.
• Continue to read and clarify the rest of the poem in the same manner.

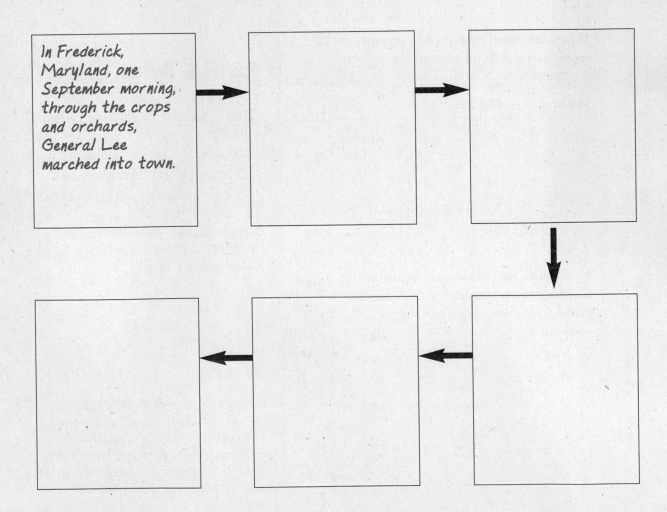

In Frederick, Maryland, one September morning, through the crops and orchards, General Lee marched into town.

Literary Analysis SkillBuilder

Poetic Form: Couplet

A rhymed pair of lines in a poem is called a **couplet.** Sometimes the author has to arrange the words within these lines in different ways so that the lines will rhyme. Sometimes that makes the meaning harder to grasp. Select several couplets from the poem, and write them in the chart, noting the end rhymes of the words. Then write a new couplet using the same rhymes. An example has been done for you.

Original Couplet	New Couplet
Fair as the garden of the Lord To the eyes of the famished rebel horde,	I tied the key to a golden cord, And hung it upon a wooden board.

Academic and Informational Reading

In this section you'll find strategies to help you read all kinds of informational materials. The examples here range from magazines you read for fun to textbooks to bus schedules. Applying the simple and effective techniques you learn will help you be a successful reader of the many texts you encounter every day.

Reading a Magazine Article

A magazine article is designed to catch and hold your interest. Learning how to use the headings and features on a magazine page will help you read even the most complicated articles. Look at the sample magazine article on the right as you read each strategy below.

A Read the **title** and other **headings** to get an idea of the article's topic. The title will often try to grab your attention with a question, an exclamation, or a play on words.

B Study **visuals**—photos, pictures, maps—together with their **captions.** Visuals help bring the topic to life.

C Note text that is set off in some way, such as in a **bulleted list.** Bullets often highlight or summarize important information.

D Pay attention to **terms** in different typeface, such as **italics** or **boldface.** Look for definitions or explanations before or after these terms.

E Look for **special features,** such as charts or graphs, that provide more detailed information on the topic.

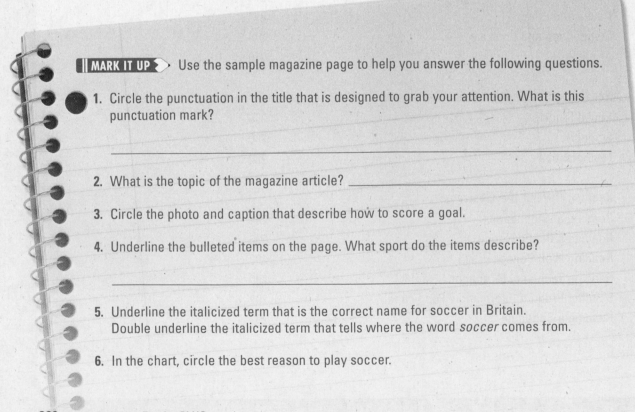

MARK IT UP Use the sample magazine page to help you answer the following questions.

1. Circle the punctuation in the title that is designed to grab your attention. What is this punctuation mark?

   _____

2. What is the topic of the magazine article? _____

3. Circle the photo and caption that describe how to score a goal.

4. Underline the bulleted items on the page. What sport do the items describe?

   _____

5. Underline the italicized term that is the correct name for soccer in Britain. Double underline the italicized term that tells where the word *soccer* comes from.

6. In the chart, circle the best reason to play soccer.

A What a Kick!

C Okay, sports fans, name this sport:

- It is known as football in much of the world.
- The World Cup is its greatest prize.
- It is the world's most popular team sport.

If you guessed soccer, you're right. Millions of people in more than 140 countries play soccer. A form of the sport was probably played in China as early as 400 B.C. The modern game was developed in Britain in the 1800s. Basic play is simple: two teams of 11 players try to kick or head the ball into each other's goal. The team that scores the most goals wins.

E **TOP 5 REASONS TO PLAY SOCCER**

5. It's great exercise.
4. It can be played almost anywhere.
3. It uses body parts other sports ignore.
2. It's exciting.

And the number 1 reason to play soccer:

1. It's a lot of fun.

Although soccer took a while to catch on in the United States, it is now one of the fastest-growing sports in the country. But some people wonder why we call it soccer. After all, the correct name for the sport in Britain is *association football*. D

Well, as it turns out, the word *soccer* actually is tied to the correct term. The word comes from *assoc.*, the abbreviation for *association*.

On July 10, 1999, the U.S.A. won the Women's World Cup title.

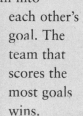

B

As this player tries to score a goal, he shows good technique by keeping his eye on the ball, aiming for a corner of the goal, and kicking with the inside of his foot.

B

The first page of a textbook lesson introduces you to a particular topic. The page also provides important information that will help guide you through the rest of the lesson. Look at the sample textbook page as you read each strategy below.

A Study any **graphics,** such as maps or time lines, placed on the page. You can use a time line to figure out the lesson's time period.

B Preview the **title** and **headings** to find out the lesson's topic.

C Read the **main idea** or **objectives** that often appear near the title. These objectives may be stated in the form of a question. The objectives establish a purpose for your reading.

D Look for a list of **vocabulary words**. These words will be identified—usually in boldface—and defined throughout the lesson.

E Examine **visuals** and **captions** that help bring the topic to life.

F Find words set in special type, such as **italics** or **boldface.** For example, respellings of unfamiliar words are often set in italics and enclosed in parentheses. Use the respellings to say the words aloud.

G Notice text on the page that is set off in some way. It may be placed within a border or printed in different type. The text may be from a primary source that gives firsthand knowledge about the topic.

MARK IT UP Use the sample textbook page to help you answer the following questions.

1. What time period does the lesson cover?_____
   Circle the part of the page where you found this information.

2. What question is this lesson supposed to answer?_____

3. Circle the vocabulary words that will be defined in the lesson.

4. What do the illustrations on the page show?_____

5. Underline the word in the text that has been respelled to help you pronounce it correctly.

6. Draw an arrow pointing to the paragraph from a primary source. Circle the lines that tell the author, title, and date of the work.

LESSON 2

B Athens: A City-State

C THINKING
FOCUS

How did democracy develop and work in Athens?

Key Terms

D
- democracy
- monarchy
- oligarchy
- tyrant
- barter

E ▼ *The ancient Greeks used these tokens to cast their votes.*

The trial promised to be one of the most important the citizens of Athens would hear all year. In 406 B.C., six navy generals were accused of abandoning hundreds of shipwrecked soldiers and leaving them to drown. Were the generals guilty of causing the deaths of these men? A jury of 2,000 Athenian citizens would decide the fate of the generals.

Early in the morning, the trial began. First the six generals took the stand. They testified that they had done all they could to save the men. The deaths were just an unfortunate turn of fate.

Next, witnesses testified, including a survivor who had floated to shore in a flour barrel. He claimed that the spirits of his drowned comrades urged him to testify against the generals.

Professional mourners, dressed in black, made their way through the crowd. They hoped to convince the jurors to convict the generals.

Xenophon **F** (*ZEHN uh fuhn*), a Greek historian, told of a public crier who announced how the jury would decide:

G Let every one who finds the generals guilty of not rescuing the heroes of the late sea-fight deposit his vote in one urn. Let him who is of the contrary opinion deposit his vote in the other urn. Further, in the event of the aforesaid generals being found guilty, let death be the penalty.

Xenophon, *Hellenica, Book I*
c. 400 B.C.

The jurors' tokens were counted. The generals were found guilty and sentenced to death.

Reading a Chart

Charts can help you understand a lot of information in a little space. These tips can help you read a chart quickly and accurately. Look at the example as you read each strategy in this list.

A First, read the **title** to understand what the chart is about.

B Check out the **heading** on each row (read left to right) and column (read top to bottom) so that you know what is being compared. To find specific information, find the place where a row and column intersect.

C Make sure you understand any **symbols** or **abbreviations,** such as *NA* ("not available," or "not applicable").

D Check the **credit** to see if the information is up-to-date and from a respected source.

Insects are among the most plentiful forms of life on Earth. They are also some of the most nutritious. In fact, some people consider them nature's perfect food. As the table below shows, some insects are high in protein, calcium, and iron and lower in fat than lean red meat.

A

Nutritional Value of Various Insects (per 100 grams)					
B	PROTEIN (g)	FAT (g)	CARBOHYDRATES (g)	CALCIUM (mg)	IRON (mg)
GIANT WATER BEETLE	19.8	8.3	2.1	43.5	13.6
CRICKET	12.9	5.5	5.1	75.8	9.5
SMALL GRASSHOPPER	20.6	6.1	3.9	35	25.0
BEEF (86% LEAN GROUND)	25.3	14	**C** NA	NA	2.3

D **Source:** *The Food Insects Newsletter,* July 1996 (Vol. 9, No. 2, ed. by Florence V. Dunkel, Montana State University); *Bugs in the System,* by May Berenbaum; and USDA Handbook 8–13, 1990.

‖ MARK IT UP Use the chart to answer the following questions.

1. According to the title, what does the chart show?_____

2. Circle the column that shows protein value. Underline the name of the insect with the least protein.

3. If you want to cut your fat intake, are you better off eating ground beef (a hamburger) or a bowl of crickets? _____ Box the information that supports your answer.

Reading a Map

To read a map correctly, you have to identify and understand its elements. Look at the example as you read each strategy in this list.

A Scan the **title** to find the main idea of the map.

B Interpret the **key,** or **legend,** to find out what the symbols and colors on the map stand for.

C Study **geographic labels** to understand specific places on the map.

D Look at the **scale** to determine distance.

E Look at the **pointer,** or **compass rose,** to figure out direction.

‖ MARK IT UP ❯ Use the map to answer the following questions.

1. What area does this map show?

_____

2. What does the symbol ☆ mean?

_____

3. Underline the geographic labels *Bristow Prairie, Bulldog Creek,* and *Bear Camp* on the map.

4. Circle the lake closest to Bulldog Rock on the map.

5. Draw a straight line between this lake and Bulldog Rock. Approximately how far apart are these places in miles?

_____

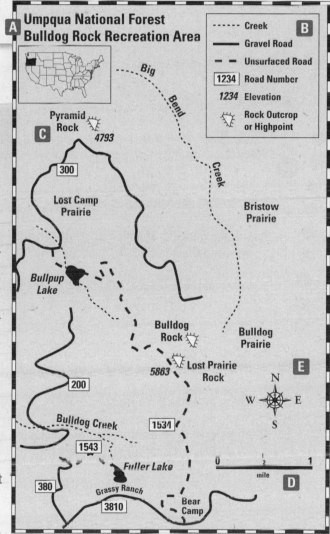

A Umpqua National Forest
Bulldog Rock Recreation Area

B
----- Creek
——— Gravel Road
– – Unsurfaced Road
1234 Road Number
1234 Elevation
☆ Rock Outcrop or Highpoint

Big
Bend
Creek

C Pyramid Rock ☆ *4793*

300

Lost Camp Prairie

Bristow Prairie

Bullpup Lake

Bulldog Rock ☆

Bulldog Prairie

E

5863 ☆ Lost Prairie Rock

200

N
W · E
S

Bulldog Creek

1531

1543

Fuller Lake

0 ½ 1
mile

D

380

Grassy Ranch

3810

Bear Camp

Reading a Diagram

Diagrams combine a picture with a few words to provide a lot of information. Look at the example on the opposite page as you read each of the following strategies.

A Look at the **title** to get a quick idea of what the diagram is about.

B Study the **images** closely to understand each part of the diagram.

C Look at the **caption** and **labels** for more information.

D Look for **arrows** or other markers that may show relationships between different parts of the diagram.

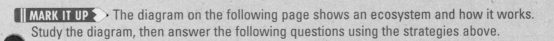 The diagram on the following page shows an ecosystem and how it works. Study the diagram, then answer the following questions using the strategies above.

1. What is an ecosystem? _____
   Circle the definition on the diagram.

2. Using a pencil or highlighter, trace the arrows showing the movement of energy between the sun and the marten.

3. What do these arrows tell you about the squirrel and the marten?

   _____

4. What are producers and what do they do? _____
   Underline this information on the diagram.

5. Circle all of the primary consumers.

6. In general, what do the primary consumers eat? _____
   Circle this information on the diagram.

7. Draw a box around the part of the diagram that shows what happens to plant and animal remains.

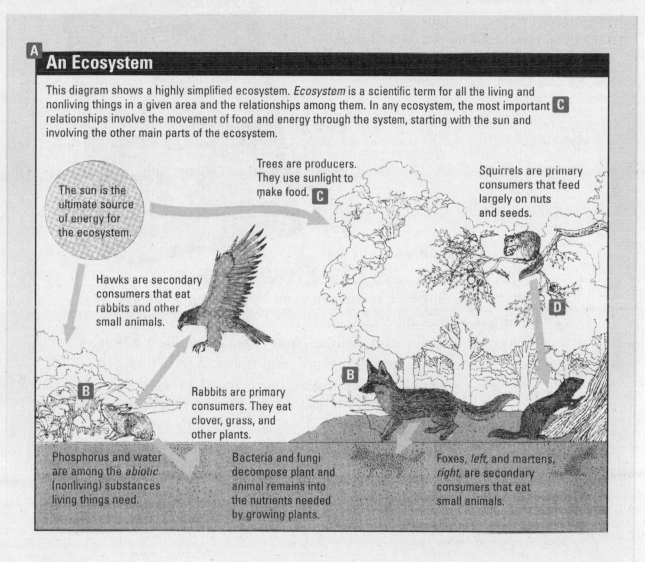

An Ecosystem

A

This diagram shows a highly simplified ecosystem. *Ecosystem* is a scientific term for all the living and nonliving things in a given area and the relationships among them. In any ecosystem, the most important **C** relationships involve the movement of food and energy through the system, starting with the sun and involving the other main parts of the ecosystem.

The sun is the ultimate source of energy for the ecosystem.

Trees are producers. They use sunlight to make food. **C**

Squirrels are primary consumers that feed largely on nuts and seeds.

Hawks are secondary consumers that eat rabbits and other small animals.

D

Rabbits are primary consumers. They eat clover, grass, and other plants.

B

B

Phosphorus and water are among the *abiotic* (nonliving) substances living things need.

Bacteria and fungi decompose plant and animal remains into the nutrients needed by growing plants.

Foxes, *left*, and martens, *right*, are secondary consumers that eat small animals.

Main Idea and Supporting Details

The main idea in a paragraph is its most important point. Details in the paragraph support the main idea. Identifying the main idea will help you focus on the paragraph's key point.

- Look for the **main idea** in the first sentence in a paragraph, which is where it often appears.

- Use the main idea to help you **summarize** the point of the paragraph.

- Identify specific **supporting details** that develop the main idea.

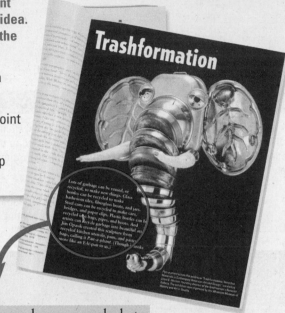

Trashformation

Main idea — Lots of garbage can be reused, or recycled, to make new things. Glass bottles can be recycled to make bathroom tiles, fiberglass boats, and jars. Steel cans can be recycled to make cars, bridges, and paper clips. Plastic bottles

Details — can be recycled into bags, pipes, and boots. And artists can recycle garbage into beautiful art. Jim Opasik created this sculpture from recycled kitchen utensils, pans, and pastry bags, calling it *Pan-a-phant*. (Though it looks more like E-le-pan to us.)

from Muse

‖ MARK IT UP › Read the following paragraph. Underline the main idea. Number each supporting detail.

As heaps of trash pile up in garbage dumps, communities are trying to cut back on the amount of trash that is thrown away. Many cities pick up plastic, glass, and paper for recycling. They encourage people to donate usable furniture, toys, and clothes to charities. Local grocery stores help by switching from plastic bags to brown, recyclable bags. Can you think of other ways your community can control the build-up of trash?

Problem and Solution

Does the proposed solution to a problem make sense? In order to decide, you need to look at each part of the text. Use the following strategies to read the text below.

- Look at the beginning or middle of a paragraph for the **statement of the problem.**

- Look for the **details** that explain the problem and why it is important.

- Look for the **proposed solution.**

- Identify the **supporting details** for the proposed solution.

- Think about whether the solution is a good one.

Bikes vs. Skates

By Tyler Clark

Statement of problem — Kettle Springs has a serious safety problem along the riverfront path. In the past five years, the number of accidents between in-line skaters and bike riders has doubled.

Details about the problem — Each summer, the emergency room staff treats dozens of broken arms and legs, scraped knees, and concussions. It is difficult for bike riders and skaters to share a path. The skaters can move quickly, and riders often don't see them coming. If riders can't get out of the way, they hit the skaters head-on.

Proposed solution — Bicycle riders and skaters must pay more attention to each other. The park district has proposed frequent ten-minute

Details about the solution — safety lessons along the path for the first three weekends of summer. These lessons would make people think about safe riding and skating. With a little help, both riders and skaters can easily build safe habits.

MARK IT UP > After reading the text above, answer these questions.

1. In the second paragraph, underline the part of a sentence that explains the proposed solution.

2. Circle a detail that supports the solution.

3. Do you think the solution is a good one? Why or why not? _____

Sequence

It's important to understand the sequence, or order of events, in what you read. That way you know what happens and why. Use the following tips when you read to make sure a sequence is clear to you.

- Read through the passage. Think about the **main steps** or **events.** In some cases, each step is presented in a separate paragraph or shown as numbered items.

- Look for words that **signal order:** *first, then, the next step is, after that, before.*

- Look for words that **signal time:** *Tuesday, after 20 minutes, later.*

MARK IT UP The article on the next page describes how you can make your own movies. Use the information from the article and the tips above to answer the questions.

1. Underline phrases in the passage that tell the five main steps. The first one is done for you.

2. Circle words that signal time or order. The first one is done for you.

3. Sometimes you can use a flowchart to help you understand a sequence of events. Use the information from the article to complete this flow chart.

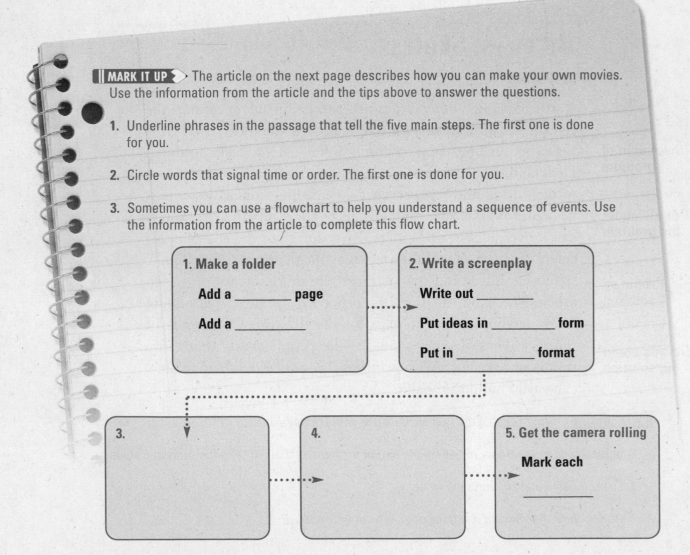

1. Make a folder

Add a _____ page

Add a _____

2. Write a screenplay

Write out _____

Put ideas in _____ form

Put in _____ format

3.

4.

5. Get the camera rolling

Mark each

_____

Step Aside, Steven Spielberg

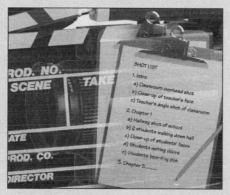

I have a lot of fun making flicks. And if you have the time and a loaded video camera, you can too! Here are tips to film like the pros.

(Before) you get rolling, <u>make up a folder</u> with all the important stuff about your film. First, stick in the cover page, which includes the title of the film and author of the screenplay: you! Next, put in a summary (just a short paragraph that briefly tells the story of your film).

Then comes the screenplay, a.k.a. the script. Although you may think a screenplay is just dialogue between actors, it has tons more detail than just the words. . . .

I first write out my ideas, and then put them in short story form. When I have enough stuff on paper, I put it in the screenplay format. . . .

After your screenplay is written, make up a shot list: a list of every shot in your film and how it'll look. Each scene will have several shots. For example, in a classroom scene, you might have a loose shot on the teacher; the teacher is the focus of the shot, but you can see some things going on around her. In the same scene, you could have a wide shot of the classroom with kids goofing off. . . .

To keep filming going smoothly, make a shooting schedule: a list of scenes in the order you plan to shoot them.

Get the camera rolling! Since you're doing scenes according to your shooting schedule, mark each scene at the start so you'll recognize it when you edit.

by Cherish Wise, age 11
excerpted from *Girls' Life*

Cause and Effect

A cause is an event. An effect is something that happens as a result of that event. Identifying causes and effects helps you understand how events are related. The tips below can help you find causes and effects in any reading.

- Look for an action or event that answers the question "What happened?" This is the **effect.**

- Look for an action or event that answers the question "Why did it happen?" This is the **cause.**

- Identify words that **signal** causes and effects, such as *because, as a result, consequently,* and *since.*

|| MARK IT UP > Read the cause-and-effect passage on the next page. Then answer the following questions.

1. Circle words in the passage that signal causes and effects. The first one is done for you.

2. Underline each cause in the passage once. Underline its effect twice. The first ones are shown for you.

3. Use three of the causes and effects in the last two paragraphs to fill in the following diagrams.

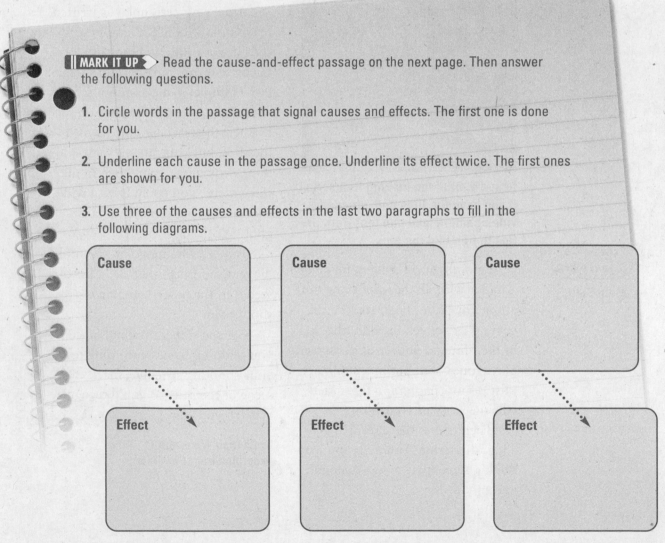

| Cause | Cause | Cause |

| Effect | Effect | Effect |

When Volcanoes Blow Their Tops

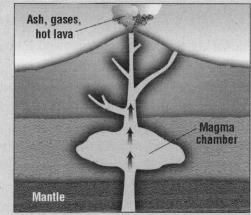

Ash, gases, hot lava

Magma chamber

Mantle

Signal word

Cause

Effect

Deep within the earth is a layer of rock called the mantle. Because the mantle is so hot, some rocks there melt like chocolate in the sun. Melted rock is lighter than the solid rock around it. As a result, the melted rock, or magma, rises. It pushes through cracks in the earth and erupts, or bursts.

Magma that has erupted is called lava. Lava can flow out of a volcano, or it can explode from it. Since flowing lava moves slowly, people can get out of its way. However, exploding lava can cause death and destruction because ash, gases, and hot lava blast from a volcano.

The ash from the eruption in 1980 of Mount St. Helens in Washington, for instance, was very dangerous. Winds carried the thick ash to a campsite twelve miles from Mount St. Helens. Consequently, two men suffocated and died from the ash. Winds also carried ash to Yakima, a city in eastern Washington. Because so much ash fell there, lights had to be turned on all day. It took ten weeks to remove the ash from Yakima's streets.

Comparison and Contrast

Comparing two things means explaining how they are the same. *Contrasting* means explaining how two things are different. Comparisons and contrasts are often used in science and history to make ideas clearer. Use the tips below to help you understand comparison and contrast in any kind of writing, including the article on the right.

- Look for **direct statements** of comparison and contrast: "This is the same as . . . " or "One difference is. . . ."

- Pay attention to **words and phrases that signal comparisons,** such as *also, too, like, similarly,* and *in the same way.*

- Notice **words and phrases that signal contrasts.** Some of these are *however, unlike, but,* and *on the other hand.*

MARK IT UP Read the article on the opposite page. Then use the information from the article and the tips above to answer the questions.

1. Circle the words and phrases that signal comparisons. The first one is done for you.

2. Underline the words and phrases that signal contrasts. The first one is done for you.

3. A Venn diagram shows how two subjects are similar and how they are different. Complete this diagram, which uses information from the article to compare and contrast the space suits of the 1960s with modern space suits. Add at least one similarity and two differences.

Old Space Suits
could wear inside spacecraft

Both
protect astronauts

New Space Suits
can wear outside or inside spacecraft

Getting Suited Up for Space

As space travel has improved, space suits have (too.) by Kathy Chaveriat

Comparison

Contrast

Why Wear a Space Suit?

Space suits are uncomfortable <u>but</u> important. Unlike Earth, there is no oxygen in space. That means the suit must give the astronaut air to breathe. A space suit must also protect against the heat and cold of space.

Space Suits of the Early 1960s

The space suits of the early 1960s were much like the flight suits worn by some pilots. These suits were not strong enough to let astronauts walk outside the spacecraft. They were so stiff that it was hard for the astronauts to bend

1960 astronaut

their knees and elbows or pick up small objects.

Space Suits of Today

The biggest difference in today's space suits is that astronauts can wear them on space walks outside of the spacecraft. The new space suits give the same kind of protection as the old ones. However, they also protect against *micrometeoroids*, tiny rocks in space that crash into the space suit.

Like the older space suits, today's suits can be hard to move around in. However, scientists have found many ways to make them more comfortable. New space suits let each

astronaut change the size of his or her suit. A new type of glove lets astronauts hold small objects more easily.

1995 astronaut

Space suits keep getting better. If you visit Mars someday, your suit will be much more comfortable than the ones shown here!

Argument

An argument is an opinion backed up with reasons and facts. Examining an opinion and the reasons and facts that back it up will help you decide if the opinion makes sense. Look at the argument on the right as you read each of these tips.

- Look for words that **signal an opinion:** *I believe, argue,* or *claim; you should* or *must.*

- Look for reasons, facts, or expert opinions that **support** the argument.

- Ask yourself if the argument and reasons **make sense.**

- Look for overgeneralizations or other **errors in reasoning** that may affect the argument.

- Think about the **accuracy** of the information.

║ MARK IT UP ▷ Read the argument on the next page and then answer the questions below.

1. Circle any words that signal an opinion. The first one is done for you.

2. Underline the words or phrases that give the writer's opinion.

3. Draw a box around the statement that is not supported by reasons or facts.

4. The author presents both sides of the argument. In the chart below, write both opinions and the reasons or facts that support each opinion. The first reason has been done for you.

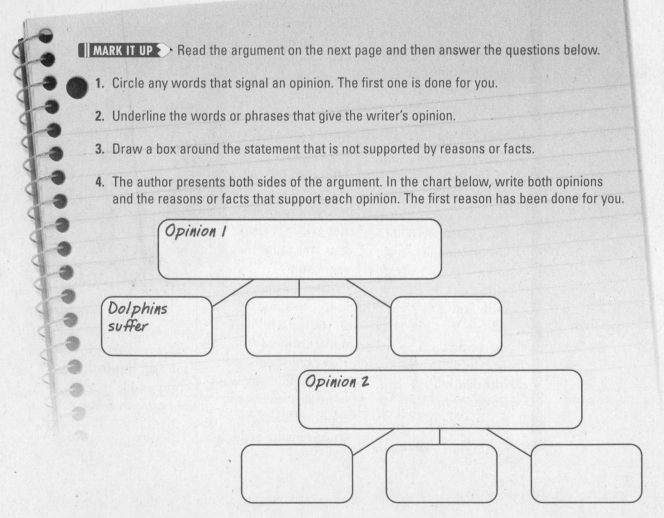

Opinion 1

Dolphins suffer

Opinion 2

Freeing the Dolphins

(Signal word)

We **must** stop capturing dolphins just to display them for our entertainment. Millions of people a year visit aquariums and sea parks to shout in delight as friendly dolphins perform entertaining tricks. We all love these wonderful creatures of the sea, but what about the harm we are doing to them? The dolphins suffer when they are taken from the sea and shipped inland. They may die from shock, or they may not adjust to their new diet of dead fish. In the wild, they can swim 100 miles a day and dive to depths of 1000 feet. When captured, they are often kept in small tanks, unable to swim and dive freely. They sometimes become ill and are not able to produce babies.

Dolphin trainers, on the other hand, claim that dolphins are thrilled to entertain the public. They tell us that dolphins are friendly animals who like being around people. They also enjoy learning new tricks that will please the crowds. Dolphins like the attention and the applause. Trainers believe that sea parks and aquariums support the well-being of dolphins. But are the dolphins really healthy, or are they physically stressed by the long hours they must perform?

Talking to dolphin trainers is useless. We need to act now. We can stop the suffering by making it illegal to take dolphins from the sea and display them for our entertainment.

Social Studies

Your social studies textbook combines words with pictures and graphics to help you learn about a particular period in time. Look at the example on the opposite page as you read each strategy on the list.

A First, read the **title.** It will tell you what the whole section is about. Some pages also have subheads that break the text into parts.

B Find the **goals** or **objectives** for the lesson. Sometimes these are stated as questions.

C Pay attention to any boldfaced or underlined **vocabulary terms.** Look for definitions of these words in the text.

D Look for **display text**—words that are enlarged, in a box, or a different color. These signals tell you to pay close attention.

E Look at **pictures** and read their **captions** to get more information.

F Study any **time lines, charts, graphs,** or **maps** on the page to see how different facts in the text fit together.

G Look for ways the text tells you the **time frame** of the lesson. Dates and time sequences in history texts are important ways of helping readers understand the causes and effects of historical events.

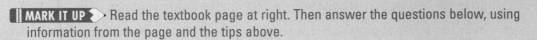 **MARK IT UP** Read the textbook page at right. Then answer the questions below, using information from the page and the tips above.

1. Put a star next to the part of the page that tells what main questions will be answered.

2. Circle each vocabulary word. Then underline the parts of the text that tell you what each word means.

3. What happened in about 700 B.C.? _____
   Double underline the two places on the page where this question is answered.

4. Why do we know so much about the everyday life of the Greeks? _____
   _____
   Draw a box around the sentence that gives the answer to this question.

5. Draw a wavy line under two groups of words that show a clear time sequence.

A The Rise of City-States

Focus *What were Greek city-states, and how did* B *they function?*

After the Trojan War, trade came to a standstill and poverty increased. There are few architectural remains from this period, and written language all but disappeared as people became isolated in separate villages. Little is known about this period. G By the mid-900s B.C., Greece began to prosper again. Town marketplaces, or agoras, became crowded. Women carried water in pitchers on their heads, shoppers argued noisily over prices, and poets recited verses aloud. This was the time when Homer lived and wrote. Greece was now made up of many independent communities, composed of villages and surrounding farmland. Called a **polis** in Greek (the root of the word "politics"), a city-state was governed by groups of powerful landowners. These nobles paid for armor, horses, and the army. This form of government by the nobility is known as an **aristocracy.** C

As members of a polis, all citizens had rights as well as responsibilities. They had to obey the laws and take part in religious ceremonies. They were also expected to fight in the event of a war. Citizens **sponsored,** or paid for, athletic games, religious festivals, and drama contests.

By the 700s B.C., the Greeks developed a system of government called **democracy,** from the Greek words *demos* (people) and *kratos* (rule). Now all male citizens — not just nobles — were allowed to play an active role in decision making. The Greeks were proud of their system, as expressed by Aristotle (AR ihs taht l), one of their philosophers.

> **"T**his is the polis. It has come into being in order, simply, that life can go on; but now it exists so as to make that life a good life.**"** D

What transformed these separate city-states into one people we call the Greeks? They all spoke Greek, with some variations. They also worshiped the same group of gods and goddesses. Most important, perhaps, they believed that the polis was the best way to live.

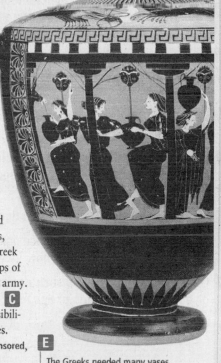

E

The Greeks needed many vases for carrying wine, water, and oil. Grain was shipped in jars, too. This detail of a vase is decorated with a painting of women filling water pots. Greeks painted many scenes from everyday life, and it is because of this practice that we know so much about them. Arts: *Find and describe the horizontal band on this vase called Greek Key.*

Events in Ancient Greece F

1200 B.C.	1000 B.C.	800 B.C.	600 B.C.	400 B.C.	200 B.C.
c. 1200 B.C. Fall of Troy	950 B.C. Aristocracies in Greece	700 B.C. Democracy in Athens	490-480 B.C. Persian Invasions	c. 450 B.C. Athens's height of power	431-404 B.C. Peloponnesian Wars

Science

Reading in science will be easier when you understand how the explanations, drawings, and special terms work together. Use the strategies below to help you better understand your science textbook. Look at the examples on the opposite page as you read each strategy in this list.

A Preview the **title** and **headings** on the page to see what science concepts will be covered.

B Look for **boldface** and **italic** words that appear in the text. Look for **definitions** of those words.

C Look for familiar text structures, such as **process description** or **cause and effect.** Many science pages also break information down into categories.

D Look for references to numbered **figures** in the text.

E Then look in the margin for these figures, which are **diagrams** or **pictures** with **captions.** See how they illustrate and explain the text.

F Look for **special features** such as notes or sidebars. These may give special information or tips.

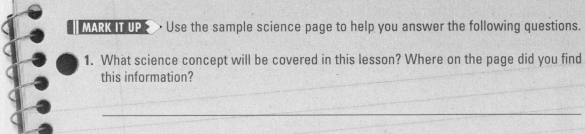

|| MARK IT UP › Use the sample science page to help you answer the following questions.

1. What science concept will be covered in this lesson? Where on the page did you find this information?

   _____

2. Write a definition for **zone of saturation.**

   _____

3. Circle the paragraph that explains what happens to the water that falls to the earth. Underline the topic sentence of this paragraph.

4. In the text, underline the reference to Figure 21-9.

5. Look at the diagram. What two zones are shown in the circle?

   _____

The Water Table **A**

Think about what would happen if you started pouring water into a bucket of sand. The bucket fills with water from the bottom upward, just as it would without the sand. Gravity pulls the water down through the sand until the water reaches the bottom of the bucket. The water cannot pass through the bucket, because the bucket is impermeable. The water fills the pore spaces in the sand. If you keep pouring water into the bucket, you fill more and more of the spaces. Eventually, you can fill all the spaces between sand grains with water. The sand is saturated with water. If you add more water, the bucket will overflow. **D**

How does this model of groundwater relate to what happens inside Earth? Look at Figure 21-9. The water that falls to Earth soaks into the ground and is pulled downward by gravity until it reaches an impermeable layer. This impermeable layer may be a bed of shale, or unweathered, nonporous bedrock. The water, unable to continue soaking downward, starts to fill the pores in the rock or soil. The area of rock or soil where the pores are completely filled by groundwater **B** is called the **zone of saturation.** The top of the zone of saturation is called the **water table.** As more water soaks into the ground, the zone of saturation gets thicker and the water table rises, getting closer to Earth's surface.

Not all groundwater is stored in the zone of saturation. Some water is left behind in the soil and rock as the water moves downward. This water is trapped where grains are in contact and is therefore not pulled downward by gravity. This water is only removed by evaporation or by plant roots. The layer of rock or soil above the water table is called the **zone of aeration** [ar ā′ shən]. *Aerate* means "to add air to something."

E Figure 21-9 The water table separates the zone of aeration from the zone of saturation. In which zone are the pore spaces filled with water?

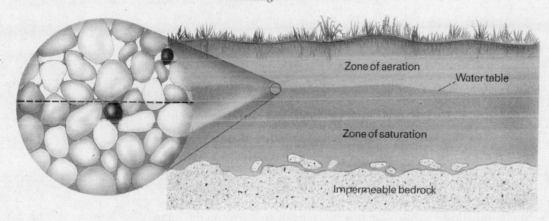

Zone of aeration

Water table

Zone of saturation

Impermeable bedrock

Mathematics

Reading a math book requires different skills than reading history, literature, or science. The tips below can help you learn these skills. As you read the tips, look at the sample math page on the right.

A First, look at the lesson **title** and any **subheads** on the page, so you know what topics will be covered.

B See if there are **objectives** for the lesson. These will tell you the most important points to know.

C Read **explanations** carefully. Sometimes the same concept is explained in more than one way to make sure you understand it.

D Look for **special features** such as study or vocabulary tips. These provide more help or information.

E Study any **worked-out solutions** to sample problems. These are the key to understanding how to do the homework assignment.

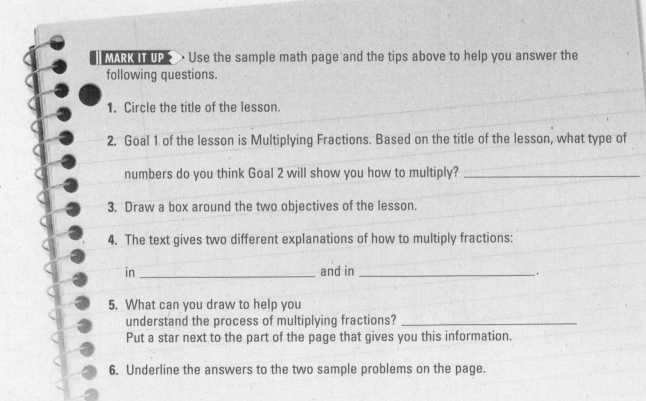

MARK IT UP Use the sample math page and the tips above to help you answer the following questions.

1. Circle the title of the lesson.

2. Goal 1 of the lesson is Multiplying Fractions. Based on the title of the lesson, what type of numbers do you think Goal 2 will show you how to multiply? _____

3. Draw a box around the two objectives of the lesson.

4. The text gives two different explanations of how to multiply fractions:

   in _____ and in _____.

5. What can you draw to help you understand the process of multiplying fractions? _____ Put a star next to the part of the page that gives you this information.

6. Underline the answers to the two sample problems on the page.

3.4 Multiplying Fractions and Mixed Numbers

A

Goal 1 MULTIPLYING FRACTIONS

In Developing Concepts 3.4, page 124, you used an area model to multiply fractions.

B In this lesson you'll:
▶ Solve problems involving multiplication of positive fractions.
▶ Explain the meaning of multiplication of fractions.

A EXAMPLE **1** Multiplying Fractions

Use an area model to find the product $\frac{3}{5} \times \frac{1}{2}$.

E **Solution**

Shade half of the rectangle in one direction and $\frac{3}{5}$ in the other direction. Since 3 of the 10 parts are doubly shaded, the product is $\frac{3}{10}$.

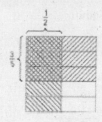

D Student Help

▶**STUDY TIP**
Drawing a model can help you understand the process of multiplying fractions.

MULTIPLYING FRACTIONS

In Words   To multiply any two fractions, multiply the numerators to get the numerator of the product, and multiply the denominators to get the denominator of the product.

C

In Algebra $\frac{a}{b} \cdot \frac{c}{d} = \frac{ac}{bd}$ where b and d are not equal to 0.

EXAMPLE **2** Calculating Length of Time

SOCCER Your gym class lasts $\frac{3}{4}$ of an hour. You play soccer for $\frac{2}{3}$ of the class. How long do you play soccer?

E **Solution**   To find $\frac{2}{3}$ of $\frac{3}{4}$, multiply $\frac{2}{3}$ and $\frac{3}{4}$.

$$\frac{2}{3} \cdot \frac{3}{4} = \frac{2 \cdot 3}{3 \cdot 4}$$ Use rule for multiplying fractions.

$$= \frac{6}{12}$$ Simplify numerator and denominator.

$$= \frac{1}{2}$$ Simplify fraction.

ANSWER ▶ You play soccer for $\frac{1}{2}$ hour.

Reading an Application

Reading and understanding an application will help you fill it out correctly. Use the strategies below to help you understand any application. Look at the example on the next page as you read each strategy.

A **Begin at the top.** Scan the application to see what the different sections are.

B Watch for sections **you don't have to fill in** or **questions you don't have to answer.**

C Notice any **special markings** such as dividing lines, boxes, or boldface type.

D Pay special attention to any part of an application that calls for **your signature.**

MARK IT UP Let's say you want to apply for a library card. Read the application on the next page. Then answer the following questions.

1. On the application, number the three different sections.

2. Cross out any parts you are not supposed to fill out.

3. Draw an arrow pointing to the section that should be filled out only by the parents or guardians of young people.

4. Why do you think one section has a box drawn around it? _____

_____

5. Circle the agreement that calls for your signature.

6. **ASSESSMENT PRACTICE** What promise do you make to the library when you sign this application?
   A. To read as many books as you can
   B. To be responsible for any library materials you borrow
   C. To become a full-time college or university student
   D. To bring a parent or guardian every time you visit the library

7. Fill out the application as best you can.

A MILLWOOD PUBLIC LIBRARY CARD APPLICATION

(for office use only) CARD NO._____ **B**

Please print clearly.

NAME_____
        Last   First   Middle

LOCAL ADDRESS _____

CITY _____ STATE _____ ZIP CODE _____

HOME PHONE (____)_____ WORK PHONE (____)_____

SEX _____ _____   BIRTH DATE _____ / _____ / _____
      Male   Female   Month   Day   Year

I agree to be responsible for all materials borrowed from the Millwood Public Library in my name.

D SIGNATURE_____ DATE _____

C

> If applicant is 14 years old or under, parent or guardian must sign and supply printed name.
>
> I agree to be responsible for all materials borrowed from the Millwood Public Library in my child's name.
>
> Parent Signature _____ Date _____
>
> Parent's Printed Name _____

for office use only

STAFF INITIALS _____ REGISTRATION CLASS_____

MI   CH   NS   OTHER   FEE STAFF   ISU   KE   NL   TE

Reading a Public Notice

Public notices can give important information about events in your community. Here are some tips for reading all kinds of public notices. Look at the example on the opposite page as you read each tip.

A Ask yourself, **"Who is this notice for?"** If the information in it might be important to you, your family, or someone you know, then you should pay attention to it.

B Look for **instructions**—things the notice is asking or telling you to do.

C See if there is any information about **who created** the notice.

D Look for details that tell you how you can **find out more** about the topic.

E Check out any **special features** designed to make the notice easier to understand, such as instructions in more than one language.

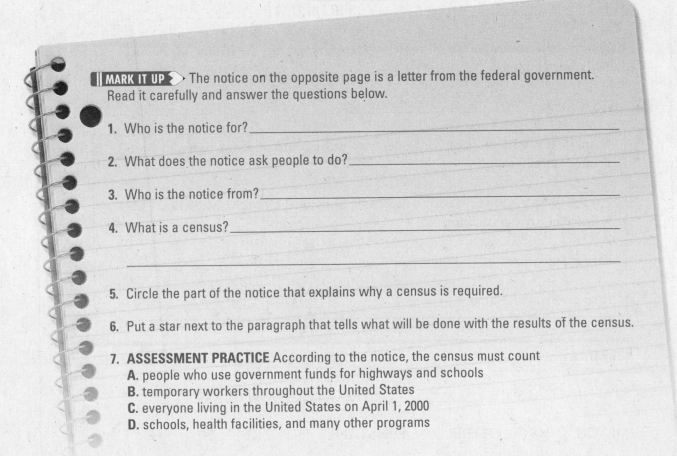

‖ MARK IT UP ⟩ The notice on the opposite page is a letter from the federal government. Read it carefully and answer the questions below.

1. Who is the notice for? _____

2. What does the notice ask people to do? _____

3. Who is the notice from? _____

4. What is a census? _____

    _____

5. Circle the part of the notice that explains why a census is required.

6. Put a star next to the paragraph that tells what will be done with the results of the census.

7. **ASSESSMENT PRACTICE** According to the notice, the census must count
    A. people who use government funds for highways and schools
    B. temporary workers throughout the United States
    C. everyone living in the United States on April 1, 2000
    D. schools, health facilities, and many other programs

UNITED STATES DEPARTMENT OF COMMERCE
Bureau of the Census
Washington, DC 20233-2000

OFFICE OF THE DIRECTOR

C

March 6, 2000

17031-0484706-88-110-421-12

A 159487366 AUTO ********** 5-DIGIT 60202

TO RESIDENT AT   01087

11120 ELMWOOD AVE
EVANSTON, IL 60202-1203

Illltlll.....llll....llll....ll.ll.llll....ll...ll.llll....llll

B **About one week from now, you will receive a U.S. Census 2000 form in the mail.**

B When you receive your form, please fill it out and mail it in promptly. Your response is very important. The United States Constitution requires a census of the United States every 10 years. Everyone living in the United States on April 1, 2000, must be counted. By completing your census form, you will make sure that you and members of your household are included in the official census count.

Official census counts are used to distribute government funds to communities and states for highways, schools, health facilities, and many other programs you and your neighbors need. Without a complete, accurate census, your community may not receive its fair share.

You can help in another way too. We are now hiring temporary workers throughout the United States to help complete the census. Call the Local Census Office near you **D** for more information. The phone number is available from directory assistance or the Internet at www.census.gov/jobs2000.

B With your help, the census can count everyone. Please do your part. Thank you.

Sincerely,

Kenneth Prewitt

Kenneth Prewitt
Director   **C**
Bureau of the Census

Enclosure

Por favor, vea el otro lado de esta página.
請翻到此頁背面。
본 페이지 뒷면을 보십시오.   **E**
Xin xem mặt sau của trang này.
Basahin ang nasa likod ng pahinang ito.

United States
Census
2000

D–5(L)

Reading Web Pages

The World Wide Web can be a source of interesting and useful information—if you know how to navigate it! Look at the examples on the opposite page as you read each of the following strategies.

A Find out where you are by looking at the page's **Web address,** sometimes called a URL.

B Look for the **title** of the page. This is usually at the top, but not always.

C Check out **menu bars** that tell you about features of the site or give you different categories of information. These are usually along the top, bottom, or side of the page.

D Look for **links** to related pages. Links are often underlined words.

E Check out **interactive areas** where you can type in a question, take part in a survey, or e-mail your comments about a site.

∥ MARK IT UP ▷ On the next page are two Web sites—a search engine with responses to a student's search, and a site linked to one of those responses. Read both carefully. Then use information from the sites and the tips above to answer the questions.

1. Circle the part of each site that shows its Web address.

2. Underline the part of the "LookQuick" site that shows how many pages match the search terms.

3. On the "Pyramids—The Inside Story" site, which link would you click on if you wanted information about the excavation?

_____

4. What kind of building did the archaeologists excavate in 1997? _____
Put a box around the part of the "Pyramids—The Inside Story" site that gives you this information.

5. **ASSESSMENT PRACTICE** The "Pyramids—The Inside Story" site has information about
   A. the Great Pyramid
   B. Egypt
   C. the pharaohs
   D. all of the above

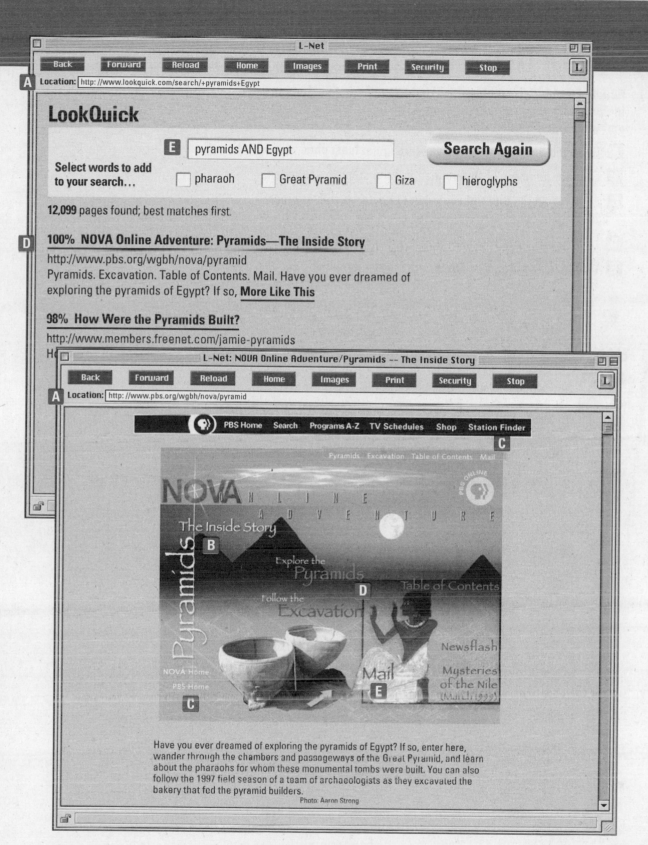

LookQuick

E | pyramids AND Egypt | **Search Again**

Select words to add to your search…
☐ pharaoh ☐ Great Pyramid ☐ Giza ☐ hieroglyphs

12,099 pages found; best matches first.

100% NOVA Online Adventure: Pyramids—The Inside Story

http://www.pbs.org/wgbh/nova/pyramid
Pyramids. Excavation. Table of Contents. Mail. Have you ever dreamed of exploring the pyramids of Egypt? If so, **More Like This**

98% How Were the Pyramids Built?

http://www.members.freenet.com/jamie-pyramids

L-Net: NOVA Online Adventure/Pyramids -- The Inside Story

Location: http://www.pbs.org/wgbh/nova/pyramid

PBS Home Search Programs A-Z TV Schedules Shop Station Finder

Have you ever dreamed of exploring the pyramids of Egypt? If so, enter here, wander through the chambers and passageways of the Great Pyramid, and learn about the pharaohs for whom these monumental tombs were built. You can also follow the 1997 field season of a team of archaeologists as they excavated the bakery that fed the pyramid builders.

Photo: Aaron Strong

Reading Technical Directions

Reading technical directions will help you understand how to use the products you buy. Here are some strategies to help you read multiple-step directions.

A Read the **directions** all the way through at least once.

B Look for **numbers** or **letters** that give the steps in sequence.

C Look for **words that tell you what to do**, for example: *press, close, select.*

D Look at **pictures** or **visuals** to help you understand and follow steps.

E Watch for **warnings** or **notes** with more information.

MARK IT UP Answer the questions below using the tips above and the directions for loading film into a camera.

1. What is the first thing you must do when you load film into a camera?

_____

2. What do the instructions recommend you use to remove dust or dirt from the lens?

_____ Box your answer.

3. What should you do before you close the back cover?

_____

_____

4. What does it mean when the exposure counter blinks **E**?

_____

_____

5. **ASSESSMENT PRACTICE** Once you insert the film cartridge, the film should
   A. face sideways
   B. lie flat
   C. stand upright
   D. bend

A # Loading the Film

B
1. **Slide the back cover release upwards to open the back cover.**

   Note: Do not touch the inside of the camera, especially the **E** lens. If there is dust or dirt on the lens, remove it with a blower brush.

D
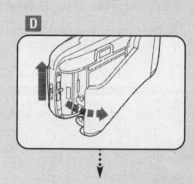

C
2. **Insert the film cartridge, making sure the film is lying flat.**

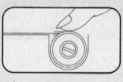

Correct
The film should be lying flat before you close the back cover.

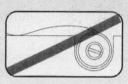

Incorrect
If the film is not lying flat, the film cartridge will not load properly.

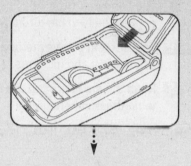

3. **Make sure the film leader is lined up with the red mark.**

   Close the back cover and wait for the film to automatically load to first frame.

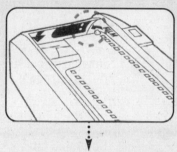

4. **Press the power switch button. The exposure counter should read "1".**

   If "E" blinks in the counter, as shown, the film is not loaded properly. Follow steps 1-4 again and reload the film.

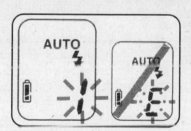

AUTO

AUTO

Product Information: Food Label

Information about a food's nutritional value usually appears in a label on its package. Learning to read nutritional labels will help you eat right. Look at the example label as you read each strategy below.

A Check the serving size carefully. The serving size listed on many products is often smaller than the serving most people eat.

B The "Percent Daily Value" tells you percentage (%) of the recommended daily amount of a nutrient is in one serving.

C This section shows the amounts and percent daily values of such nutrients as fat and sodium. Amounts are measured in grams (g) and milligrams (mg). Notice that Total Fat and Total Carbohydrates include one or more nutrients.

D The Food and Drug Administration has not come up with a percent daily value for added sugars or protein.

E This section shows the percent daily values of nutrients such as vitamins and minerals.

F Read the small print at the bottom of the label to understand what the numbers mean.

Nutrition Facts

A Serving Size 4 cookies (31g)
Servings Per Container about 9

Amount Per Serving

Calories 160	Calories from Fat 80

B **% Daily Value***

Total Fat 9g	13%
Saturated Fat 6g	28%
C **Cholesterol** 0mg	0%
Sodium 140mg	6%
Total Carbohydrate 20g	7%
Dietary Fiber 1g	5%
Sugars 11g	
Protein 1g **D**	

E

Vitamin A 0%	•	Vitamin C 0%
Calcium 0%	•	Iron 2%

F * Percent Daily Values are based on a 2,000 calorie diet. Your daily values may be higher or lower depending on your calorie needs.

‖ MARK IT UP ▸ Read the nutrition label to help you answer these questions.

1. How many cookies are in two servings? _____
   Circle the line that helped you figure out the number.

2. Circle the nutrient on the label with the highest percent daily value.

3. Saturated fat is a kind of fat. What kind of nutrient is sugar? _____
   Draw a line connecting Sugars to your answer.

4. What percent daily value of iron is contained in a serving? _____
   On the label, underline where you found the answer.

5. The percent daily values are based on a diet of how many calories? _____
   On the label, underline where you found the answer.

6. **ASSESSMENT PRACTICE** How many servings of cookies are contained in this box?
   A. 160
   B. 80
   C. about 9
   D. 4

Reading a Schedule

Knowing how to read a schedule accurately will help you get to places on time. Look at the example as you read each strategy in this list.

A Scan the **title** to find what the schedule is about.

B Look at labels with **dates or days of the week** to find what months, weeks, or days are listed on the schedule.

C Study **event names** to understand specific activities and places on the schedule.

D Look at **expressions of time** to know what hours or minutes are listed on the schedule.

MARK IT UP Use the schedule to the right to answer the following questions.

1. What is the purpose of this schedule?

_____

_____

2. Is this a daily, weekly, or monthly schedule?

_____

Circle the parts of the schedule that give you this information.

A **Large Gym Schedule** **B** Week of October 5, 2004

Time	Monday	Tuesday	Wednesday	Thursday	Friday	Saturday	Sunday
8 AM	Open 8–9	Open 8–9	Open 8–9	Open 8–9	Open 8–9	Open 8–9	
9	Preschool Classes 9–12	Preschool Classes 9–12	Preschool Classes 9–12	Preschool Classes 9–12	Preschool Classes 9–12	Tae Kwon Do 9–12	Adult Open 8–12
10							
11							
12 PM	**C** Adult Open 12–3:30	Adult Open 12–3:30	Adult Open 12–3:30	Adult Open 12–3:30	Adult Open 12–3:30	Basketball Clinic 12–2:30	Birthday Parties 12–2
1							
2							
3	Youth Open 3:30–6	Youth Open 3:30–6	Youth Open 3:30–6		Youth Open 3:30 6	Youth Open 2:30–6	Youth Open 2–5
4							
D 5				Youth Open 3:30–9			
6	Tae Kwon Do 6–9	Football Clinic 5–7:30	Tae Kwon Do 6–9		Volleyball 6–9	Adult Open 6–9	
7		Volleyball **D** 7:30–9					
8							

3. Underline the label Tae Kwon Do each time it is listed on the schedule.

4. Circle the hours for each Tae Kwon Do class listed on the schedule. Put an "X" by the weekend Tae Kwon Do class.

5. **ASSESSMENT PRACTICE** What activity is scheduled for Friday between 6:00 P.M. and 9:00 P.M.?
   A. Basketball Clinic
   B. Volleyball
   C. Football Clinic
   D. Tae Kwon Do

Test Preparation Strategies

In this section you'll find strategies and practice to help you with many different kinds of standardized tests. The strategies apply to questions based on long and short readings, as well as questions about charts, graphs, and product labels. You'll also find examples and practice for revising-and-editing tests and writing tests. Applying the strategies to the practice materials and thinking through the answers will help you succeed in many formal testing situations.

Test Preparation Strategies

You can prepare for tests in several ways. First, study and understand the content that will be on the test. Second, learn as many test-taking techniques as you can. These techniques will help you better understand the questions and how to answer them. Following are some general suggestions for preparing for and taking tests. Starting on page 300, you'll find more detailed suggestions and test-taking practice.

Successful Test Taking

 Study Content Throughout the Year

1. **Master the content of your language arts class.** The best way to study for tests is to read, understand, and review the content of your language arts class. Read your daily assignments carefully. Study the notes that you have taken in class. Participate in class discussions. Work with classmates in small groups to help one another learn. You might trade writing assignments and comment on your classmates' work.

2. **Use your textbook for practice.** Your textbook includes many different types of questions. Some may ask you to talk about a story you just read. Others may ask you to figure out what's wrong with a sentence or how to make a paragraph sound better. Try answering these questions out loud and in writing. This type of practice can make taking a test much easier.

3. **Learn how to understand the information in charts, maps, and graphic organizers.** One type of test question may ask you to look at a graphic organizer, such as a spider map, and explain something about the information you see there. Another type of question may ask you to look at a map to find a particular place, such as the Arctic setting of the biography "Matthew Henson at the Top of the World." You'll find charts, maps, and graphic organizers to study in your literature textbooks. You'll also find charts, maps and graphs in your science, mathematics, and social studies textbook. When you look at these, ask yourself, What information is being presented and why is it important?

4. **Practice taking tests.** Use copies of tests you have taken in the past or in other classes for practice. Every test has a time limit, so set a timer for 15 or 20 minutes and then begin your practice. Try to finish the test in the time you've given yourself.

☑ Reading Check

In what practical way can your textbook help you prepare for a test?

5. **Talk about test-taking experiences.** After you've taken a classroom test or quiz, talk about it with your teacher and classmates. Which types of questions were the hardest to understand? What made them difficult? Which questions seemed easiest, and why? When you share test-taking techniques with your classmates, everyone can become a successful test taker.

 ## Use Strategies During the Test

1. **Read the directions carefully.** You can't be a successful test taker unless you know exactly what you are expected to do. Look for key words and phrases, such as *circle the best answer, write a paragraph,* or *choose the word that best completes each sentence.*

2. **Learn how to read test questions.** Test questions can sometimes be difficult to figure out. They may include unfamiliar language or be written in an unfamiliar way. Try rephrasing the question in a simpler way using words you understand. Always ask yourself, What type of information does this question want me to provide?

3. **Pay special attention when using a separate answer sheet.** If you accidentally skip a line on an answer sheet, all the rest of your answers may be wrong! Try one or more of the following techniques:

   - Use a ruler on the answer sheet to make sure you are placing your answers on the correct line.

   - After every five answers, check to make sure you're on the right line.

   - Each time you turn a page of the test booklet, check to make sure the number of the question is the same as the number of the answer line on the answer sheet.

   - If the answer sheet has circles, fill them in neatly. A stray pencil mark might cause the scoring machine to count the answer as incorrect.

4. **If you're not sure of the answer, make your best guess.** Unless you've been told that there is a penalty for guessing, choose the answer that you think is likeliest to be correct.

5. **Keep track of the time.** Answering all the questions on a test usually results in a better score. That's why finishing the test is important. Keep track of the time you have left. At the beginning of the test, figure out how many questions you will have to answer by the halfway point in order to finish in the time given.

✔ **Reading Check**
What are at least two good ways to avoid skipping lines on an answer sheet?

Understand Types of Test Questions

Most tests include two types of questions: multiple choice and open-ended. Specific strategies will help you understand and correctly answer each type of question.

A **multiple-choice question** has two parts. The first part is the question itself, called the stem. The second part is a series of possible answers. Usually four possible answers are provided, and only one of them is correct. Your task is to choose the correct answer. Here are some strategies to help you do just that.

1. Read and think about each question carefully before looking at the possible answers.

2. Pay close attention to key words in the question. For example, look for the word *not,* as in "Which of the following is not a cause of the conflict in this story?"

3. Read and think about all of the possible answers before making your choice.

4. Reduce the number of choices by eliminating any answers you know are incorrect. Then, think about why some of the remaining choices might also be incorrect.

   • If two of the choices are pretty much the same, both are probably wrong.

   • Answers that contain any of the following words are usually incorrect: *always, never, none, all,* and *only.*

5. If you're still unsure about an answer, see if any of the following applies:

   • When one choice is longer and more detailed than the others, it is often the correct answer.

   • When a choice repeats a word that is in the question, it may be the correct answer.

   • When two choices are direct opposites, one of them is likely the correct answer.

   • When one choice includes one or more of the other choices, it is often the correct answer.

   • When a choice includes the word *some* or *often,* it may be the correct answer.

☑ **Reading Check**

What words in a multiple-choice question probably signal a wrong answer?

- If one of the choices is *All of the above,* make sure that at least two of the other choices seem correct.

- If one of the choices is *None of the above,* make sure that none of the other choices seems correct.

An **open-ended test item** can take many forms. It might ask you to write a word or phrase to complete a sentence. You might be asked to create a chart, draw a map, or fill in a graphic organizer. Sometimes, you will be asked to write one or more paragraphs in response to a writing prompt. Use the following strategies when reading and answering open-ended items:

1. If the item includes directions, read them carefully. Take note of any steps required.

2. Look for key words and phrases in the item as you plan how you will respond. Does the item ask you to identify a cause-and-effect relationship or to compare and contrast two or more things? Are you supposed to provide a sequence of events or make a generalization? Does the item ask you to write an essay in which you state your point of view and then try to persuade others that your view is correct?

3. If you're going to be writing a paragraph or more, plan your answer. Jot down notes and a brief outline of what you want to say before you begin writing.

4. Focus your answer. Don't include everything you can think of, but be sure to include everything the item asks for.

5. If you're creating a chart or drawing a map, make sure your work is as clear as possible.

✔ **Reading Check**
What are at least three key strategies for answering an open-ended question?

Reading Test Model
LONG SELECTIONS

DIRECTIONS Here is a selection entitled "The Lost City of Akrotiri" by Jennifer Burton Bauer. Read the selection carefully. The notes in the side columns will help you prepare for the kinds of questions that are likely to follow readings like this. You might want to preview the questions on pages 303 and 304 before you begin reading.

Reading Strategies for Assessment

Think about the title. What questions do you have after reading the title? Jot down your questions and try to answer them as you read further.

Consider the author's purpose. Think about why the author wrote this article. Is her reason to entertain, describe, inform, or persuade? How do you know?

Notice comparisons. Explain what the comparison in the last sentence helps you understand about the archaeologists' process of learning about Akrotiri.

The Lost City of Akrotiri
by Jennifer Burton Bauer

Imagine that one day a volcano erupted near your home and covered your town with layers of thick ash. Now picture that thousands of years later, your city is discovered buried deep beneath the earth. What clues do you think would be left behind to tell people how you lived? What you ate? What you did for fun?

This actually happened more than 3,500 years ago on Thera, an island located off the coast of Greece. At the time, Thera served as an important Minoan trading center. But one day, the earth, like a waking giant, began to shake and rumble. Suddenly, like a cork popping from a bottle, a volcano exploded, spewing ash and pumice miles into the air. Lava flowed, giant tidal waves drenched the land, and ash fell like rain in one of the largest eruptions in recorded history.

The island, now called Santorini, is a popular tourist stop, but buried deep beneath the island's rocky surface lie clues to its remarkable past. These clues lie in the ancient city of Akrotiri, which was hidden for thousands of years under thick layers of ash and pumice. Scientists, called archaeologists, study the remains of the city. They've pieced together, like a giant jigsaw puzzle, a picture of everyday life in Akrotiri.

Housing

Akrotiri is open to visitors. Let's take a tour through the city. First, you will notice narrow, winding streets lined with houses made of a mixture of stone, mud, and straw. A typical house is two or three stories high with staircases made of stone or wood. The bottom story consists of a workshop and storeroom for keeping food. Almost all the houses have a stone mill for grinding corn or other grains to make bread. There were no stores like those we have today so people had to keep enough food to last many months. You can almost smell the corn and grains once stored in the clay pots scattered throughout these rooms.

The living quarters are upstairs. If we were to walk upstairs, we'd see large rooms once filled with tables, chairs, beds, and looms for making cloth. While no actual furniture remains, scientists have made molds of furniture by pouring plaster of Paris into hollows in the ash. The most interesting are the molds of a small, wooden bed and a three-legged table. Beautiful wall paintings were found decorating these rooms.

Wall Paintings

The wall paintings are what truly tell the story of Akrotiri's past. The ash from the volcano kept them from flaking away, and many still appear much the same as when they were first painted. In one, a fisherman proudly displays a bunch of fish. In another, two boys are boxing. Perhaps their long, curly hair is the style worn by young boys of the time. A fleet of ships gives details of sailing and of warriors clad in boar-tusk helmets. Paintings of ladies in Minoan-style dresses, large earrings, and bracelets show the fashions of the time.

Food

What did the Akrotirians eat? Grains found in storage jars tell archaeologists that barley and other grains were grown to make bread. Sheep, goat, pig, and fish bones left behind show what animals they ate. Pots were found that once contained fine wines, tasty olive oil, and sweet honey. Larger clay pots filled with the shells of a familiar garden pest reveal their favorite treat—snails!

Notice details. Pay attention to the details provided by the author. What can you conclude about the Akrotirians' daily lives and work?

Draw conclusions. Why are the wall paintings valuable to archaeologists? Underline what can be learned from them.

Notice supporting details. How do archaeologists know what the Akrotirians ate and drank? Circle the evidence they used to draw their conclusions.

The Eruption

The layers of earth at Akrotiri reveal to scientists the events leading up to the eruption. Earthquakes came first. Then falling ash darkened the sky. When this occurred, most of the people grabbed their valuable belongings and left. No human bones have been found so the islanders must have had enough time to leave before the final eruption. Where they went is a mystery.

We do know, however, that Akrotiri offers many clues about history and how people lived long ago.

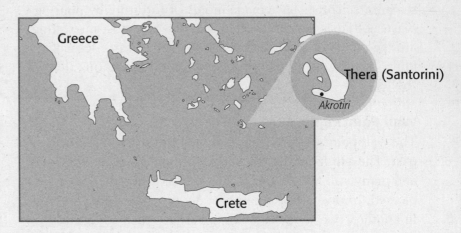

The part of ancient Greece that included Thera was known as the Minoan world after King Minos of Greece.

Note causes and effects. The sequence of events is signaled by words such as *first, then,* and *when.* There is also a cause-and-effect relationship in this paragraph. What happened as a result of the earthquakes and falling ash?

_____

_____

_____

Analyze visual aids. What facts do you learn about Thera and Akrotiri from the map and caption?

Infer word meanings. You have already seen the word *Minoan* in the article. Look for a word with a similar spelling in this caption. Write a definition of *Minoan.*

_____

_____

Now answer questions 1 through 6. Base your answers on the article "The Lost City of Akrotiri." Then check yourself by reading through the side-column notes.

1 What does the title, "The Lost City of Akrotiri," suggest about the main idea of the article?

    A. that it will include a map of Akrotiri

    B. that Akrotiri no longer exists

    C. that Akrotiri is hard to find

    D. that Akrotirians have bad senses of direction

2 Archaeologists haven't found any human bones on Akrotiri because

    E. the Akrotirians had enough time to leave before the eruption.

    F. the cemetery was destroyed in the eruption of the volcano.

    G. the events happened so long ago that no bones remain.

    H. the scientists don't know what Akrotirians or their bones looked like.

3 One conclusion you can draw from the wall paintings is that Akrotiri

    A. was not a peaceful place.

    B. didn't have any barbers.

    C. depended on sailing and fishing.

    D. paid artists very well.

4 Read the following sentence from the article.

    Larger clay pots filled with the shells of a familiar garden pest reveal their favorite treat—snails!

    What is the "familiar garden pest"?

    E. weeds

    F. shellfish

    G. rabbits

    H. snails

Answer Strategies

Revisit the title. Now that you have read the article, the meaning of the title should be clear. Which answer explains how the title reflects the main idea of the article?

Look for cause-and-effect relationships. Reread the part of the article that deals with the eruption of the volcano. What do scientists believe happened when the ash began to fall?

Draw conclusions. A conclusion must be supported by details in the text. There is no evidence for D or for B (the boys' long hair is thought to have been the style). Warriors are pictured but not in battle, making A questionable. This leaves C, supported by two details from the paintings.

Analyze details. The structure of the sentence indicates that the familiar garden pest and the favorite treat are the same. Therefore, if snails are the treat, they are also the pest.

Answers: 1.B, 2.E, 3.C, 4.H

5 What information in the map or its caption do you need to understand a word used in the article?

A. the meaning of the word *Akrotiri*

B. the name of the island where Akrotiri is located

C. the definition of the word *Minoan*

D. the name of the most important king of Crete

6 Read the following sentence from the passage.

> They've pieced together, like a giant jigsaw puzzle, a picture of everyday life in Akrotiri.

In your own words, explain how the ruins of Akrotiri are like and different from a giant jigsaw puzzle. Use details and information from the article to support your answer.

Sample short response for question 6:

Both the ruins and the puzzle have many pieces. However, the pieces of a jigsaw puzzle are all made of cardboard and are about the same size. If you put them together correctly, they make a whole picture. On the other hand, the ruins of Akrotiri come in all shapes and sizes. The article says that there are wall paintings, animal bones, pots, and other objects. Many of the pieces of the puzzle of Akrotiri may not even be there. Also, archaeologists don't have a picture on a box to tell them what the ancient city looked like.

Reading Test Practice
LONG SELECTIONS

DIRECTIONS Now it's time to practice what you've learned about reading test items and choosing the best answers. Read the following selection, "Girls (Even the Young Ones) Think of Everything: Becky Schroeder" by Catherine Thimmesh. Use the side columns to make notes about the important parts of this selection: main ideas, cause and effect, comparisons and contrasts, difficult vocabulary, supporting details, and so on.

Girls (Even the Young Ones) Think of Everything: Becky Schroeder

by Catherine Thimmesh

A person has to be sixteen to drive, seventeen to see certain movies, and eighteen to vote. People can get terrific discounts on all sorts of stuff—provided they're over sixty-five. Everywhere we look there are age limits that define what people can and can't do. But creativity has no boundaries, no limitations. Anyone can invent. And they do. Inventors are popping up at the youngest of ages.

Sitting in the car waiting for her mom to return from shopping, Becky decided she might as well try to finish her math homework. But it was growing dark and getting hard to see the paper.

"I didn't have a flashlight, and I didn't want to open the car door because then the whole car would light up," recalled Becky. "So I thought it would be neat to have my paper light up somehow, and that's when the idea came to me."

It isn't every day that a ten-year-old invents a product eagerly sought by several businesses, but that's exactly what Becky Schroeder did when she created a tool that enabled people to write in the dark.

Her invention? The Glo-sheet.

That night Becky went home trying to imagine different ways of making her paper glow in the dark. She remembered all sorts of glow-in-the-dark toys—like balls and Frisbees—

and wondered how they were made. She was determined to find a solution. So the very next day, Becky's dad took her on an outing to the hardware store. They returned with a pail of phosphorescent paint. She took the paint and stacks of paper into the darkest room in the house—the bathroom. There, she experimented.

"I'd turn on the light, turn it off, turn it on," said Becky. "My parents remember me running out of the room saying, 'It works, it works! I'm writing in the dark!' "

She used an acrylic board and coated it with a specific amount of phosphorescent paint. She took a complicated idea and made it work rather simply. When the coated clipboard is exposed to light, it glows. The glowing board then illuminates, or lights up, the paper that has been placed on top. Two years after her initial inspiration, in 1974, Becky became the youngest female ever to receive a U.S. patent.

She didn't actively market her Glo-sheet. She didn't need to. *The New York Times* wrote an article about an incredible invention—patented by a twelve-year-old—and the inquiries and orders streamed in. Professionals who needed to write in the dark started ordering her Glo-sheet: photographers for their darkrooms, critics who took notes in darkened theaters, emergency medical people for use in ambulances.

"Some of the Glo-sheets I was handmaking and some I had a company manufacture for me," Becky explained. "There were more expensive versions and less expensive ones— electric-operated and light-activated models."

Several large companies offered to buy her patent rights, but Becky and her father decided to sell the Glo-sheet on their own. What began as a personal project, just for fun, blossomed into a business, with Becky as the president of the company. Proof that success can come at any age with a good idea and a little imagination.

Your Turn

Suppose you have an invention of your own. It's different, it's new, it's neat. Now what? Obtaining a patent may be an important first step. A patent is the legal document issued by the government to protect an idea. Utility patents are for inventions that are either mechanical or electrical in nature. Design patents cover inventions that are new and original designs of existing products.

To patent an invention, you must prove that it is new and useful and that you are the very first person to have invented the item. It is important that you apply for a patent immediately, and you are required to use a patent attorney or patent agent to do so. A patent application must be complete with diagrams, notes, and models. If your invention proves to be unique, you pay the fees and are assigned a patent number. Your invention is then legally protected for twenty years (from the date of filing), and you alone have the right to profit from it.

Not all inventions, however, will benefit from having a patent. The patent process can be extremely expensive, and depending on the invention, might not be really necessary. A good patent attorney should be able to advise you on the merits of obtaining a patent for your specific invention.

For more information on the patent process, contact:
U.S. Patent and Trademark Office
Washington, D.C. 20231
(800) 786-9199
www.uspto.gov

NOTES

Now answer questions 1 through 7. Base your answers on the article "Girls (Even the Young Ones) Think of Everything: Becky Schroeder."

1 The main information you learn from reading the first paragraph is that

A. age limits are unfair.

B. young people are more creative than older people.

C. inventing things will keep you young.

D. people of any age can be inventors.

2 How did Becky get the idea for the Glo-sheet?

E. She was trying to avoid doing her math homework.

F. She was trying to do her math homework in a dark car.

G. She fell asleep while doing her homework and dreamed about it.

H. She read about it in her math book.

3 What does the word *phosphorescent* mean in the following sentence?

They returned with a pail of phosphorescent paint.

A. light-colored

B. glow-in-the-dark

C. shiny blue

D. bubbly white

4 Read the following sentence from the article.

Becky became the youngest female ever to receive a U.S. patent.

A *patent* is

E. something shiny that glows in the dark.

F. a legal document issued by the government.

G. a successful invention.

H. the right to advertise a product.

5 In the second paragraph under "Your Turn," how is the information about applying for a patent organized?

A. by main idea and supporting details

B. by cause and effect

C. in question-and-answer format

D. step by step, in chronological order

6 What was the author's main purpose for writing this article?

E. to encourage other young inventors

F. to explain how Glo-sheets work

G. to get people to buy Glo-sheets

H. to explain why patents are necessary

7 Why was the Glo-sheet such a successful invention? Use details and information from the article to support your answer.

THINKING IT THROUGH

The notes in the side columns will help you think through your answers. See the key at the bottom of the page. How well did you do?

Reread the first paragraph. Which answer choice uses slightly different language to express the same idea found at the end of the paragraph?

1 The main information you learn from reading the first paragraph is that

A. age limits are unfair.

B. young people are more creative than older people.

C. inventing things will keep you young.

D. people of any age can be inventors.

Skim the first few paragraphs of the article to find the specific source of Becky's inspiration.

2 How did Becky get the idea for the Glo-sheet?

E. She was trying to avoid doing her math homework.

F. She was trying to do her math homework in a dark car.

G. She fell asleep while doing her homework and dreamed about it.

H. She read about it in her math book.

The sentence does not give any clues to the word's meaning. Therefore, you need to reread the paragraph in which the sentence is found. Notice that one of the choices is used elsewhere in that paragraph, making it the correct answer.

3 What does the word *phosphorescent* mean in the following sentence?

> **They returned with a pail of phosphorescent paint.**

A. light-colored

B. glow-in-the-dark

C. shiny blue

D. bubbly white

Use the context clues of *receive* and *U.S.* to narrow your choices. *Receive* means "to be given," eliminating E and G, since Becky was not given either. *U.S.* suggests an association with the government, which points to F.

4 Read the following sentence from the article.

> **Becky became the youngest female ever to receive a U.S. patent.**

A *patent* is

E. something shiny that glows in the dark.

F. a legal document issued by the government.

G. a successful invention.

H. the right to advertise a product.

Answers: 1.D, 2.F, 3.B, 4.F

5 In the second paragraph under "Your Turn," how is the information about applying for a patent organized?

A. by main idea and supporting details
B. by cause and effect
C. in question-and-answer format
D. step by step, in chronological order

Eliminate organizational patterns that are obviously not used, such as cause-and-effect and question-and-answer. Check to see if time-order words are used, such as *immediately* or *then*. If so, it is chronological order.

6 What was the author's main purpose for writing this article?

E. to encourage other young inventors
F. to explain how Glo-sheets work
G. to get people to buy Glo-sheets
H. to explain why patents are necessary

Skim the article, paying particular attention to the first and last paragraphs. What does the author emphasize?

7 Why was the Glo-sheet such a successful invention? Use details and information from the article to support your answer.

The Glo-sheet was a successful invention for many reasons. First, the Glo-sheet was useful to a variety of people who needed to write in the dark, such as photographers, theater critics, and emergency medical workers. Second, the Glo-sheet was not very complicated. This meant that it was not difficult for Becky or a manufacturer to make the Glo-sheets to sell. Third, customers could buy cheaper or more expensive versions of the Glo-sheet, depending on what they could afford and which model they wanted.

This response received a top score because it
- explains three reasons for the success of the Glo-sheet.
- includes details from the article.
- is clearly written.

Reading Test Model
SHORT SELECTIONS

DIRECTIONS This reading selection is a brief story. The strategies you have just used can also help you with this shorter selection. As you read the selection, respond to the notes in the side column.

When you've finished reading, you'll find four multiple-choice questions. Again, use the side-column notes to help you understand what each question is asking and why each answer is correct.

Pandora and the Box

Long ago, a young boy named Epimetheus lived alone in a cottage. Another child came to live with him. Her name was Pandora. When she arrived at the cottage, the first thing she saw was a large box. She asked, "Epimetheus, what is in that box?"

Epimetheus answered, "That is a secret, and you must not ask any questions about it. The box was left here for safekeeping, and even I don't know what is inside."

The children went out to play, but Pandora's thoughts were drawn back to the box in the cottage. "How did the box get there?" she asked Epimetheus.

"An old man with a cap of feathers left it at the door, not long before you arrived."

"I know that gentleman," said Pandora. "No doubt he meant for me to have the box. There must be pretty clothes for me, or toys for us to play with."

"That may be so," answered Epimetheus, "but until he returns to tell us so, we have no right to open the box."

The children continued to live in the cottage for several years, but the elderly person never returned. One day, Epimetheus went out without asking Pandora to go with him. He went to gather nuts and fruit, but perhaps he also wished to get away from Pandora's constant questions about the box. While he was gone, Pandora eased close to the box and studied its rich carvings. She admired the shape of a face in the center of the lid. As she stared at the finely-drawn mouth, she seemed to hear it speak these words: "What do you fear, Pandora? Never mind what Epimetheus says. Open the box and see the beautiful things inside!"

Reading Strategies for Assessment

Analyze conflict. As you read the story, find out how Pandora's attitude toward the box differs from that of Epimetheus. What do you think she wants to do when she asks this question?

Infer meanings from context. Write a synonym for *drawn* as it is used in this sentence.

Evaluate symbolism. What do you think the box represents in the story? Underline what Pandora thinks it tells her to do.

Pandora's curiosity tugged at her. She placed her hand on the lid and tried to lift it, but it didn't budge. She noticed a thin, finely woven cord encircling the box, holding it closed. Her fingers brushed against the silken strands. Before she realized what she was doing, her fingers had found the ends of the silken cord and were twisting apart its braided strands . . .

1 Which event is most likely to happen next in the story?

A. Pandora opens the box.

B. Pandora goes looking for Epimetheus.

C. Epimetheus says, "Don't do it!"

D. The old man arrives.

2 Pandora's placing her hand on the lid of the box is part of which story element?

E. characterization

F. setting

G. plot

H. point of view

3 Which states a main theme of the story?

A. The world is filled with wonderful things.

B. People are tempted to do what is forbidden.

C. Loneliness is an unhappy state.

D. It is important to keep a secret.

4 The word *drawn* in the third paragraph is closest in meaning to which of the following?

E. sketched

F. ripped

G. torn

H. pulled

Predict the end of the story.
Highlight each action Pandora takes in the last paragraph. Then predict what you think she will do next.

Answer Strategies

Make predictions. Reread the ending of the story and then the answers. Which choice is closest to your prediction?

Analyze story elements. Why is this action important in the story? Is it necessary to reveal character or to show when and where the story is set? Does it move the plot forward to the next important event? Does it identify the narrator?

Recall symbols. The main theme of a story is sometimes revealed through symbols. Think about the symbolism of the box to help you answer this question.

Infer meanings. Find the sentence in the third paragraph that includes *drawn*. Try substituting each of these words for *drawn*. Eliminate those that change the meaning of the sentence.

Answers:
1.A, 2.G, 3.B, 4.H

from How to Tell the Wild Animals

by Carolyn Wells

The true Chameleon is small,
   A lizard sort of thing;
He hasn't any ears at all,   3
   And not a single wing.
If there is nothing on the tree,
'Tis the Chameleon you see.   6

5 What is the form of the passage?

   A. poem

   B. story

   C. essay

   D. drama

6 To what does "He" in line 3 specifically refer?

   E. a lizard

   F. a wild animal

   G. the Chameleon

   H. the poet

7 What is the author's main purpose in the passage?

   A. to report

   B. to amuse

   C. to persuade

   D. to inform

8 Which statement best explains lines 5 and 6 of the passage?

   E. The Chameleon is an unimportant animal.

   F. The Chameleon appears to be part of a tree.

   G. The Chameleon does not live in a tree.

   H. The Chameleon is a wild animal.

Reading Test Practice
SHORT SELECTIONS

DIRECTIONS Use the following to practice your skills. Read each passage and circle the key ideas. Then answer the multiple-choice questions that follow.

1. Which line from the passage uses emotional appeal?
   A. Be the First on Your Block to Own One!
   B. Available only at My Man Music, Main Street.
   C. Only one copy to a customer.
   D. First come, first served.

2. Which states an opinion?
   E. Get your pre-sale copy . . .
   F. Be cool with a B-Kool Boys CD!
   G. Available only at My Man Music . . .
   H. Bring this ad for a 10% discount . . .

3 What is the purpose of this passage?

   A. to entertain the reader

   B. to persuade the reader to be cool

   C. to persuade the reader to buy a product

   D. none of the above

Motor Cars

by Rowena Bastin Bennett

From a city window, 'way up high,
I like to watch the cars go by.
They look like burnished beetles black,   3
That leave a little muddy track
Behind them as they slowly crawl.
Sometimes they do not move at all   6
But huddle close with hum and drone
As though they feared to be alone.
They grope their way through fog and night   9
With the golden feelers of their light.

4 To what are the cars compared?

   E. beetles

   F. ants

   G. windows

   H. tracks

5 To what do the "golden feelers" in line 10 refer?

   A. reflectors

   B. fog

   C. burnished beetles

   D. headlight beams

6 What type of writing is this passage?

   E. an essay

   F. a drama

   G. a short story

   H. a poem

THINKING IT THROUGH

The notes in the side column will help you think through your answers.
Check the key at the bottom of the page. How well did you do?

1 Which line from the passage uses emotional appeal?

  A. Be the First on Your Block to Own One!
  B. Available only at My Man Music, Main Street.
  C. Only one copy to a customer.
  D. First come, first served.

2 Which states an opinion?

  E. Get your pre-sale copy . . .
  F. Be cool with a B-Kool Boys CD!
  G. Available only at My Man Music . . .
  H. Bring this ad for a 10% discount . . .

3 What is the purpose of this passage?

  A. to entertain the reader
  B. to persuade the reader to be cool
  C. to persuade the reader to buy a product
  D. none of the above

4 To what are the cars compared?

  E. beetles
  F. ants
  G. windows
  H. tracks

5 To what do the "golden feelers" in line 10 refer?

  A. reflectors
  B. fog
  C. burnished beetles
  D. headlight beams

6 What type of writing is this passage?

  E. an essay
  F. a drama
  G. a short story
  H. a poem

> An emotional appeal stirs the reader's feelings. Eliminate choices that are just statements of fact.

> Distinguish between fact and opinion by deciding which choices can be proven right or wrong. The choice that remains is a personal belief or opinion.

> Because persuasive techniques are used throughout the passage, you can narrow your choices to B, C, or D. What action is the reader meant to take as a result of this persuasion?

> Return to line 3. A comparison is signaled by the use of the word *like*. What do the cars look like?

> Keep in mind the central comparison from line 3 and the function of feelers on insects. Which parts of cars similarly help them find their way through the fog or night?

> Consider the passage's rhyme, arrangement of lines, and use of figurative language in making your choice.

Functional Reading Test Model

DIRECTIONS Study the following warranty information for a binocular. Then answer the questions that follow.

Functional Reading Test Model

Reading Strategies for Assessment

Identify significant details. Read the first paragraph carefully. Underline the conditions under which the warranty is valid. Circle what someone must do to have a defective instrument repaired or replaced.

Find the main idea. Summarize the conditions that make the warranty invalid.

_____

_____

Notice exceptions and exclusions. If you own a Behold Extendable Binocular, what does the last line tell you?

Answer Strategies

> The key words in this question are *would be repaired*. Eliminate choices that the second paragraph says would make the warranty invalid or that are excluded from the protection of the warranty.

BINOCULAR LIMITED WARRANTY
*BEHOLD BINOCULARS**

This binocular is warranted to be free of defects in materials and workmanship for a period of **10 Years.** This warranty is for the benefit of the original retail purchaser only. During this warranty period Behold Binoculars and Optical Instruments will repair or replace, at Behold's option, any warranted instrument that proves to be defective provided it is returned postage paid to Behold Warranty Repair, 21 Panorama, Vista Village, MN 21777. If your product is not registered, proof of purchase (such as a copy of the original invoice) is required.

This warranty does not apply if, in Behold's judgment, the instrument has been abused, mishandled, self-repaired, or modified, nor does it apply to normal wear and tear. This warranty gives you specific legal rights, and you may also have other rights, which vary from state to state. For further warranty service information, contact Customer Service, Behold Binoculars and Optical Instruments, P.O. Box 1815, Starlight, CA 92220; phone 800-555-1234.

* Behold Extendable Binoculars excluded.

---

1 Which of the following types of damage would be repaired under this warranty?

A. the shattering of the lenses as a result of dropping the binocular

B. the inability to focus the binocular after taking it apart and putting it back together again

C. a crack in the central focusing wheel noticed soon after purchase

D. a scratched lens on a Behold Extendable Binocular

Answer:
1. C

2 Which of the following conditions would make the warranty invalid?

    E. the passage of eight years from date of purchase

    F. a different owner from the purchaser of the binocular

    G. prepaid shipment of the binocular to the repair center

    H. damage resulting from improper workmanship

Check each choice against the conditions in the first paragraph. Which answer does not fall within the warranty's restrictions?

3 What does the phrase *at Behold's option* mean?

    A. The company will replace or repair anything defective without questions.

    B. The company will automatically send a new binocular to replace the old.

    C. The company will decide whether to repair or replace the damaged parts.

    D. The company will give the customer the choice of having the binocular repaired or replaced.

Read the choices carefully. If three of them express similar ideas, then look at the fourth or different answer more closely. In this case, three describe the company's willingness to repair or replace the binocular without question. What does the fourth choice suggest that the company will do?

Answers:
2. F 3. C

Functional Reading Test Practice

DIRECTIONS Study the prescription medicine label below. Circle the information that you think is the most important. Answer the multiple-choice questions that follow.

Davis Pharmacy
1700 West Wilson
Chicago, IL 60640
800-555-1234

Dr. JUNE SUMMERS   05/11/03
RX: 576-00598
ROBERT HANSEN

PLAQUENIL 200 MG TABLETS
QTY: 90
Mfg: Watson
TAKE ONE TABLET BY MOUTH THREE TIMES DAILY
No Refills   Dr. Authorization Needed
KEEP OUT OF REACH OF CHILDREN
TAKE WITH FOOD OR MILK

---

1 How many milligrams of Plaquenil must Robert take daily?

   A. 200 mg

   B. 400 mg

   C. 600 mg

   D. 900 mg

2 How many days will this prescription last?

   E. 90 days

   F. 270 days

   G. 15 days

   H. 30 days

3 In order to follow the directions on the prescription, what should Robert do if he normally doesn't eat lunch?

A. take two tablets at once either at breakfast or dinner

B. take one tablet in the middle of the day with a glass of milk

C. take only two tablets a day for a greater number of days

D. take one tablet in the middle of the day with a glass of water

THINKING IT THROUGH

The notes in the side column will help you think through your answers. Check the key at the bottom of the page. How well did you do?

1 How many milligrams of Plaquenil must Robert take daily?

A. 200 mg

B. 400 mg

C. 600 mg

D. 900 mg

> Look at what the question is asking. If each tablet is 200 milligrams and Robert takes 3 tablets a day, then multiplying the two numbers will result in his total daily milligrams.

2 How many days will this prescription last?

E. 90 days

F. 270 days

G. 15 days

H. 30 days

> The quickest way to answer this question is to divide 90, the total number of pills, by 3, the number that Robert takes each day.

3 In order to follow the directions on the prescription, what should Robert do if he normally doesn't eat lunch?

A. take two tablets at once either at breakfast or dinner

B. take one tablet in the middle of the day with a glass of milk

C. take only two tablets a day for a greater number of days

D. take one tablet in the middle of the day with a glass of water

> Reread the directions carefully. They state that Robert must take one tablet three times a day, thus eliminating A and C. Further directions explain that the tablets must be taken with food or milk.

Answers: 1. C, 2. H, 3. B

Revising-and-Editing Test Model

DIRECTIONS Read the following paragraph carefully. Then answer the multiple-choice questions that follow. After answering the questions, read the material in the side columns to check your answer strategies.

¹ There are many differences between the book and the movie version of *Father, Dancing.* ² The book has stronger characters, who's personalities are fully developed. ³ The director of the movie must of thought that having big-name actors would make up for weak characters. ⁴ The plot of the book is also more better than the movie's, because some scenes they leave out are important. ⁵ On the other hand, the movie has flashy special effects however, effects have less meaning than plot. ⁶ In my opinion, the book is more interesting than the movie, even though the movie was the most expensive production in the history of Hollywood.

1 Which of the following is the correct spelling of *who's* in sentence 2?

A. whos'
B. whose
C. whose'
D. who's

2 What is the correct verb phrase in sentence 3?

E. must think
F. must of been thinking
G. must have thought
H. must thought

Reading Strategies for Assessment

Watch for common errors. Highlight or underline errors such as incorrect punctuation, spelling, or capitalization; incomplete or run-on sentences; and missing or misplaced information.

Answer Strategies

Possessive Pronouns A possessive pronoun is needed in sentence 2. Possessive pronouns are not spelled with apostrophes.
For help, see Pupil Edition, p. R73* Grammar, Usage, and Mechanics Book, pp. 52–54

Verb Tenses The word *of* is a preposition and does not belong in a verb phrase. It is sometimes used incorrectly to replace *have.*
For help, see Pupil Edition, p. R76 Grammar, Usage, and Mechanics Book, pp. 94–96

Answers:
1. B. 2. G

*Pages listed are for the Grammar Handbook in *The Language of Literature* Pupil Edition and the *Grammar, Usage, and Mechanics Book.*

3 In sentence 4, which of the following is the correct form of the comparative adjective?

    A. more better

    B. most better

    C. best

    D. better

> **Comparative Adjectives** *Good* is an irregular adjective. The comparative form is *better*, and the superlative is *best*.
> *For help, see Pupil Edition, pp. R78–R80*
> *Grammar, Usage, and Mechanics Book, pp. 112–114*

4 What is the best way to rewrite the second part of sentence 4?

    E. because some scenes the movie leaves out are important

    F. because some scenes the book leaves out are important

    G. because some left-out scenes are important

    H. because some scenes are important that are left out

> **Pronoun References** Avoid unclear and inaccurate pronoun references by repeating the noun when necessary. Does the movie or the book leave out scenes?

5 In sentence 5, what does the transitional phrase *On the other hand* suggest about sentences 4 and 5?

    A. that their messages are similar

    B. that their messages are different

    C. that their messages are related as cause and effect

    D. that their messages are related as main idea and supporting details

> **Transitions** Transitions show relationships between ideas. *On the other hand* signals a contrast or change.

6 Which sentence in the paragraph is a run-on sentence?

    E. sentence 3

    F. sentence 4

    G. sentence 5

    H. sentence 6

> **Run-on Sentences** A run-on is two or more complete thoughts joined without correct punctuation. Often the word *however* in the middle of a sentence without a preceding semicolon is a clue that the sentence is a run-on.
> *For help, see Pupil Edition, p. R67*
> *Grammar, Usage, and Mechanics Book, pp. 28–30*

Answers: 3.D, 4.E, 5.B, 6.G

Revising-and-Editing Test Practice

DIRECTIONS Read the following paragraph carefully. As you read, circle each error that you find and identify the error in the side column—for example, *misspelled word* or *not a complete sentence*. When you have finished, circle the letter of the correct choice for each question that follows.

¹ The gods odin in norse mythology and zeus in Greek mythology are very different from each other. ² Odin don't eat with the other gods and goddesses. ³ He sits quietly, and thinks about the advice of his two ravens, whose names are Thought and Memory. ⁴ Furthermore, Odin is willing to pursue wisdom even if he has to suffer. ⁵ When Odin learns that he will have to sacrifice one of his eyes to gain the knowledge he seeks, he makes it. ⁶ In your opinion, do you think that wisdom is worth such a price? ⁷ Zeus certainly wouldn't think so.

1 What is the correct capitalization in sentence 1?

A. The Gods odin in Norse mythology and zeus in Greek mythology

B. The gods Odin in norse mythology and Zeus in Greek mythology

C. The gods Odin in Norse Mythology and Zeus in Greek Mythology

D. The gods Odin in Norse mythology and Zeus in Greek mythology

2 What is the correct verb phrase in sentence 2?

E. do not eat

F. don't eats

G. doesn't eat

H. doesn't eats

3 What change, if any, should be made in sentence 3?

A. change *Thought* and *Memory* to *thought* and *memory*

B. change *quietly, and* to *quietly and*

C. change *the advice of his two ravens* to *the advise of his two Ravens*

D. no change

4 Which sentence in this paragraph is NOT a declarative sentence?

   E. sentence 2

   F. sentence 3

   G. sentence 4

   H. sentence 6

5 What is the best replacement for *it* in sentence 5?

   A. his goal

   B. the knowledge he seeks

   C. the sacrifice

   D. one of his eyes

6 What is the best way to rewrite sentence 6?

   E. In your opinion, do you believe wisdom is worth such a price?

   F. Do you, in your opinion, think that wisdom is worth such a price?

   G. Do you think that wisdom is worth such a price?

   H. Do you think, in your opinion, that wisdom is worth such a price?

7 On the basis of this paragraph's first and last sentences and main topic, what would you expect the main topic of the next paragraph to be?

   A. the knowledge Odin gains

   B. the Greek god Zeus

   C. Odin's lost eye

   D. all the gods of Greek mythology

THINKING IT THROUGH

Use the notes in the side columns to help you understand why some answers are correct and others are not. Check the answer key on the next page. How well did you do?

Remember that proper names and proper adjectives are capitalized. Common nouns, such as the word *gods*, are not capitalized.
For help, see Pupil Edition, pp. R66, R81–R82*
Grammar, Usage, and Mechanics Book, pp. 148–150

1 What is the correct capitalization in sentence 1?

   A. The Gods odin in Norse mythology and zeus in Greek mythology

   B. The gods Odin in norse mythology and Zeus in Greek mythology

   C. The gods Odin in Norse Mythology and Zeus in Greek Mythology

   D. The gods Odin in Norse mythology and Zeus in Greek mythology

Odin is singular, so the helping verb in the verb phrase must be singular.
For help, see Pupil Edition, p. R68
Grammar, Usage, and Mechanics Book, pp. 133–135

2 What is the correct verb phrase in sentence 2?

   E. do not eat

   F. don't eats

   G. doesn't eat

   H. doesn't eats

Eliminate A and C by recalling that proper names are capitalized and common nouns are not. To decide between B and D, keep in mind that a comma is not necessary between the two parts of a compound verb.
For help, see Pupil Edition, pp. R64–R65, R66
Grammar, Usage, and Mechanics Book, pp. 148–150

3 What change, if any, should be made in sentence 3?

   A. change *Thought* and *Memory* to *thought* and *memory*

   B. change *quietly, and* to *quietly and*

   C. change *the advice of his two ravens* to *the advise of his two Ravens*

   D. no change

Look at the punctuation and the function of each sentence listed. A declarative sentence ends in a period and makes a statement.
For help, see Pupil Edition, p. R95
Grammar, Usage, and Mechanics Book, pp. 16–18

4 Which sentence in this paragraph is NOT a declarative sentence?

   E. sentence 2

   F. sentence 3

   G. sentence 4

   H. sentence 6

*Pages listed are for the Grammar Handbook in *The Language of Literature* Pupil Edition and the *Grammar, Usage, and Mechanics Book*.

⑤ What is the best replacement for *it* in sentence 5?

   A. his goal

   B. the knowledge he seeks

   C. the sacrifice

   D. one of his eyes

Replace *it* with each of the choices to see which makes sense. *For help, see Pupil Edition, p. R73 Grammar, Usage, and Mechanics Book, pp. 49–51*

⑥ What is the best way to rewrite sentence 6?

   E. In your opinion, do you believe wisdom is worth such a price?

   F. Do you, in your opinion, think that wisdom is worth such a price?

   G. Do you think that wisdom is worth such a price?

   H. Do you think, in your opinion, that wisdom is worth such a price?

Notice that only one of the four choices does not include *in your opinion*. Consider what *in your opinion* means. Is the phrase necessary or redundant when used with *do you think*?

⑦ On the basis of this paragraph's first and last sentences and main topic, what would you expect the main topic of the next paragraph to be?

   A. the knowledge Odin gains

   B. the Greek god Zeus

   C. Odin's lost eye

   D. all the gods of Greek mythology

The first sentence sets up a comparison between Odin and Zeus. After Odin is described, what should be discussed next in order to complete the comparison?

Answers:
1.D, 2.G, 3.B, 4.H, 5.C, 6.G, 7.B

Writing Test Model

DIRECTIONS Many tests ask you to write an essay in response to a writing prompt. A writing prompt is a brief statement that describes a writing situation. Some writing prompts ask you to explain what, why, or how. Others ask you to convince someone about something.

As you analyze the following writing prompts, read and respond to the notes in the side columns. Then look at the response to each prompt. The notes in the side columns will help you understand why each response is considered strong.

Analyzing the Prompt

Identify the focus. What issue will you be writing about? Circle the focus of your essay in the first sentence.

Understand what's expected of you. Circle what you must do first. Then identify your audience. What kinds of details will convince this audience?

Answer Strategies

Capture readers' attention. The writer shows her view of the proposal and hooks her readers by describing a realistic classroom scene that could result from the change.

State the position clearly. By stating her opinion early in the essay, the writer has a chance to develop her argument fully.

Keep the audience in mind. Knowing that the school board is concerned mostly with education, the writer addresses the effect of the proposal on students' school work first.

Prompt A

The school board in your community has decided to begin school 30 minutes earlier each day.

Think about how this change would affect you. Now write to convince the school board to accept your point of view. Be sure to provide support for your argument.

Strong Response

It's 1:15 on a Thursday afternoon at Central Middle School. Ms. Lee is explaining about percents at the front of the room. But only a small percentage of the students are listening. The rest are asleep at their desks. It's not that Ms. Lee is a boring teacher, though. As hard as they try, the students haven't been able to stay awake in class since the school board decided to start the school day 30 minutes earlier. This is only one negative effect this decision will have. Starting school half an hour earlier will be very harmful to students for a number of reasons.

The major result of beginning school 30 minutes earlier would be that students would not do as well in their classes. We are at an age when we need all the sleep we can get. After-school activities and homework keep many of us up past 10:00 every night. Having to wake up half an hour earlier would not give us the rest we need to do our best. I'm sure this is not what you want your change in the schedule to accomplish.

You might say that we could go to sleep 30 minutes earlier to make up for having to get up earlier. However, this would force us to give up a half hour of some activity. I'm sure you wouldn't want it to be our homework. What about after-school activities like clubs and sports, you ask? These activities are an important part of our education. We need them because they help make us well-rounded people.

Also, to be well-rounded, healthy people, we need some time to just relax, too. Doctors keep saying how bad stress is for adults. Think of what it must do to growing children! In addition to school and activities related to it, most of us have chores and music or other kinds of lessons that take up our time. There's hardly a minute just to sit and enjoy life.

In conclusion, I believe that beginning the school day 30 minutes early will have bad effects on students and their education. I urge you as members of the school board to think about the well-being of the school's students and to vote against this change.

Address opposing views. The writer makes her argument more effective by anticipating the other side's suggestions and explaining why they won't work.

Develop the argument with strong reasons and specific details. Specific examples strongly support each of the writer's three reasons.

Restate opinion. The writer leaves the school board with a clear restatement of her view.

Analyzing the Prompt

Consider your approach. First narrow your focus. Which holiday will you choose? Then think about the kinds of details you will include. Will you tell a story or describe the sights and sounds associated with the day?

Answer Strategies

Create a strong introduction. The writer gives a clue to the holiday he chose and the reason it is special by opening his essay with a quotation.

Include specific details. By naming and describing several family members, the writer *shows* readers what his Thanksgiving is like rather than just telling them.

Choose an effective organization. The writer explains the most important part of the holiday first.

Develop the main idea fully. The writer elaborates on his second reason with specific details and examples that appeal to the senses.

Prompt B

Everyone has a favorite holiday. Think about which holiday is your favorite. Now explain why you like that holiday the most.

Strong Response

"We gather together." There's Grandpa sitting on the sofa like a king on his throne. Here come Uncle Joe and Aunt Diane. And who's this? Cousin Jason? He's gotten so big, I hardly recognize him. Before I can even say hello, my twin step-sisters Kyra and Kyla poke their heads in the door. I make my way through the crowded room listening to parts of a dozen conversations. It's crazy, but I love it. It's Thanksgiving, my favorite holiday.

The most important part of Thanksgiving for me is being with my family. We don't get to see each other very often, and we have decided to make this holiday the annual gathering time. Sure, the kids get into arguments sometimes. Also, you can usually count on Aunt Ellen to pick a fight with my father. It's not serious, though. We all care about each other and are grateful to be together.

Of course, Thanksgiving is also about eating. I like to eat as much as anybody else does. All that eating means a lot of cooking, which I also enjoy.

On Thanksgiving, my mother lets me help in the kitchen. I even invented a special dish of sweet potatoes, oranges, and marshmallows that has become a family favorite. We also have the traditional turkey and stuffing, and there's always pumpkin pie for dessert. Most of us eat too much and wish we hadn't, but isn't that what holidays are for?

I'm really thankful for Thanksgiving. It's a special day to enjoy and be grateful for my wonderful family and good food. I don't mind that it just lasts a day, because it will come around again at the same time next year.

Present a powerful conclusion. The writer uses his concluding paragraph to bring together all the threads of his essay.

Writing Test Practice

DIRECTIONS Read the following writing prompt. Using the strategies you've learned in this section, analyze the prompt, plan your response, and then write an essay explaining your position.

Prompt C

Your parents have decided to eliminate potato chips, candy, and other "junk food" from your family's diet. Think about how this change would affect you. Now write to convince your parents to accept your point of view on this issue. Include support for your position.

Scoring Rubrics

DIRECTIONS Use the following checklist to see whether you have written a strong persuasive essay. You will have succeeded if you can check nearly all of the items.

The Prompt

☐ My response meets all the requirements stated in the prompt.

☐ I have stated my position clearly and supported it with details.

☐ I have addressed the audience appropriately.

☐ My essay fits the type of writing suggested in the prompt (letter to the editor, article for the school paper, and so on).

Reasons

☐ The reasons I offer really support my position.

☐ My audience will find the reasons convincing.

☐ I have stated my reasons clearly.

☐ I have given at least three reasons.

☐ I have supported my reasons with sufficient facts, examples, quotations, and other details.

☐ I have presented and responded to opposing arguments.

☐ My reasoning is sound. I have avoided faulty logic.

Order and Arrangement

☐ I have included a strong introduction.

☐ I have included a strong conclusion.

☐ The reasons are arranged in a logical order.

Word Choice

☐ The language of my essay is appropriate for my audience.

☐ I have used precise, vivid words and persuasive language.

Fluency

☐ I have used sentences of varying lengths and structures.

☐ I have connected ideas with transitions and other devices.

☐ I have used correct spelling, punctuation, and grammar.

Personal Word List

Use these pages to build your personal vocabulary. As you read the selections take time to mark unfamiliar words. These should be words that seem interesting or important enough to add to your permanent vocabulary. After reading, look up the meanings of these words and record the information below. For each word, write a sentence that shows its correct use.

Review your list from time to time. Try to put these words into use in your writing and conversation.

Word: _____

Selection: _____

Page/Line: _____ / _____

Part of Speech: _____

Definition: _____

_____

_____

_____

Sentence: _____

_____

_____

_____

Word: _____

Selection: _____

Page/Line: _____ / _____

Part of Speech: _____

Definition: _____

_____

_____

Sentence: _____

_____

_____

_____

Word: _____

Selection: _____

Page/Line: _____ / _____

Part of Speech: _____

Definition: _____

_____

_____

Sentence: _____

_____

_____

_____

Personal Word List

Word: _____

Selection: _____

Page/Line: _____ / _____

Part of Speech: _____

Definition: _____

_____

_____

Sentence: _____

_____

_____

_____

Word: _____

Selection: _____

Page/Line: _____ / _____

Part of Speech: _____

Definition: _____

_____

_____

Sentence: _____

_____

_____

_____

Word: _____

Selection: _____

Page/Line: _____ / _____

Part of Speech: _____

Definition: _____

_____

_____

Sentence: _____

_____

_____

_____

Word: _____

Selection: _____

Page/Line: _____ / _____

Part of Speech: _____

Definition: _____

_____

_____

Sentence: _____

_____

_____

_____

Word: _____

Selection: _____

Page/Line: _____ / _____

Part of Speech: _____

Definition: _____

_____

_____

Sentence: _____

_____

_____

_____

Word: _____

Selection: _____

Page/Line: _____ / _____

Part of Speech: _____

Definition: _____

_____

_____

Sentence: _____

_____

_____

_____

Word: _____

Selection: _____

Page/Line: _____ / _____

Part of Speech: _____

Definition: _____

_____

_____

Sentence: _____

_____

_____

_____

Word: _____

Selection: _____

Page/Line: _____ / _____

Part of Speech: _____

Definition: _____

_____

_____

Sentence: _____

_____

_____

_____

Personal Word List

Word: _____

Selection: _____

Page/Line: _____ / _____

Part of Speech: _____

Definition: _____

_____

_____

Sentence: _____

_____

_____

_____

Word: _____

Selection: _____

Page/Line: _____ / _____

Part of Speech: _____

Definition: _____

_____

_____

Sentence: _____

_____

_____

_____

Word: _____

Selection: _____

Page/Line: _____ / _____

Part of Speech: _____

Definition: _____

_____

_____

Sentence: _____

_____

_____

_____

Word: _____

Selection: _____

Page/Line: _____ / _____

Part of Speech: _____

Definition: _____

_____

_____

Sentence: _____

_____

_____

_____

Word: _____

Selection: _____

Page/Line: _____ / _____

Part of Speech: _____

Definition: _____

_____

_____

Sentence: _____

_____

_____

_____

Word: _____

Selection: _____

Page/Line: _____ / _____

Part of Speech: _____

Definition: _____

_____

_____

Sentence: _____

_____

_____

_____

Word: _____

Selection: _____

Page/Line: _____ / _____

Part of Speech: _____

Definition: _____

_____

_____

Sentence: _____

_____

_____

_____

Word: _____

Selection: _____

Page/Line: _____ / _____

Part of Speech: _____

Definition: _____

_____

_____

Sentence: _____

_____

_____

_____

Personal Word List

Word: _____

Selection: _____

Page/Line: _____ / _____

Part of Speech: _____

Definition: _____

_____

_____

Sentence: _____

_____

_____

_____

Word: _____

Selection: _____

Page/Line: _____ / _____

Part of Speech: _____

Definition: _____

_____

_____

Sentence: _____

_____

_____

_____

Word: _____

Selection: _____

Page/Line: _____ / _____

Part of Speech: _____

Definition: _____

_____

_____

Sentence: _____

_____

_____

_____

Word: _____

Selection: _____

Page/Line: _____ / _____

Part of Speech: _____

Definition: _____

_____

_____

Sentence: _____

_____

_____

_____

Word: _____

Selection: _____

Page/Line: _____ / _____

Part of Speech: _____

Definition: _____

_____

_____

Sentence: _____

_____

_____

_____

Word: _____

Selection: _____

Page/Line: _____ / _____

Part of Speech: _____

Definition: _____

_____

_____

Sentence: _____

_____

_____

_____

Word: _____

Selection: _____

Page/Line: _____ / _____

Part of Speech: _____

Definition: _____

_____

_____

Sentence: _____

_____

_____

_____

Word: _____

Selection: _____

Page/Line: _____ / _____

Part of Speech: _____

Definition: _____

_____

_____

Sentence: _____

_____

_____

_____

Personal Word List

Word: _____

Selection: _____

Page/Line: _____ / _____

Part of Speech: _____

Definition: _____

_____

_____

Sentence: _____

_____

_____

_____

Word: _____

Selection: _____

Page/Line: _____ / _____

Part of Speech: _____

Definition: _____

_____

_____

Sentence: _____

_____

_____

_____

Word: _____

Selection: _____

Page/Line: _____ / _____

Part of Speech: _____

Definition: _____

_____

_____

Sentence: _____

_____

_____

_____

Word: _____

Selection: _____

Page/Line: _____ / _____

Part of Speech: _____

Definition: _____

_____

_____

Sentence: _____

_____

_____

_____

Word: _____

Selection: _____

Page/Line: _____ / _____

Part of Speech: _____

Definition: _____

_____

_____

Sentence: _____

_____

_____

_____

Word: _____

Selection: _____

Page/Line: _____ / _____

Part of Speech: _____

Definition: _____

_____

_____

Sentence: _____

_____

_____

_____

Word: _____

Selection: _____

Page/Line: _____ / _____

Part of Speech: _____

Definition: _____

_____

_____

Sentence: _____

_____

_____

_____

Word: _____

Selection: _____

Page/Line: _____ / _____

Part of Speech: _____

Definition: _____

_____

_____

Sentence: _____

_____

_____

_____

Personal Word List

Word: _____

Selection: _____

Page/Line: _____ / _____

Part of Speech: _____

Definition: _____

_____

_____

Sentence: _____

_____

_____

_____

Word: _____

Selection: _____

Page/Line: _____ / _____

Part of Speech: _____

Definition: _____

_____

_____

Sentence: _____

_____

_____

_____

Word: _____

Selection: _____

Page/Line: _____ / _____

Part of Speech: _____

Definition: _____

_____

_____

Sentence: _____

_____

_____

_____

Word: _____

Selection: _____

Page/Line: _____ / _____

Part of Speech: _____

Definition: _____

_____

_____

Sentence: _____

_____

_____

_____

Word: _____

Selection: _____

Page/Line: _____ / _____

Part of Speech: _____

Definition: _____

_____

_____

Sentence: _____

_____

_____

_____

Word: _____

Selection: _____

Page/Line: _____ / _____

Part of Speech: _____

Definition: _____

_____

_____

Sentence: _____

_____

_____

_____

Word: _____

Selection: _____

Page/Line: _____ / _____

Part of Speech: _____

Definition: _____

_____

_____

Sentence: _____

_____

_____

Word: _____

Selection: _____

Page/Line: _____ / _____

Part of Speech: _____

Definition: _____

_____

_____

Sentence: _____

_____

_____

Personal Word List

Word: _____

Selection: _____

Page/Line: _____ / _____

Part of Speech: _____

Definition: _____

_____

_____

Sentence: _____

_____

_____

_____

Word: _____

Selection: _____

Page/Line: _____ / _____

Part of Speech: _____

Definition: _____

_____

_____

Sentence: _____

_____

_____

_____

Word: _____

Selection: _____

Page/Line: _____ / _____

Part of Speech: _____

Definition: _____

_____

_____

Sentence: _____

_____

_____

_____

Word: _____

Selection: _____

Page/Line: _____ / _____

Part of Speech: _____

Definition: _____

_____

_____

Sentence: _____

_____

_____

_____

Word: _____

Selection: _____

Page/Line: _____ / _____

Part of Speech: _____

Definition: _____

_____

_____

Sentence: _____

_____

_____

_____

Word: _____

Selection: _____

Page/Line: _____ / _____

Part of Speech: _____

Definition: _____

_____

_____

Sentence: _____

_____

_____

_____

Word: _____

Selection: _____

Page/Line: _____ / _____

Part of Speech: _____

Definition: _____

_____

_____

Sentence: _____

_____

_____

_____

Word: _____

Selection: _____

Page/Line: _____ / _____

Part of Speech: _____

Definition: _____

_____

_____

Sentence: _____

_____

_____

_____

Personal Word List

Word: _____

Selection: _____

Page/Line: _____ / _____

Part of Speech: _____

Definition: _____

_____

_____

Sentence: _____

_____

_____

_____

Word: _____

Selection: _____

Page/Line: _____ / _____

Part of Speech: _____

Definition: _____

_____

_____

Sentence: _____

_____

_____

_____

Word: _____

Selection: _____

Page/Line: _____ / _____

Part of Speech: _____

Definition: _____

_____

_____

Sentence: _____

_____

_____

_____

Word: _____

Selection: _____

Page/Line: _____ / _____

Part of Speech: _____

Definition: _____

_____

_____

Sentence: _____

_____

_____

_____

Word: _____

Selection: _____

Page/Line: _____ / _____

Part of Speech: _____

Definition: _____

_____

_____

Sentence: _____

_____

_____

_____

Word: _____

Selection: _____

Page/Line: _____ / _____

Part of Speech: _____

Definition: _____

_____

_____

Sentence: _____

_____

_____

_____

Word: _____

Selection: _____

Page/Line: _____ / _____

Part of Speech: _____

Definition: _____

_____

_____

Sentence: _____

_____

_____

_____

Word: _____

Selection: _____

Page/Line: _____ / _____

Part of Speech: _____

Definition: _____

_____

_____

Sentence: _____

_____

_____

_____

Personal Word List

Word: _____

Selection: _____

Page/Line: _____ / _____

Part of Speech: _____

Definition: _____

_____

_____

Sentence: _____

_____

_____

_____

Word: _____

Selection: _____

Page/Line: _____ / _____

Part of Speech: _____

Definition: _____

_____

_____

Sentence: _____

_____

_____

_____

Word: _____

Selection: _____

Page/Line: _____ / _____

Part of Speech: _____

Definition: _____

_____

_____

Sentence: _____

_____

_____

_____

Word: _____

Selection: _____

Page/Line: _____ / _____

Part of Speech: _____

Definition: _____

_____

_____

Sentence: _____

_____

_____

_____

Word: _____

Selection: _____

Page/Line: _____ / _____

Part of Speech: _____

Definition: _____

_____

_____

Sentence: _____

_____

_____

_____

Word: _____

Selection: _____

Page/Line: _____ / _____

Part of Speech: _____

Definition: _____

_____

_____

Sentence: _____

_____

_____

_____

Word: _____

Selection: _____

Page/Line: _____ / _____

Part of Speech: _____

Definition: _____

_____

_____

Sentence: _____

_____

_____

_____

Word: _____

Selection: _____

Page/Line: _____ / _____

Part of Speech: _____

Definition: _____

_____

_____

Sentence: _____

_____

_____

_____

Personal Word List

Word: _____

Selection: _____

Page/Line: _____ / _____

Part of Speech: _____

Definition: _____

_____

_____

Sentence: _____

_____

_____

_____

Word: _____

Selection: _____

Page/Line: _____ / _____

Part of Speech: _____

Definition: _____

_____

_____

Sentence: _____

_____

_____

_____

Word: _____

Selection: _____

Page/Line: _____ / _____

Part of Speech: _____

Definition: _____

_____

_____

Sentence: _____

_____

_____

_____

Word: _____

Selection: _____

Page/Line: _____ / _____

Part of Speech: _____

Definition: _____

_____

_____

Sentence: _____

_____

_____

_____